ENGLISH TEACHER'S
Month-by-Month
ACTIVITIES KIT

Ready-to-Use Lessons & Activities
for Grades 7-12

KEITH MANOS

**THE CENTER FOR APPLIED
RESEARCH IN EDUCATION**
Paramus, New Jersey 07652

CIP data is available from the Library of Congress

Printed in the United States of America

10 9 8 7 6 5 4 3 2 1

ISBN 0-13-089485-0

THE CENTER FOR APPLIED RESEARCH
IN EDUCATION
West Nyack, NY 10994

On the World Wide Web at http://www.phdirect.com

DEDICATION

To the hundreds of remarkable individuals
cited in this book
whose actions created history and
whose contributions influenced all our lives.
We need to teach our young people to
identify and celebrate their achievements.

ACKNOWLEDGMENTS

With appreciation to my colleagues at Richmond Heights High School who offered much needed advice and assistance during the development of this book.

Much love and gratitude to my wife Cheryl and children—Brittny, John-Morgan, and Christian—who remained patient and devoted through the hundreds of hours I spent at the computer.

ABOUT THE AUTHOR

Keith Manos, currently an English teacher at Richmond Heights (OH) High School, has taught writing to grades 7 through 12 for over 20 years at four different high schools. His students' poetry, fiction, and essays have earned them awards and recognition after being accepted for publication in local and national magazines. In 2000, Keith was named Ohio's English Teacher of the Year by the Ohio Council of Teachers of English Language Arts.

In 1993 Keith earned a Master's Degree in English (Creative Writing) from Cleveland State University. His skill as a teacher of writing has enabled him to serve as an editor of various educational newsletters and student publications. He has conducted many in-service seminars for writers, teachers, and coaches.

He is the author of many articles directed toward teachers and coaches which have appeared in national publications such as *Scholastic Coach, Wesleyan Advocate, School Library Journal, Strategies, Accent, Athletic Management, HiCall, Athletic Business, Lutheran Journal, Visions, New Earth Review,* and *Wrestling USA,* among others. *Wrestling Coaches Survival Guide* (1995), *Writing Smarter* (1998), and *Coach's and Athletic Director's Complete Book of Forms and Letters* (2000) were also published by Prentice Hall.

Currently, Keith is marketing two young adult novels while he continues to do freelance writing.

Keith is also a well-known motivational speaker for civic organizations, athletic teams, and awards programs in the Cleveland area when he isn't spending time with his wife and three children.

ABOUT THIS RESOURCE

English Teachers' Month by Month Activities Kit is directed to junior high and senior high school teachers who want easy access to creative lessons that connect past events to present day curriculum in a meaningful way. This resource contains over 800 practical and interesting learning activities that appeal to all learning styles and intelligences. Teachers can select from nearly 100 assignments and 8 to 15 reproducible worksheets per month that keep students on track for success in the areas of writing, reading, speech, and drama. Even the most veteran teachers can find fresh advice and innovative methods to enhance students' academic success and achieve curriculum goals at the same time.

English Teachers' Month by Month Activities Kit follows the typical ten months of the school year, September 1 to June 30. Each month teachers of grades 7–12 can use this resource to introduce authors, organize units, promote multicultural awareness, and celebrate historical achievements. Any teacher's lesson plan can be expanded, and cross-curriculum teaching becomes more accessible when English/ Language Arts teachers employ the learning activities in this resource on a consistent basis. It is easy to use and helpful to teachers who want to expand on their current lesson plan or create a new one. Students' interest in any subject matter is enhanced when this book is consulted on a weekly or daily basis.

This book not only is a beneficial resource for any English/Language Arts teacher on nearly any day of the school year, it can also be effectively utilized by social studies and history teachers who want quick access to key dates in history. Moreover, substitute teachers may also find the lessons and activities to be worthwhile when they are asked to cover a class on short notice.

English Teachers' Month by Month Activities Kit, in short, contains knowledge for a lifetime. It can be a welcome addition to any teacher's professional library.

HOW TO USE THIS RESOURCE

Each month the *English Teachers' Month by Month Activities Kit* begins with a one-page profile of that month's origin, holidays, gemstone, and flower, followed by a poem(s) related to that month. These background details can be applied to any of the lessons that follow.

The Table of Contents lists the various units along with the specific numbers of the learning activities that correspond to that unit. For example, if you wanted to develop a Poetry Unit in September, you could use Learning Activities #9, 10, 49, 50, and 99, together or individually.

The birthdates of famous writers, celebrities, performers, athletes, Presidents, politicians, scientists, educators, artists, musicians, military leaders, inventors, humanitarians, and businesspersons follow the Table of Contents page. In brackets by each individual's name are the numbers of the Learning Activities that correspond to that person. Keep in mind that some activities overlap. The same number, therefore, could apply to several individuals or events and appear more than once.

The Memorable Events section offers major historical events in the areas of literature, exploration, technology, athletics, education, television, science, medicine, politics, movies, business, archaeology, war, and fine arts that took place that month. Included also are historic firsts—the first balloon flight, the first woman mayor, the first intercontinental telephone calls—and the dates when states were admitted to the Union. Once again, you can find the learning activity related to each event by locating the number(s) in brackets.

Five types of Learning Activities are offered each month: Reading, Debating, Writing, Discussion, and Audio/Visual, which appeal to all learning styles and intelligences. Designed for flexibility, these learning activities can be used in sequence as part of general thematic units or as individual lessons on any subject.

Reading Activities direct you to assign students to read certain authors, books, reference materials, or *Forms*. Usually, in the case of a *Form*, a set of questions may follow.

Debating Activities are designed to generate disagreement and a brief, yet challenging exchange of opinions on the subject. The use of critical thinking skills are especially important here.

The Writing Activities could be lists, charts, sentences, paragraphs, letters, essays, or narratives. Some forms to evaluate these assignments are provided.

Discussion Activities generally can last several minutes or longer. Here, the focus is on students responding insightfully to questions that could serve as prompts to beginning or concluding larger thematic units or to improving critical thinking skills.

Audio/Visual Activities often require you to locate videotapes, recordings, pictures, or other materials, which usually are available in most libraries or video stores. Some preview work is needed before using these items.

Overall, this book contains over 800 practical and interesting learning activities in the areas of writing, reading, speech, media, and drama. Beneath some activities are boxes that contain background information or helpful explanations for easy reference.

At the end of each month are 8 to 15 reproducible Forms or Skill Sheets. Forms typically provide useful information for students, while the Skill Sheets are generally writing lessons. The Answer Key for the skill sheets follows as the final pages of each month.

Contents

SEPTEMBER

OCTOBER

INTRODUCTORY PAGE

LEARNING ACTIVITIES

REPRODUCIBLES

QUICK LOCATOR FOR OCTOBER LEARNING ACTIVITIES

NOVEMBER

Composition Skills

      Research *13, 14, 22, 27, 28, 29, 39, 52* • Prewriting *76* • Organization *32, 33, 37, 38, 39, 75, 77, 78, 79, 105* • Description *41, 42, 43, 44, 93, 94* • Reflection *48, 49* • Comparison/Contrast *26, 27, 40, 101* • Persuasion *53, 54, 58, 102, 103* • Narratives *50, 51, 52* • Dialogue *5, 45* • Character Sketch *6, 34, 35, 36, 96, 97*

News Unit   *46, 47, 86, 87, 88*

Careers Unit   *17, 21, 90*

Media Unit   *18, 19, 54, 69, 73, 86, 87, 88, 101*

Fine Arts   *91, 95*

Social Skills/Understanding Ethnic Diversity   *21, 29, 45, 51, 80, 81, 82*

DECEMBER

JANUARY

INTRODUCTORY PAGE

LEARNING ACTIVITIES

REPRODUCIBLES

QUICK LOCATOR FOR JANUARY LEARNING ACTIVITIES

FEBRUARY

INTRODUCTORY PAGE

LEARNING ACTIVITIES

REPRODUCIBLES

QUICK LOCATOR FOR FEBRUARY LEARNING ACTIVITIES

Composition Skills

MARCH

APRIL

MAY

QUICK LOCATOR FOR MAY LEARNING ACTIVITIES

Critical Thinking Skills   *1, 2, 15, 16, 17, 18, 19, 20, 21, 22, 23, 24, 25, 26, 51, 52, 53, 54, 55, 56, 57, 58, 59, 60, 61, 65, 66, 67, 70*

Fiction Unit   *8, 9, 10, 11, 22, 65, 66, 77*

Poetry Unit   *3, 4, 5, 7, 8, 19, 20, 21, 32, 49, 50, 59, 60, 61, 62, 63, 64, 80, 81*

Drama Unit   *12, 17, 22, 84*

Biography Unit   *13, 14, 31, 32, 33, 39, 72, 75*

Vocabulary/Word Choice Skills   *48, 58, 79, 80, 81, 82, 83*

Speech/Oral Presentations   *34, 35, 67*

Composition Skills
    Research *11, 21, 23, 25, 32, 33, 39, 44, 54* • Description *27, 28, 29, 30, 58, 82, 83* • Reflection *45, 46, 47, 48* • Comparison/Contrast *21, 22, 23, 24, 25, 26, 62* • Narratives *34, 37* • Dialogue *38, 39* • Character Sketch *74, 75, 76, 77, 78* • Letters *40, 41*

News Unit   *42, 43*

Careers Unit   *25, 26, 55, 57, 68, 69, 70*

Media Unit   *56, 70, 74*

Fine Arts   *80, 81*

Social Skills/Understanding Ethnic Diversity   *16, 20, 44, 72, 73*

JUNE

SEPTEMBER

SEPTEMBER

Origin: The seventh month in the old Roman calendar, September originates from the Latin *septem*, which means seven. Later, when the ancient Romans moved the beginning of the year from March 1 to January 1, September became the ninth month.

Holidays: Labor Day, the only legal holiday in the United States, comes on the first Monday of the month.

Jewish people often celebrate Rosh Hashanah, or New Year; Tzom Gedaliah, a fast day; Yom Kippur, the Day of Atonement; Sukkot, the Feast of the Tabernacles; and Simhat Torah, a day of rejoicing, in September.

Hindus begin Durga Puja, or Festival of the Divine Mother, this month.

Costa Rica, El Salvador, Guatemala, Honduras, Mexico, and Nicaragua all have national holidays in September to celebrate their independence from Spain in 1821.

Gemstone: Sapphire

Flower: Morning Glory

Poetry: The morrow was a bright September morn;
The earth was beautiful as if newborn;
There was nameless splendor everywhere,
That wild exhilaration in the air,
Which makes the passers in the city street
Congratulate each other as they meet.

> *by Henry Wadsworth Longfellow*

BIRTHDAYS

Sept. 1 Rocky Marciano, only undefeated heavyweight boxing champion (1923) [#13, 27, 100]; Lily Tomlin, actress/comedian (1939) [#52, 65, 87]; Conway Twitty, country western singer (1933) [#25]

Sept. 4 Richard Wright, author of *Black Boy* and *Native Son* (1908) [#6, 15, 16, 22, 39, 95]

Sept. 8 Patsy Cline, country western singer (1932) [#25]; Peter Sellers, actor especially noted for his role as Inspector Clouseau in the "Pink Panther" films (1925) [#88]

Sept. 9 Leo Tolstoy, author of *War and Peace* and *Anna Karenina* (1828) [#15, 22, 39, 67, 94]

Sept. 11 William S. Porter (O. Henry was his pen name), short story writer (1862) [#3, 15, 22, 60, 62]

Sept. 12 H.L. (Henry Louis) Mencken, writer/editor (1880) [#20, 26, 55, 62, 72]; Jesse Owens, winner of four gold medals in the 1936 Berlin Olympics [#13, 27]

Sept. 13 Sherwood Anderson, author of *Winesburg, Ohio* (1876) [#4, 15, 22, 39]; Roald Dahl, author of *Charlie and the Chocolate Factory* and *James and the Giant Peach* (1916) [#15, 22, 39, 80, 89]

Sept. 15 Roy Acuff, Grand Ole Opry "King of Country Music" (1903) [#25]; Agatha Christie, author of nearly one hundred books—mysteries, poetry, drama (1890) [#15, 22, 39, 56]; James Fenimore Cooper, novelist/historian (1789) [#7, 15, 22, 39]; William Howard Taft, 27th President and heaviest man to serve as President (1857) [#24]

Sept. 17 William Carlos Williams, winner of 1963 Pulitzer Prize for Poetry (1883) [#10, 49]

Sept. 18 Samuel Johnson, creator of the first dictionary of the English language (1755) [#8]

Sept. 19 William Golding, author of Lord of the Flies and winner of the Nobel Prize in 1983 (1911) [#4, 15, 22, 39]

Sept. 21 Stephen King, horror writer (1937) [#15, 16, 22, 39, 56, 57, 59, 63]; Rikki Lake, talk show host/actress (1968) [#11, 65, 66]; Bill Murray, actor/comedian (1950) [#52, 87]; Herbert George (H.G.) Wells, novelist (1866) [#4, 15, 22, 39]

Sept. 24   F. Scott Fitzgerald, novelist (1896) [#7, 15, 16, 22, 39]

Sept. 25   William Faulkner, novelist who won 1955 Nobel Prize & 1963 Pulitzer Prize (1897) [#5, 15, 16, 22, 39]; Will Smith, actor/singer (1968) [#52, 65]; Barbara Walters, television personality (1931) [#11, 20, 26, 65, 72]

Sept. 26   T.S. Eliot, poet/playwright and Nobel Prize winner (1888) [#9, 49, 50]

MEMORABLE EVENTS

Sept. 1   Emma M. Nutt Day—the first woman telephone operator began her career September 1, 1878 in Boston [#37, 48, 77].

Sept. 3   Great Britain signed the Treaty of Paris in 1783, thus ending the Revolutionary War in America [#28].

Sept. 4   Manhattan Island was discovered by British explorer Henry Hudson in 1609 [#29, 51].

George Eastman patented the Kodak camera, which was a hand held, roll-film camera, in 1888 [#53, 102].

Sept. 7   Neither Snow Nor Rain Day—to honor the opening to the public in 1914 of the New York Post Office Building which had on the front of the building the inscription copied from Herodotus: "Neither snow nor rain nor heat nor gloom of night stays these couriers from the swift completion of their appointed rounds." The legend grew that this was the motto of the U.S. Postal Service, although, in fact, they have no motto [#68, 77, 78, 97, 98].

Sept. 8   First Miss America was crowned (Margaret Gorman of Washington, DC) in 1921 in Atlantic City after a two-day pageant [#36].

"The Oprah Winfrey Show"—the first national TV show hosted by a black woman—premiered in 1986 [#11, 66].

"Star Trek" premiered in 1966, eventually prompting six motion pictures, a cartoon series, "Star Trek: The Next Generation" and "Start Trek: Deep Space Nine" [#30, 32, 93].

Sept. 9   California was admitted to the Union in 1850 as the 31st state [#17, 74, 99].

Sept. 11   911 Day—to honor all 911 emergency operators and the EMS crews who respond to the calls [#86].

Sept. 12   Video Games Day—to celebrate the fun kids have with video games [#12].

Sept. 14   Francis Scott Key wrote "The Star-Spangled Banner" during the British attack on Fort Henry in 1814 [#23, 84].

Sept. 15   Greenpeace was founded in 1971 by twelve individuals whose basic principle was to promote a green and peaceful world and bring "attention to any environmental abuse through our mere unwavering presence whatever the risk" [#14].

Sept. 16   The Pilgrims sailed from England on the *Mayflower* in 1620 [#29, 46].

National Student Day—to recognize and praise all students from preschool through postgraduate [#41, 42, 43, 44, 45, 47, 54, 76].

Sept. 17   The National Football League was formed in Canton, Ohio in 1920 [#27, 96].

Sept. 18   "The Addams Family" premiered in 1964 [#30, 32].

The United States federal government took out its first loan—negotiated by Alexander Hamilton—with the Bank of New York for $191,608.00 in 1789 to pay the salaries of the President, Senators, and Representatives to the first Congress. Repayment was completed on June 8, 1790 [#75, 79].

Sept. 21   Biosphere Day—to remind humanity of the fragility of the planet's biosphere [#14, 31].

Sept. 22   Dear Diary Day [#34, 35].

Elephant Appreciation Day—to celebrate the earth's largest land animal [#31, 81, 82].

Patent for the ice cream cone was filed in 1903. The first cone was made of paper and later from pastry to hold lemon ice [#33, 83].

Sept. 25   *Publik Occurrences Both Foreign and Domestick* became the first newspaper published in America in 1690 by Benjamin Harris in Boston [The *Boston News Letter* was later the first newspaper printed in a metropolitan area in the colonies. The *News Letter* was usually six months to one year behind in its news stories.] [#2, 18, 19, 21, 38, 69, 70, 71, 73, 90, 91, 92].

First double header in major league history was played between Providence and Worcester in 1882 [#34].

Vasco Balboa became in 1513 the first European to discover the Pacific Ocean [#29, 51].

LEARNING ACTIVITIES FOR SEPTEMBER

READING ACTIVITIES

Purpose: ***To investigate resources in a library***

1. Introduce the importance of students having a *library card*, especially as they begin the school year. Explain how the card can benefit them for their personal and school use. Use **Skill Sheet 9-1**—the "Scavenger Hunt."

Purpose: ***To analyze newspapers***

2. Have students read various newspaper articles to compare the amount and quality of foreign and domestic news they provide. Are details missing? Relate this to *Publik Occurrences Both Foreign and Domestick* and the *Boston News Letter*, the first major newspapers published in America.

Purpose: ***To begin a fiction unit***

3. Have students read the opening paragraphs of five O. Henry stories. Ask: How do these first paragraphs prompt readers to continue reading? Use **Skill Sheet 9-2.**

Purpose: ***To identify types of conflict in fiction***

4. Assign the reading of H.G. Wells' *War of the Worlds*, Sherwood Anderson's *Winesburg, Ohio*, or William Golding's *Lord of the Flies* and direct students to identify their different types of conflicts.

> **War of the Worlds** has a conflict of protagonist (humanity) vs. supernatural (Martians); **Winesburg, Ohio's** conflict is protagonist (George Willard) vs. his hopes and dreams for his community; and *Lord of the Flies* focuses on the protagonist (Ralph) against society (the other boys or Hunters on the island).

Purpose: ***To introduce the "stream of consciousness" technique in fiction***

5. Have students study the excerpt from William Faulkner's *As I Lay Dying* using **Form 9-3.**

Purpose: ***To explore characterization in fiction***

6. Have students read the excerpts from Richard Wright's story "The Man Who was Almost a Man." Use **Skill Sheet 9-4.** Preview this by asking: Why are there conflicts between adults and teens? When should teenagers expect adults to treat them as fellow adults?

What are typical signs of maturity? Could owning a gun suggest maturity? Why/why not?

> Adolescents often believe that they enter adulthood by gaining a single possession or accomplishing a single achievement; this is one of the themes of Wright's story "The Man Who was Almost a Man." David Glover, the main character, believes having a pistol will serve as a badge of manhood; however, when he kills by accident another man's mule he realizes through his frustration and fear others still consider him to be a child.

Purpose: To analyze writing styles in fiction

7. Prompt students to locate passages from novels by F. Scott Fitzgerald and James Fenimore Cooper so students can analyze their writing styles. Students should count and average the number of words per sentence and list the vocabulary used to describe characters and scenes.

> Typically, Fitzgerald and Cooper's writing styles are characterized by lengthy sentences, polysyllabic word choice, and an emphasis on melodrama.

Purpose: To improve word selection/vocabulary skills

8. Refer to Samuel Johnson and have students first skim the dictionary and then list the most interesting one, two, three, four, and five syllable words they find. Ask: How might these words be used in sentences?

Purpose: To study symbolism in poetry

9. Have students read any T.S. Eliot poems in their literature text to study the content and symbolism.

> For example, T.S. Eliot's "The Waste Land" symbolizes in part the mythological story of the quest for the Holy Grail, the cup used by Jesus at the Last Supper. Eliot's other poems offer symbols of Western history, mythology, and time.

Purpose: To study imagery in poetry

10. Have students read any William Carlos Williams poems in their literature text or available anthology to study his use of imagery. Have students focus on sensory language especially.

DEBATING ACTIVITIES

Purpose: To begin or conclude a speech unit

11. Who is the better speaker/interviewer: Rikki Lake, Oprah Winfrey, or Barbara Walters? How effectively does each discuss current issues or topics?

Purpose: To introduce critical thinking skills

12. How important are video games? Do they dominate too much of kids' leisure time and mental activity? Do they help or hurt students' academic performances? Refer to Video Games Day.

13. Refer to Jesse Owens and Rocky Marciano. Should exercise/fitness programs be mandatory for teenagers in school? Why/why not?

14. Refer to Biosphere Day and Greenpeace. Are we doing enough to conserve and protect our planet's natural resources and environment? How important is this issue?

Purpose: To begin or conclude a fiction unit

15. In works of fiction, which is most important—characters, plot, or setting? Why? Refer to the various writers who have birthdays this month.

16. In fiction we usually expect the writer to have the main character resolve the conflict at the end of the narrative. Should all stories, like those written by Fitzgerald, O. Henry, Faulkner, Wright, and King have resolutions? Why/why not?

Purpose: To introduce comparison/contrast

17. Refer to the summer vacation just completed and debate the location for the best vacation. What makes one location better than another? Refer to California as a typical vacation location.

Purpose: To explore the media

18. Refer to *Publik Occurrences Both Foreign and Domestick*, the first newspaper published in America (1690), and the *Boston News Letter*. Rate the following from Most Important to Least Important as to who *controls* the news we read: reporter, editor, publisher, advertisers, readers, and politicians.

> Reporters cover the news events and then write the articles. They have control over the article itself. The editor has control over the assignments and news events covered by the reporter. The publisher hires (and fires, if necessary) the editor and handles the business aspects of the newspaper. Advertisers pay for ads, which make up the bulk of newspaper revenue, suggesting they could influence how news events that relate to them are covered. Readers do purchase subscriptions and politicians are always in demand as interviewees and news sources.

19. Consider newspapers, television, radio, and magazines. Which type of news media is the best news source? Why is that type the best source?

> **Newspapers are typically more detailed and community-oriented; television is more visual and immediate; radio is more convenient and up-to-date; magazines are more informative and in-depth in their coverage.**

20. Refer to H.L. Mencken and Barbara Walters and ask: Who is the best news reporter that you have read? Why? Who is the best news broadcaster? What makes these people better than others?

21. Refer to *Publik Occurrences Both Foreign and Domestick* and the *Boston News Letter.* What is the most important news story *this* week?

Purpose: To introduce independent reading

22. Refer to the authors who have birthdays this month and ask: How important are books to a student's education? Are they even necessary? How should they be used in this class?

> **Consider Ralph Waldo Emerson's quote: "If we encounter a man of rare intellect, we should ask him what books he reads." Others may point to the power of experience, of practice, over reading.**

Purpose: To improve word selection/vocabulary skills

23. Does the "Star Spangled Banner" promote war? Do the lyrics convey a glorification of battle or do they simply praise our soldiers' efforts at the battle of Fort McHenry?

Purpose: To introduce a careers unit

24. Refer to the various occupations held by William Howard Taft in his life. Which was the most impressive and/or important? [United States Solicitor General (the country's top lawyer); Dean of the University of Cincinnati Law School; Governor-General of the Philippines; Secretary of War (now called Secretary of Defense); Chief Justice U.S. Supreme Court; President of the United States]

WRITING ACTIVITIES

Purpose: To introduce comparison/contrast

25. Refer to Patsy Cline, Conway Twitty, and Roy Acuff and have students write an essay that compares the rhythm, lyrics, and instruments of country western music to other types of music, such as rap.

26. Refer to H.L. Mencken and Barbara Walters and have students write a brief essay that compares television news to written news. They should refer to any specific news story to compare and contrast these two news sources.

Purpose: To teach brainstorming as a prewriting technique

27. Consider Jesse Owens, Rocky Marciano, and players in the National Football League. Have students brainstorm the physical and mental skills required of outstanding athletes.

Purpose: To teach organization in writing

28. Consider Great Britain and the United States signing the Treaty of Paris in 1783, ending the Revolutionary War. Have students write a treaty between two conference schools that ends all competition between them.

29. Have students compose a diary entry of a crew member on the Mayflower in 1620, Henry Hudson's ship in 1609, or Vasco Balboa's ship in 1513, listing the events that occurred in order on that day.

Purpose: To explore the importance of titles

30. Consider how "Star Trek" and "The Addams Family" caught the attention of viewers and have students list creative titles of current television programs. Then discuss the importance of titles in stories, essays, and plays.

Purpose: To practice writing effective introductions

31. Have students write the first paragraph—a "catchy," dramatic beginning—for an editorial essay on Elephant Appreciation Day or Biosphere Day.

Purpose: To practice writing description

32. Have students write a paragraph describing the physical appearance of the most interesting character on television, like one of the family members of the "3rd Rock" or an alien on "Star Trek—Deep Space Nine."

33. Have students list the sensory words people used after they ate the first ice cream cone in 1903 (The first cone was made of paper and later from pastry to hold lemon ice).

> **Consider sight (yellow crystals), sound (smacking of lips), taste (sweet, lemon), touch (chilly, damp) and the smell (lemon, crisp).**

Purpose: To teach reflective writing

34. Refer to Dear Diary Day and have students compose the diary entry of a teenager who has just seen the first baseball double-header, played between Providence and Worcester in 1882.

35. Have students write a diary entry to document the significant events of their day. Then ask: How do these events compare to others in your life? Why should we record the events of our days? How can diaries benefit writers? Refer to Dear Diary Day.

Purpose: *To introduce evaluation criteria for essays*

36. Refer to Margaret Gorman, the first Miss America, and have students list the criteria or create the evaluation instrument for selecting a Miss America or Mr. America. Then relate this to **Form 9-5,** an essay evaluation form.

Purpose: *To explore the news media*

37. Have students write a newspaper article (a feature, if necessary) about Emma M. Nutt.

> **Traditional news articles are organized based on Who (Who is involved?); What (What happened to make this a newsworthy event?); Where (Where did this event happen?); When (When did this news event happen?); and Why (Why did this happen?).**

38. Refer to *Publik Occurrences Both Foreign and Domestick* and H.L. Mencken and have students complete a survey on news writing—**Skill Sheet 9-6.** What do they know about news?

Purpose: *To begin a fiction unit*

39. Refer to the novelists who have birthdays this month and distribute **Skill Sheet 9-7** to discover what students know about fiction.

40. Have students compose a critical response to any novel they read over the summer declaring its merits or faults. Then present this to the dean of the English Department.

Purpose: *To introduce the course*

41. Have students list their expectations for the course and of the teacher. Ask: What do you want to learn? What helps you learn best? What are your expectations of me? Refer to National Student Day.

42. Have students predict in one or two paragraphs events that will take place during the coming school year. Use this also to investigate the students' attitudes and perceptions toward school and the course. Refer to National Student Day.

43. To establish a sense of unity and cooperation in the classroom, have students interview each other (**Skill Sheet 9-8**). When they finish, they can share the results of their interviews and introduce their interviewee to the entire class. Refer to National Student Day.

Purpose: To practice persuasive writing

44. Have students write an editorial about any school rule, policy, or program they think should be changed. Submit their final copies to the principal. Refer to National Student Day.

45. Refer to National Student Day and have students construct a proposal for promoting school spirit. Submit this to the principal or student council advisor.

46. Have students write the advertisement that encouraged pilgrims to journey on the Mayflower to the New World.

47. Refer to National Student Day and have students write brief letters to fellow students persuading them to do their best in the class.

Purpose: To introduce writing fiction

48. Have students write a character sketch or brief narrative describing Emma Nutt on her first day on the job in 1878.

DISCUSSION ACTIVITIES

Purpose: To begin a poetry unit

49. Refer to T.S. Eliot and William Carlos Williams and ask: Who are the popular poets today?

50. What does T.S. Eliot mean when he says, "Immature poets imitate; mature poets steal"? What kind of a poet are you?

Purpose: To introduce critical thinking skills

51. What is the purpose of exploration? Consider Hudson and Balboa. What possibly were their intents or goals? If exploration involves danger or risks, should we continue? Why/why not? What risks can we take as writers?

52. Why do we idolize celebrities like Lily Tomlin, Bill Murray, or Will Smith? Why are we interested in their personal lives? How could one of us become a celebrity?

53. Consider George Eastman and his Kodak camera, which was a hand held, roll-film camera, in 1888. Guess the image that appeared on the first photograph. Why do you think Eastman used that for his first picture? What would you select as the subject for your first picture? Why?

54. If most students begin the school year in September with excitement and interest, why do some drop out? What can be done about the dropout rate, especially in urban high schools? Are there problems with the school's system of evaluation? Refer to National Student Day.

55. What does H.L. Mencken mean when he says, "A celebrity is one who is known to many persons he is glad he doesn't know"? What does he mean when he says, "Conscience is the inner voice that warns us somebody may be looking."

Purpose: To begin a fiction unit

56. Consider Agatha Christie and Stephen King. Should a story leave the reader in suspense? Why or why not? How might writers of fiction create suspense with their titles? Use **Form 9-9.**

57. What are your favorite Stephen King books, stories, or movies? Why those? Why is he such a popular author? What makes his books so special or unique? Use **Form 9-9** to examine various titles.

58. Note the major novelists born this month. Then ask: Who are some of the major authors from our century? Who are some from this decade?

59. Refer to Stephen King and explain how a best-seller is determined. Then ask: Who are some other best-selling authors today?

> Best-sellers are determined by several variables which can vary from one best-seller list to another. For example, Borders and Barnes & Noble have their best-seller lists which are determined by the number of books sold over a given time period, typically a week or a month. Newspapers like the *Cleveland Plain Dealer* and the *San Francisco Chronicle* also provide weekly best-seller lists based on the total sales of books in selected stores in their areas.
>
> The traditional, and national, best-seller list comes from the *New York Times*, which began listing best-sellers in 1942 from the cumulative sales from selected book stores across the country. Although these store names are supposed to be kept secret, their identities and locations are often uncovered by some publishers who then send agents there to buy all the copies of their books so they make the best-seller list—in short, buying their way onto a best-seller list.
>
> Other best-seller lists, like those given by *USA Today* and *Publishers Weekly*, are as important, and less likely to be manipulated. Some lists are based on surveys; bookstore, drugstore, and airport sales; and even online sales. There are paperback vs. hardcover sales, quick sales (like when an author appears for a book signing) vs. long sales (for example, *Gone With the Wind* has sold over 11 million copies all time), and summer sales vs. holiday sales. In fact, some books by famous authors, like a Stephen King or a John Grisham, are "targeted" as best-sellers, sometimes even before they are published.
>
> Clearly, there are no established industry standards for determining which books end up on best-seller lists.

60. Explain O. Henry's (William Sidney Porter) background and ask: Other than to make money, what are the other benefits of writing fictional stories?

> O. Henry did not actively begin publishing short fiction until his late thirties when he was imprisoned for bank embezzlement in the Ohio Penitentiary. There he used the pseudonym O. Henry to begin writing his stories, which dealt in much part with the experiences he had in Texas, in Central America where he lived before turning himself into authorities, and in prison. In just over a span of a decade he published nearly one story a week in a variety of magazines and periodicals and ten story collections, becoming the most widely read story writer in America. In 1919 the Society of Arts and Sciences founded the O. Henry Memorial Awards to recognize the best American short stories published each year.

61. Consider the influence teenagers have on the publishing industry. What are some books—fiction and nonfiction—about teens? What are some just for teens? Ask students to browse the shelves of local bookstores and libraries to find books for and about teenagers.

62. Refer to H.L. Mencken and O. Henry and ask: How are news stories unlike fictional stories in terms of format?

> Fiction does not follow the "five Ws" format; nor are the stories expected to follow at all times the rules of standard English. News feature articles, however, sometimes resemble fictional writing in terms of format.

63. Refer to Stephen King and the literary genres of Horror and Gothic literature. What are some examples of each type? What makes them entertaining to read? How might they prompt nightmares?

> Horror focuses on the grotesque, mysterious, and/or supernatural in terms of its setting and characters; Gothic literature focuses on gloomy settings and supernatural events, which could be retained in the subconscious and cause a nightmare.

Purpose: To introduce speech/listening skills

64. What are the characteristics of effective listening? How can we encourage effective listening? What could ruin effective listening in the classroom? Who can demonstrate good listening?

> **During active, unlike passive, listening, the listener is face to face with the speaker and attentive. Listeners should be prepared to paraphrase the speaker's comments, as in "What I hear you saying is . . ." Distractions, other conversations, daydreaming, and doodling all can ruin effective listening.**

65. Consider talk show hosts, like Barbara Walters and Rikki Lake, and celebrities, like Lily Tomlin and Will Smith. It seems interviewers continually seek their opinions. At home, when are you asked to voice *your* opinion? How does this make you feel? In school, when are you asked to voice your opinion? How does this make you feel?

66. Have a talk show with one student serving as a real (Rikki Lake, Oprah Winfrey) or imaginary host. Guests could be students acting as imaginary persons or actual celebrities. Students prepare questions, the roles of each member, and the talk show format. Permit the "studio audience" (the other students) to ask questions, make appropriate comments, or assess the effectiveness of the interviews.

Purpose: To begin a composition unit

67. What does Leo Tolstoy mean when he says, "Without feeling, one cannot write anything decent." How accurate is this statement? What prompts successful writing?

68. Write on the board the quote from Herodotus: "Neither snow nor rain nor heat nor gloom of night stays these couriers from the swift completion of their appointed rounds." Then point out the use of the conjunction *nor* to connect the four nouns in a *coherent* and *parallel* way in the sentence.

Purpose: To explore the news media

69. Refer to *Publik Occurrences Both Foreign and Domestick* and the *Boston News Letter.* Is it right for the press to publish rumors? Why/why not?

70. Explain that some authorities define news as "major and recent events that affect the majority of people." Then ask: What is meant by *major?* What determines the *majority of people?* How recent does the news item have to be?

> **A news item is deemed major when it affects the economic, political, or social well-being of the public. Newspaper, radio, and television companies consider the demographics of their audience and cater to their needs and interests. For example, the "majority" for the *Akron Beacon Journal* will certainly differ from that of the *New York Times.***

71. Refer to *Publik Occurrences Both Foreign and Domestick*, the *Boston News Letter*, and to a study that reveals that today Americans ages 18–29 care less about the news than any generation in the past fifty years. Why is that? How can reading the newspaper benefit you in your education? How can reading the newspaper benefit you in your career?

72. How often do you read the newspaper? Why are newspapers important? What sections appeal to you? Why? What are some popular news magazines and newspapers? What if news reporting and broadcasting ceased to exist?

73. Explain that news reporters, like H.L. Mencken and Barbara Walters, are sometimes said to be cynical people. Ask: Why? Explain the origin of the term.

> **The Cynics were a group of ancient Greek philosophers who followed the teachings of Antisthenes of Athens (444–371 BC) who believed that human happiness consisted in trying to be virtuous, and in order to be virtuous a person had to reduce his dependence on the outside world. This involved living in poverty, scorning pleasure, and ignoring social conventions, in an idealistic but also negative manner. Soon, the Cynics were sneering at people and their motives. Today, news reporters and broadcasters write or speak about so many negative events each day—crimes, corruption, deaths—they can become cynical about life.**

Purpose: To teach comparison/contrast

74. Who has visited California? Favorite places? What are the state's attractions? Why is it a popular state for tourists? How does it compare to our state? How is it different?

75. Refer to the first loan by the federal government with the Bank of New York for $191,608.00 in 1789 which was repaid one year later. Then ask: How does this compare to any loan you've ever transacted? How does this compare with today's home mortgages or car loans? What other loans do people typically have?

Purpose: To introduce the course

76. What are the typical costs of school supplies? How do you make a school budget? What are some other expenditures a student would have to make for school? Refer to National Student Day.

Purpose: To begin or conclude a careers unit

77. Refer to Emma M. Nutt. Ask: Why was *she* selected to be the first telephone operator? What skills or background did she possess? What typically do employers expect of high school students?

78. Refer to Neither Snow Nor Rain Day and ask: Why is this motto attached to postal carriers? What qualifications does one need to work for the postal service? What are the advantages/disadvantages of working for the postal service?

79. Refer to the Bank of New York, which made the first loan to the United States government in 1789, and assign students to visit (possible field trip) a local bank to identify the various positions and jobs associated with the banking profession.

AUDIO/VISUAL ACTIVITIES

Purpose: To practice writing description

80. Show a scene from Tim Burton's film *James and the Giant Peach* and have students select and describe any character or predict the next event. Refer to Roald Dahl.

81. Show selected scenes from the movie *Dumbo* or from *Malaika* starring John Laughlin, which portrays four children who hide an injured pet elephant from ruthless hunters. Use this as a descriptive writing exercise or to generate student sympathy for the plight of elephants and refer to Elephant Appreciation Day.

82. Refer to Elephant Appreciation Day and show picture(s) or illustrations of elephants. Then have students write a detailed paragraph profiling them.

83. Refer to the first ice cream cone and ask students to write a paragraph describing their favorite ice cream product or shop, using sensory language.

Purpose: To improve word selection/vocabulary skills

84. Play a tape/CD of someone singing "The Star-Spangled Banner" and have students list the lines or phrases they find most important, patriotic, or inspiring.

85. Play a tape of rap or rock-n-roll music or, if they are available, distribute the song lyrics and ask how well the lyrics meet the criteria established for standard English.

86. Have selected students role-play the dialogue between a 911 dispatcher and the friend of an accident victim—a fire, for example. Refer to 911 Day and point out problems in clarity and conciseness.

Purpose: To analyze humor in literature

87. Show a brief clip from a videotape of any Lily Tomlin or Bill Murray movie and ask students to explain the humor. Also ask: What are some examples of humor in fiction?

88. Show selected scenes from the movie *Pink Panther* starring Peter Sellers and have students analyze the type of comedy (much slapstick). Ask: How would you describe in writing the scene we just watched?

89. Show selected scenes from the movie *Charlie and the Chocolate Factory*. Then ask: How would you classify this movie—Fantasy? Comedy? Drama? Why? Refer to Roald Dahl.

Purpose: *To analyze the news media*

90. Clip and mount two news articles from any newspaper, other than a tabloid, that are *not* newsworthy. They could be "sensational" articles or even media hype. Discuss why news editors chose them as important news events.

91. Have students clip ten headlines from newspapers or news magazines to evaluate: Do they attract the reader's attention? Are they part of an effective lead? How do they announce the news event? Then students could create their own news headlines.

92. Refer to *Publik Occurrences Both Foreign and Domestick*, the first newspaper published in America, and show selected scenes from the movie *The Paper* starring Michael Keaton and Glenn Close, especially the scenes where the editors are discussing what news stories to place on the front page. Ask: How do editors determine the front page news items?

Purpose: *To introduce science fiction*

93. Show selected scenes from any "Star Trek" movie. Use this to introduce or review the genre of science fiction. Ask: What makes this science fiction? What do readers/viewers usually expect from science fiction? What is your favorite science fiction show or movie? Why?

Purpose: *To conclude the reading of a Tolstoy novel*

94. Show selected scenes from the movie *Anna Karenina* starring Vivien Leigh to introduce or review the novel by Leo Tolstoy.

Purpose: *To conclude the reading of Native Son*

95. Show selected scenes from the movie *Native Son* starring Victor Love. Use this to introduce or review the novel by Richard Wright and the moral issue of bigotry. Ask: How would you describe this protagonist? Is he heroic in any way? Why/why not?

Purpose: *To develop students' skills at characterization*

96. Ask selected students to role-play the five men who met in Canton, Ohio in 1920 to form—with a $100 fee each—the new American Professional Football Association (now called the National Football League). Have students consider such items for discussion as rules, players, their salaries, and the schedule.

Teams for the American Professional Football Association were based in the midwestern cities like Canton (Bulldogs), Green Bay (Packers), McKeesport (Olympics), and Pittsburgh (Duquesnes). Jim Thorpe was the president of the league in its first year.

Purpose: To begin a letter writing unit

97. Refer to Neither Snow Nor Rain Day which honors the 1914 opening to the public of the New York Post Office Building. Play a recording of "The Letter" by the Box Tops and/or "Mr. Postman" by Gladys Horton and the Marvelettes. Ask: How do the songs portray the importance of the postal service in our personal lives?

98. Show selected scenes from the movie *The Postman* starring Kevin Costner, especially the scene where he pretends to be a postman for the first time, and ask: Why are letters so important to us? What makes receiving a letter a special experience? What have been some of the best letters you have received?

Purpose: To explore lyrical poetry

99. Refer to California gaining statehood and play recordings of songs, like "California Dreaming" by the Mamas and the Papas or any songs by the Beach Boys. Have students listen and copy the lyrics that praise the state.

Purpose: To introduce writing character sketches

100. Show selected scenes from the movie *Somebody Up There Likes Me* starring Paul Newman as boxer Rocky Marciano. Have students write a characterization of Marciano. What kind of a man was he? Why did he succeed as a boxer? How did he prepare himself to be the world champion?

Purpose: To introduce the course

101. Show selected scenes from the movies *Blackboard Jungle, Up the Down Staircase, To Sir with Love,* and *Dead Poets' Society* and have students analyze the behavior of the students in classroom scenes. Ask: Why do the students act that way? How should the teacher respond? Use this to initiate a discussion on class rules.

102. Refer to George Eastman and his Kodak camera and ask students to bring in pictures of themselves to place on the bulletin board. Use these later for a writing exercise.

Name _____

Library Orientation—Scavenger Hunt

_____   Write the *title* of a short story anthology that has at least one story that relates to a personal interest of yours, such as sports, music, traveling, etc.

_____

_____   Write the *title* and *author* of any book that deals with the life of a President.

_____

_____   Write the *title* and *author* of a book that describes the life of someone who lived before 1900.

_____

_____   Write the *title* and *author* of a book that describes *your personality*.

_____

_____   Write the *title* and *author* of a fictional book written by an author who has the same name *initials* as you (or same last name or first name).

_____

_____   Write the *title* and *author* of any book that deals with your *ethnic* background.

_____

_____   Write the *title* of a magazine that deals with language arts (reading, art, music, history, literature, etc.).

_____

_____   Write the *title* of a book that deals with American poetry.

_____

_____   Write the *title* and *author* of a nonfiction book that deals directly or indirectly with either one of your parent/guardian's current occupation.

_____

Name _____

O. Henry and His Stories

Directions: Read the following opening paragraphs of several O. Henry stories and then determine how each engages readers into the story.

1. "The Caballero's Way"

   The Cisco Kid had killed six men in more or less fair scrimmages, had murdered twice as many (mostly Mexicans), and had winged a larger number whom he modestly forbore to count. Therefore a woman loved him.

2. "The Ethics of a Pig"

   On an east-bound train I went into the smoker and found Jefferson Peters, the only man with a brain west of the Wabash River who can use his cerebrum and cerebellum, and medulla oblongata at the same time.

3. "The Fourth in Salvador"

   On a summer's day, while the city was rocking with the din and red uproar of patriotism, Billy Casparis told me this story.

4. "The Gift of the Magi"

   One dollar and eighty-seven cents. That was all. And sixty cents of it was in pennies. Pennies saved one and two at a time by bulldozing the grocer and the vegetable man and the butcher until one's cheeks burned with the silent imputation of parsimony that such close dealing implied. Three times Della counted it. One dollar and eighty-seven cents. And the next day would be Christmas.

5. "He Also Serves"

   If I could have a thousand years—just one little thousand years—more of life, I might, in that time, draw near enough to true Romance to touch the hem of her robe.

Stream of Consciousness

Directions: Read and study the following excerpt from Faulkner's novel, *As I Lay Dying*, for its demonstration of the stream of consciousness technique used in fiction.

Stream of consciousness = a rambling soliloquy by a character, first used in the late 19th century, revealing that character's feelings and thoughts. It often lacks the unity and selectivity of direct thought.

Background: The story here is told from the point-of-view of several characters, primarily the members of the Bundren family as they transport by wagon their dead mother Addie to her own family's cemetery. The following excerpt is from an early chapter where the mother lies sick and nearly dead and the father Adze constructs her coffin. This chapter is entitled "Jewel," who is the daughter.

And now them others sitting there, like buzzards.
Waiting, fanning themselves. Because I said if you
wouldn't keep on sawing and nailing at it until a
man can't sleep and her hands laying on the quilt
like two of them roots dug up and tried to wash and
you couldn't get them clean. I can see the fan and
Dewey Dell's arm. I said if you'd just let her alone.
Sawing and knocking, and keeping the air always moving
so fast on her face that when you're tired you can't
breathe it, and that Adze going One lick less. One
lick less. One lick less until everybody that passes
in the road will have to stop and see it and say what
a fine carpenter he is.

Name _____

Richard Wright

Directions: Read the following paragraphs from Richard Wright's short story "The Man Who was Almost a Man" and then answer the questions that follow.

A. "He poured his plate full of molasses and sopped it up slowly with a chunk of corn-bread. When his father and brother had left the kitchen, he still sat and looked again at the guns in the catalogue, longing to muster courage enough to present his case to his mother. Lawd, ef Ah only had tha pretty one! He could almost feel the slickness of the weapon with his fingers. If he had a gun like that he would polish it and keep it shining so it would never rust. N Ah'd keep it loaded, by Gawd!"

B. "The first movement he made the following morning was to reach under his pillow for the gun. In the gray light of dawn he held it loosely, feeling a sense of power. Could kill a man with a gun like this. Kill anybody, black or white. And if he were holding his gun in his hand, nobody could run over him; they would have to respect him."

1. What do you believe to be the age of the character here? Why?

2. What is his background (family, education)?

3. Why is he so interested in owning a gun?

4. What advice would you give him?

5. What plot events do you think occur in the story?

Name _____

Essay Evaluation Form

Points		Criteria

PREWRITING

5   _____   The writer performed brainstorming, webbing, or another prewriting strategy.

5   _____   The essay appeals effectively to a specific reader. It reflects a definitive "angle."

ORGANIZATION

5   _____   The introduction captures the reader's interest and leads effectively into the thesis statement.

5   _____   There is an effective thesis statement.

5   _____   The essay has complete, well structured paragraphs, each with a topic sentence that is fully developed.

5   _____   These paragraphs have unity and coherence.

5   _____   The essay has unity—all sentences relate directly to the thesis—and key points are thoroughly developed.

5   _____   Transitional words and strategies are used.

5   _____   The conclusion is a forceful summary of the main points and re-states the thesis.

DICTION

5   _____   Is there specific wording (concrete language) throughout the essay? There are no unclear phrases or references.

5   _____   The writer uses no clichés.

5   _____   Wordiness has been eliminated (there is economy in writing)—such as repetition.

5   _____   Are there any shifts in diction (formal, for example, mixed with slang)?

GRAMMAR

5   _____   Proper sentence structure?

5   _____   Punctuation errors?

5   _____   Spelling errors?

5   _____   Were words omitted? Faulty phrasing?

5   _____   Improper verb or pronoun usage?

MANUSCRIPT FORM

5   _____   Proper title page (Creative title and name, class, and period placed correctly)

5   _____   General neatness (paragraphs indented, double-spaced)

100   _____   Total

Name _____

What Do You Know About the News?

Directions: Answer each question in detail.

1. What are the most popular news magazines?

2. Who are the most popular news broadcasters nationally?

3. What are some current news topics?

4. What were the major news topics six months ago?

5. What can you anticipate being the major news topic six months in the future?

6. Where would you find an article about a teenage shoplifter?

7. Where would you find an article about a teenage chess master?

8. Why are newspapers arranged into sections?

9. How can we be certain the news we receive is accurate?

10. How would you define *news*?

11. *Who* determines what is published or broadcasted as news?

Name _____

What Do You Know About Fiction?

Directions: Circle the letter of the correct answer.

1. Fiction can be based on actual experience.

   A. TRUE   B. FALSE

2. Professional writers revise or edit their fiction, sometimes several times.

   A. TRUE   B. FALSE

3. A short story can be nonfiction.

   A. TRUE   B. FALSE

4. It is best to introduce a story's conflict as soon as possible when writing fiction.

   A. TRUE   B. FALSE

5. Ideas for writing fiction can come from

   A. newspaper articles.

   B. magazine pictures.

   C. a relative's experience.

   D. all of the above.

6. The most important elements for developing fiction are

   A. humor and conflict.

   B. description and tone.

   C. plot and characterization.

   D. character's feelings and the writer's theme.

7. Dialogue reveals how characters

   A. feel and behave.

   B. make friends.

   C. respond to conflicts.

   D. do all of the above.

8. When writing dialogue, the writer should

   A. have the characters say dramatic things.

   B. make it realistic and natural.

   C. have it only be a little part of the story.

   D. do all of the above.

9. A protagonist in fiction is

   A. the enemy of the main character.

   B. the main character in a story.

10. The antagonist in fiction is

   A. the enemy of the main character.

   B. the main character in a story.

Name _____

Classmate Interview

I am interviewing (full name) _____

1. Where were you born?

2. Who are your brothers and sisters?

3. What is your favorite school subject?

4. What is your usual after school activity?

5. What is your favorite snack food?

6. What kind of music do you like?

7. Who is your favorite performer or actor?

8. What is your favorite all-time movie?

9. What is your favorite television program?

10. What do you want to learn this year in English?

Name _____

Comparing Titles of Agatha Christie and Stephen King

Directions: Read the following novel titles from Agatha Christie and Stephen King. How do they prompt suspense or mystery? How do these titles suggest the events in the novels?

Agatha Christie	**Stephen King**
Body in the Library	*The Dead Zone*
Death on the Nile	*The Dark Tower*
Murder of Roger Ackroyd	*Insomnia*
Murder on the Orient Express	*Night Shift*
Ten Little Indians	*The Stand*
Mirror Crack'd	*Skeleton Crew*
And Then There Were None	*Pet Sematary*
After the Funeral	*Misery*
Appointment with Death	*The Eyes of the Dragon*

SEPTEMBER
Answer Key

#6 SKILL SHEET 9-3—RICHARD WRIGHT

1. David is a young teenager because he feels a lack of respect, and he isn't allowed to buy a gun.

2. By his inarticulate speech he seems uneducated. We know he has a father and brother, and they all seem to be poor rural farmers. Plus, he seems somewhat alienated from them.

3. He thinks the gun will provide him a sense of power, courage, even authority. Others will see him as powerful, mature, a *man*.

4. Answers will vary.

5. Answers will vary.

#38 SKILL SHEET 9-6—WHAT DO YOU KNOW ABOUT THE NEWS?

1. The most popular news magazines include *Time, Newsweek, U.S. News and World Report*, among others.

2. The most popular news broadcasters nationally are from the major broadcast companies and include Peter Jennings, Dan Rather, Tom Brokaw, Jim Lehrer, Ted Koppel, Barbara Walters, Wolf Blitzer, among others.

3. Answers will vary.

4. Answers will vary.

5. The major news events in the future certainly would include the President of the United States and other political leaders along with major sports events and international conferences already scheduled.

6. An article about a teenage shoplifter usually would be found in the newspaper's local or metro section, if at all.

7. An article about a teenage chess master would probably appear as a feature article or in the sports section.

8. Newspapers are arranged into sections as a convenience for the reader and to suggest the departments of the newspaper company.

9. We can be certain the news we receive is accurate by checking other news sources' reports on the same news event.

10. Answers will vary.

11. Editors, publishers, and reporters primarily determine what is published or broadcasted as news.

#39 SKILL SHEET 9-7—WHAT DO YOU KNOW ABOUT FICTION?

1. A	2. A	3. B	4. A	5. D
6. C	7. D	8. B	9. B	10. A

OCTOBER

OCTOBER

Origin: October comes from the Latin word for eight, but later became the tenth month when the ancient Romans moved the beginning of the year from March 1 to January 1.

Holidays: Columbus Day is celebrated on the second Monday of the month to honor the arrival of Christopher Columbus in the New World.

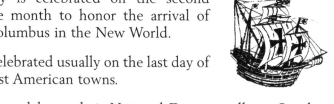

Halloween is celebrated usually on the last day of October in most American towns.

Chinese citizens celebrate their National Day annually in October to commemorate the founding of the People's Republic of China in 1949.

Icelanders celebrate Leif Erickson Day to honor his discovery of North America in the year 1000.

Gemstone: Opal

Flower: Calendula

Poetry:
October gave a party;
The leaves by hundreds came;
The ashes, oaks, and maples,
And those of every name.
   by George Cooper

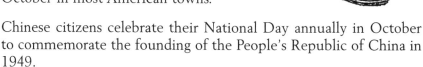

There is something in October sets the gypsy
   blood astir;
We must rise and follow her,
When from every hill of flame,
She calls, and calls each vagabond by name.
   by Bliss Carman

BIRTHDAYS

Oct. 2 Mohandas Karamchand (Mahatma) Gandhi, Indian political and spiritual leader (1869) [#3, 42, 88]; Don McLean, singer of "Miss American Pie" (1945) [#79]

Oct. 4 Rutherford B. Hayes, 19th President (1822) [#40, 47]; Frederick Remington, painter of frontier scenes, especially American Indians, cowboys, and horses (1861) [#69]; Damon Runyon, journalist/author (1884) [#17, 52, 60]

Oct. 5 Chester A. Arthur, 21st President (1829) [#40, 47]; Jonathan Edwards, colonial theologian, leader of the "Great Awakening," and later president of Princeton University (1703) [#34]

Oct. 6 Thor Heyerdahl, Norwegian adventurer and author *(Kon-Tiki)* who sailed across the ocean on a raft (1914) [#26, 28]

Oct. 8 Jesse Jackson, civil rights leader and one time Presidential candidate (1941) [#65, 93]; R.L. Stine, author of *Goosebumps* and *Fear Street* series (1943) [#7]

Oct. 9 John Lennon, songwriter and musician—"The Beatles"—(1940) [#17, 76]

Oct. 12 Charles Gordone, first black playwright to win the Pulitzer Prize for his play *No Place to be Somebody* (1925) [#19, 68]; Luciano Pavarotti, opera singer (1935) [#74, 84]

Oct. 14 Dwight D. Eisenhower, 34th President (1890) [#40, 47]

Oct. 16 William O. Douglas, U.S. Supreme Court Judge who served a 36-year term, longest of any other justice (1898) [#75]; Eugene O'Neill, Pulitzer Prize and Nobel Prize winning playwright (1888) [#8]; Oscar Wilde, Irish poet/playwright (1854) [#17, 45, 46]; Noah Webster, educator who compiled *Webster's Dictionary* (1758) [#18, 27, 31, 50, 55]

Oct. 17 Arthur Miller, playwright—*Death of a Salesman* (1915) [#8, 19, 38, 92]

Oct. 18 Shel Silverstein, cartoonist/author (1932) [#77]

Oct. 21 Samuel Taylor Coleridge, English poet—"The Rime of the Ancient Mariner" (1772) [#5, 58, 59]

Oct. 27 Theodore Roosevelt, 26th President (1858) [#40, 47]; Dylan Thomas, Welsh poet/playwright (1914) [#4, 6]

Oct. 28   Bill Gates, multibillionaire owner of Microsoft (1955) [#23, 43, 72]; Jonas Salk, American physician who developed the vaccine for polio (1914) [#30]

Oct. 30   John Adams, 2nd President (1735) [#40, 47]; Charles Atlas, bodybuilder (Angelo Siciliano) (1893) [#57, 74]; Emily Post, writer of *Etiquette: The Blue Book of Social Usage*, the bible of manners (1922) [#10, 62]; Ezra Pound, poet and only American poet tried for treason (1885) [#16, 58]

Oct. 31   John Keats, English poet (1795) [#5, 58]; Juliette Low, founder of the Girl Scouts (1912) [#12]

MEMORABLE EVENTS

Oct. 1 Major League baseball's first World Series was played between Boston and Pittsburgh, a series won by Boston, 5 games to 3 [#82].

Henry Ford put on sale his Model-T Ford, or "Tin Lizzie," in 1908 at a price of $850 [#32, 81].

Oct. 2 Thurgood Marshall, first Black associate justice on the Supreme Court, sworn in (1967) [#36, 68].

"Twilight Zone" premiered in 1959 [#2, 61].

Oct. 4 "Leave it to Beaver" premiered in 1957. The situation-comedy involved Jerry Mathers as the "Beaver" and his misadventures. Hugh Beaumont played Ward Cleaver, the Beaver's patient father; Barbara Billingsly played June, his well-dressed, all-knowing mother; and Tony Dow was Wally, his good-natured brother [#14, 38, 44].

The Sputnik (which means "fellow traveler of earth") was launched in 1957, becoming the first successful man-made earth satellite and prompting a greater emphasis on the teaching of science in American classrooms [#13].

Oct. 10 Tuxedo was created by Griswold Lorillan of Tuxedo Park, New York in 1886 [#56, 80].

Oct. 11 "Saturday Night Live" premiered in 1975 [#49].

Oct. 12 Christopher Columbus landed on the New World in 1492. In actuality, a Dutch sailor Piet de Stuini persuaded Columbus to change the ship's log from October 13 to October 12, believing the actual date would cause superstitious fears in other sailors [#9, 13, 29, 39, 48].

Oct. 14 Martin Luther King was awarded the Nobel Peace Prize in 1964, the youngest recipient ever at the time [#22].

Oct. 16 First department store—Zion's Co-operative Mercantile Institution—opened in Salt Lake City in 1868. It is still in operation [#21, 53].

World Food Day—to increase awareness of world hunger [#37].

Oct. 19 Thomas A. Edison demonstrated the electric light bulb in 1879 [#83].

British General Lord Cornwallis surrendered to General George Washington in 1781 at Yorktown, Virginia, thus ending the Revolutionary War [#33].

Oct. 24 United Nations was established in 1945 [#41, 63, 71, 86, 87].

Oct. 28   The Statue of Liberty, the sculpture constructed by Frederic Bartholdi, was dedicated as "Liberty Enlightening the World" on Bedloe's Island in New York's harbor in 1886 [#1, 15, 64, 65, 71, 87, 89, 90].

Harvard University was founded in Cambridge, MA in 1636 [#73].

Helen Eugenie Moore Anderson was sworn in by President Truman as the first woman U.S. Ambassador (to Denmark) in 1949 [#35].

Oct. 30   "War of the Worlds" was broadcast on the radio in 1938 by Orson Welles. This Halloween drama caused near panic in New Jersey when listeners believed it to be true that Martians had invaded [#20, 78].

Oct. 31   National Magic Day—to honor the anniversary of the death of Harry Houdini [#54, 91].

Mount Rushmore was completed, featuring the facial likenesses of Presidents Washington, Jefferson, Lincoln, and Theodore Roosevelt, in 1941 [#11].

Nevada was admitted to the Union as the 36th state in 1864 [#85].

LEARNING ACTIVITIES FOR OCTOBER

READING ACTIVITIES

Purpose: To improve skills at analysis/interpretation

1. Have students interpret the sentences written on the base of the Statue of Liberty. Use **Skill Sheet 10-1.**

2. Have students read Rod Serling's opening monologue for "The Twilight Zone" Use **Skill Sheet 10-2.**

3. Have students study the quotes by Mahatma Gandhi, one of the world's greatest peacemakers. Use **Skill Sheet 10-3.**

Purpose: To improve skills at analyzing poetry

4. Distribute the final stanza from the poem "Do Not Go Gentle into that Good Night" by Dylan Thomas (**Skill Sheet 10-4**) to analyze his creative use of language, the references to emotion (i.e., rage and grief) common in poetry, and his use of imagery.

5. Have students read the poetry of Samuel Taylor Coleridge and John Keats found in their literature textbook or an available anthology to study the poets' cryptic meanings and their emphasis on the power of the imagination. Use **Form 10-5.**

6. Have students locate and read the poetry of Dylan Thomas and another 20th century poet found in a literature text or available anthology to compare the language in their poems.

> The poetry of Dylan Thomas was known for its verbal imagery and dynamic language. Often, his lines celebrated natural beauty in a surrealistic manner.

Purpose: To improve skills at analyzing fiction

7. Use **Form 10-6**—paragraphs from R.L. Stine novels (some from the Fear Street series). Use this to analyze his use of suspense (especially the use of indefinite pronouns) to engage the reader.

Purpose: To improve skills at analyzing drama

8. Have students read and review the dialogue from a play by Eugene O'Neill or Arthur Miller found in a literature text or available anthology. Ask: Is it interesting, engaging, and realistic? Why is dialogue often more important in stage productions than in movies? How effective is the dialogue seen in this play?

Eugene O'Neill and Arthur Miller wrote a variety of plays, but their characters and dramas share a focus on colloquial language, interior monologues, and psychological discourse.

DEBATING ACTIVITIES

Purpose: To promote critical thinking skills

9. Should Leif Erikson or Christopher Columbus (or neither) receive the credit for discovering the New World? Why?

10. Consider the social rules of etiquette established by Emily Post. Should they be followed strictly? What rules are the most often ignored or neglected by teenagers? How important are good manners in today's society?

11. Mount Rushmore was completed in 1941, featuring the facial likenesses of Presidents Washington, Jefferson, Lincoln, and Theodore Roosevelt. Why these Presidents? Are any others more deserving? Possibly allow students to do research before debating.

12. Consider the Boy Scouts and Girl Scouts, which were founded by Juliette Low in 1912. Should there be one scouting organization or two separate groups? Is this a situation of sexism?

13. Which was the more important historical event: Christopher Columbus landing on the New World in 1492 or the launch of the Sputnik space capsule in 1957?

14. Consider "Leave it to Beaver." What is the *ideal* family? Should there be a certain standard families should expect to follow on a daily basis? Students could locate any news and magazine articles that deal with families to use as evidence.

15. Consider Emma Lazarus's message on the Statue of Liberty. It welcomes immigrants coming to America who are "tired . . . poor, . . . yearning to breathe free, the wretched refuse of your teeming shore. Send these, the homeless . . ."

    Should there be limits now on immigration? Does illegal immigration harm the United States? What is our government's policy on immigration now? Possibly allow students to research this before debating.

16. Should Ezra Pound, who was simply a poet and a broadcaster on a foreign radio station, have been tried as a traitor? Read the brief biography **(Form 10-7)** and debate his indictment for treason. Use this also to connect writers to historical events.

Purpose: To begin a composition unit

17. Consider writers like Damon Runyon (journalist), Oscar Wilde (playwright), and John Lennon (song writer). Why did they write and for whom? Should our writing just please the teacher who, of course, is the primary evaluator, or others?

18. Define slang for students and then ask: Should Noah Webster have permitted slang to be included in his first (or later) dictionaries? Should slang be permitted in conversation but not in any expository writing?

> Typically, slang is fad language, or "street talk." Unlike formal diction, slang frequently changes (consider the term *groovy*), yet could be adopted into standard English if it becomes widespread—*jazz* is an example. Although slang does have a certain vitality, not everyone understands nor appreciates it. Therefore, slang is unacceptable in formal writing. However, if the audience understands and enjoys slang, the writer can use it.

Purpose: To begin or conclude a drama unit

19. Who contributed more to modern American drama: Charles Gordone or Arthur Miller? Students could read excerpts from their plays or research the backgrounds of these two important playwrights.

WRITING ACTIVITIES

Purpose: To begin a fiction unit

20. Consider the fictional radio drama "War of the Worlds," written and produced by Orson Welles, and distribute the Survey—**Skill Sheet 10-8**—to explore the often close connection between fiction and reality.

Purpose: To review brainstorming as a prewriting activity

21. Have students compose a shopping list, where money is or is not a concern, for purchases at the local department store. Refer to the first department store—Zion's Co-operative Mercantile Institution.

22. Have students list what they believe to be the criteria for selecting the annual Nobel Peace Prize winner. Refer to Martin Luther King and ask: What would be the background and traits of the Nobel Peace Prize winner?

Purpose: To practice writing characterizations

23 Refer to Bill Gates and have students write a one page character sketch about any wealthy person, real or imaginary. Ask: What are the traits and characteristics of the wealthiest person you know?

24. Refer to Halloween and the scary costumes and movies often associated with this holiday. Ask: What would be the general appearance of someone who is afraid? Have students write a one-page character sketch.

Purpose: ***To practice writing short fiction***

25. Refer to Halloween and have students create a brief narrative using in any order the following words: skeleton, candy, pumpkin, witch, bonfire, pavement, clouds, costume, dirt, and window. Challenge their creativity.

26. Refer to Thor Heyerdahl and have students create a brief story of one day of his adventure on the Pacific Ocean. Remind them to use sensory language and strong verbs.

Purpose: ***To introduce organizational skills in writing***

27. Have students list the steps taken by Noah Webster to list every word in his first dictionary. How did he compile these thousands of words? Or have students make a dictionary of their own slang terms.

> **Webster began his project due to his profound dismay over the continued use of British textbooks and dictionaries in American schools after the United States had become independent from Great Britain. Motivated by national pride, Webster published in 1828 his American dictionary which contained over 12,000 words that were not listed in any other dictionary, many of them "Americanisms," that is, expressions coined and used only by Americans. He produced a second edition in 1840 that is updated yearly.**

28. Have students write a journal entry by Thor Heyerdahl, the Norwegian adventurer who sailed across the Pacific ocean on the raft Kon-Tiki in 1947. He departed from Callao, Peru and traveled 4300 miles before landing at the Tuamotu Archipelago of Polynesia. Assign them different days of of his voyage (a day for as many students in the class) and then collate the finished copies into one manuscript.

29. Assign each student a different log entry of Christopher Columbus on his journey to the New World in 1492. Then collate the final copies into a finished manuscript.

> **Columbus's three ships—the *Santa Maria*, *Nina*, and *Pinta*—sailed from Palos de la Frontera, Spain on August 3, 1492, seeking a sea route to the Asian continent. He was forced to stop at the Canary Islands to repair the *Pinta*'s mast. They set sail again on September 6 heading due west until October 7 when it was suggested they sail southwest, which he did, arriving on Guanahani, Bahamas on October 13. He returned to Spain in January, 1493 and arrived at Palos de la Frontera in March.**

Purpose: To improve vocabulary/word selection skills

30. Consider Jonas Salk's many medical procedures during the course of his battle against polio, a disease which affects the spinal cord. Have students write Salk's notes about his research, using as many medical and technical terms as they can, including descriptive references to patients.

31. Consider how new words are added to Webster's Dictionary. Have students list the nomination procedures and acceptance criteria for a new word to be admitted to the dictionary. Use this to prompt a discussion on the importance of word choice to any rubric for writing.

32. Refer to Henry Ford's Model T and the advertisements for cars found in magazines and have students create an advertisement for their favorite car.

33. Have students create the dialogue that took place between General George Washington and the British commander Lord Cornwallis when Cornwallis surrendered in 1781 at Yorktown, Virginia, thus ending the Revolutionary War.

34. Consider Jonathan Edward's use of a description of Hell as a pit of fire in his sermon "Sinners in the Hands of an Angry God." Have students brainstorm terms they think describe his congregation of Puritans as they listened to this sermon, which also presented God as full of rage against mankind.

Purpose: To teach reflective writing

35. Have students write Helen Eugenie Moore Anderson's diary entry after she was sworn in by President Truman as the first woman U.S. Ambassador (to Denmark) in 1949.

> **One form of expository writing is reflection. Here, the writer simply reflects on an issue, an event, or an idea and adopts a viewpoint about it. The format can be essay, diary, journal, or editorial.**

36. Have students write Thurgood Marshall's diary entry the night after he was sworn in as the first black justice to the Supreme Court. Ask: What were his emotions, fears, and thoughts? Also use this to teach the connection between history, politics and writing.

37. Refer to World Food Day and have students write a brief editorial on the problem of world hunger, especially in impoverished countries.

Purpose: To practice letter writing skills

38. Refer to the Loman family in Arthur Miller's *Death of a Salesman* and the Cleaver family of "Leave it to Beaver." Have students write a letter to a parent/guardian explaining their feelings about a family issue that upset or inspired them. Students must avoid using dull words and generalizations. Possibly mail this letter as a means to teach writing for a genuine audience.

Purpose: To practice speech skills

39. Have students write the speech Columbus used to convince King Ferdinand V and Queen Isabella of Spain, who eventually funded his journey, and others that the world was indeed not flat and that he and his crew would not sail off the end of the earth.

40. Have students write the acceptance speech of a real or imaginary candidate who has just obtained a political office. Refer to the Presidents who have birthdays this month and the inauguration speech they make in January.

Purpose: To introduce social skills

41. Consider the new United Nations, which was established in 1945 directly after WW II, and have students list 10 to 15 mandates (e.g., all nations must settle conflicts in a peaceful manner). Then have students compare those by-laws to the ones that appear in their school student handbook that explain the behaviors expected of students.

DISCUSSION ACTIVITIES

Purpose: To promote critical thinking skills

42. Refer to Mahatma Gandhi who was originally labeled as a criminal by British authorities in India. How have criminal acts turned some people into celebrities? Other examples?

43. Consider Bill Gates and ask: What is the connection between money, fame and success? Why does our society value wealth and fame so much? What do you think mainly influenced his personal success?

> **Bill Gates dropped out of Harvard in his junior year to develop Microsoft. His idea was to develop and promote the sale of personal computers to individuals, not just companies and institutions, and to create a computer language (Windows) that all customers could use. By 2000 he has amassed a personal fortune of nearly $80 billion.**

44. Consider Jerry Mathers who could never disassociate himself as an actor or person with the character Beaver Cleaver after appearing in the series "Leave it to Beaver." Ask: How has television affected the celebrity status of some people?

45. What did Oscar Wilde mean when he said, "Discontent is the first step in the progress of a man or a nation"? What examples can you cite to prove he is correct? What examples indicate he is wrong?

46. What does Oscar Wilde suggest with his quote: "History is merely gossip"? How would a history teacher react to this? What are your attitudes toward gossip? Can we always trust the information provided in history textbooks?

47. Consider Presidents Chester A. Arthur, Rutherford B. Hayes, Dwight D. Eisenhower, John Adams, and Theodore Roosevelt. Examine their main achievements as Presidents. Use **Skill Sheet 10-9** and have students list all the things they would do if they could be President.

48. Refer to Columbus discovering the New World and then offer students Jacque Cousteau's quote: "What I admire in Columbus is not his having discovered a world, but his having gone in search for it on the faith of an opinion." Ask: What is Cousteau's attitude toward Columbus? What impresses Cousteau most about Columbus's journey across the Atlantic? When have you depended on your opinion?

Purpose: To introduce the literary terms parody, satire, and hyperbole

49. Introduce and explain parody, satire, and hyperbole. Then ask: How are these often seen on "Saturday Night Live"? What skits demonstrate satire or parody? When might a comedian use hyperbole?

> **Parody: a form of literature intended to mock or ridicule for comic effect another type of literature, art work, or event.**
>
> **Satire: used to ridicule or make fun of politics, vices, and beliefs, often with the intent to correct or change the behavior or policy.**
>
> **Hyperbole: an exaggeration; overstating the real truth.**

Purpose: To improve word selection/vocabulary skills

50. Refer to Noah Webster and ask: Should profanity be listed in the dictionary? Who, if anyone, is the appropriate audience for profanity?

51. Why is using formal diction usually better for a composition? Why is nonstandard diction unacceptable?

> **Formal diction shows the writer has approached the topic in an intelligent and organized manner. Formal diction is the language deemed acceptable by educated persons and is the type of diction expected in all formal documents.**

52. Explain clichés' and why story and poetry writers avoid them. Then explain: Why are expressions like *flat as a pancake* and *light as a feather* a sign of a poor writer? Challenge students to locate clichés from famous writers, like Damon Runyon.

> **Clichés are overused phrases or trite statements such as "light as a feather," "crystal clear," "strong as an ox."**

53. Refer to the first department store—Zion's Co-operative Mercantile Institution which opened in Salt Lake City in 1868. Then ask: What kind of language would a store clerk use with a customer? [polite, cheerful, flattery]. What terms or language have clerks used with you?

54. Refer to National Magic Day. What are the differences between allusion and illusion?

> **Allusion = a reference to historical/mythological person or event.**
>
> **Illusion = an unreal, deceptive, or misleading appearance or image**

55. What is the longest word in the dictionary? What is the most technical term? What is the most confusing definition? Refer to Noah Webster.

56. Refer to the tuxedo, which was created by Griswold Lorillan of Tuxedo Park, New York in 1886. What would be the most appropriate writing style in an essay or language in a speech for an audience dressed in tuxedos? What about an audience in heavy metal T-shirts? How should any writer or speaker determine the word choice for an essay or a speech? (by determining the age, background, and interests of his/her reader/audience).

57. What terms would you use to describe a bodybuilder? How would you explain their attitude on stage during a contest? What technical terms can be applied to their training methods?

Purpose: To begin or conclude a poetry unit

58. Consider poets like Coleridge, Keats, and Pound. What are the best methods for interpreting poetry and poetic diction?

> **When analyzing poetry the reader should study the figurative language, the poem's format (its type of verse), content (what actually is being said), and the historical significance of the poet's time period to help determine meaning.**

59. Refer to Samuel Taylor Coleridge's definition of poetry: "I wish our clever young poets would remember my homely definitions of prose and poetry; that is, prose = words in their best order; poetry = the *best* words in the best order." Ask: How effective is this definition? What is your definition of poetry?

Purpose: To begin or conclude a composition unit

60. Refer to "Twilight Zone," and Rod Serling's opening monologue, to introduce parallelism in writing. First, explain parallelism and then ask students to identify how Serling used it.

> **If two or more ideas are expressed in a sentence, they should be expressed in parallel form—that is, single words should be balanced with single words, adjective-noun constructions with another adjective-noun, phrases with phrases, clauses with clauses. A prime example would be Thomas Jefferson's "In matters of principle, stand like a rock; in matters of taste, swim with the current."**
>
> **Serling's examples of parallelism are "as vast as space and as timeless as infinity," "light and shadow, science and superstition," and "between the pit of man's fear and the summit of his knowledge."**

61. How could the following "c" terms relate to writing: collect, classify, construct? Refer to Damon Runyon.

> **Collect = gathering data, brainstorming or clustering ideas, prewriting;**
> **Classify = organizing these details, constructing an outline;**
> **Construct = composing a first draft, writing paragraphs based on the outline.**

Purpose: To improve social skills and cultural awareness

62. Consider Emily Post and her book *Etiquette: The Blue Book of Social Usage.* What prewriting do you think she did before writing this book? What was her research? Why does the public still consider her the expert on social manners? Use **Skill Sheet 10-10** to examine her rules for proper social behavior.

63. What rules or regulations in the school student handbook should be eliminated? Which are rarely enforced? Relate this to the charter of the United Nations and review the importance of following rules in school, especially those related to social behavior.

64. Refer to the Statue of Liberty and ask: What do you think it's like for foreign travelers in the United States? What do you think it would be like to live in another country?

65. Why was America once known as the "Melting Pot"? (People from all different nationalities and cultures intermingled much like different food ingredients in pot). What term is now most commonly used? (the "American quilt," which has been used by Jesse Jackson). Why the change? Refer to the Statue of Liberty which greets all immigrants to America.

66. Refer to China's National Day and ask: What holidays do we celebrate to honor our country? Why do we do this? How do the citizens of other countries honor their nations? Why is this recognition important? How would you explain our Independence Day and/or Memorial Day to a Chinese citizen?

67. Ask students to pretend they're in a foreign country, that no one speaks their language, and someone is following them. Then ask: How would you communicate your need for help?

68. Refer to Charles Gordone, first black playwright to win the Pulitzer Prize for his play *No Place to be Somebody*, and Thurgood Marshall, first Black associate justice on the Supreme Court. What other firsts have been achieved by Black Americans? Use **Form 10-11.**

Purpose: To encourage an appreciation for the arts

69. Refer to Frederick Remington, painter of frontier scenes, especially American Indians, cowboys, and horses. Ask: Who is your favorite artist? Why? What do you like about his/her works?

70. Refer to Luciano Pavarotti, opera singer, and ask: Though most of us cannot understand the words, why does opera remain a popular form of entertainment for millions of people around the world? Who has seen/heard an opera? How do the singers add drama to their performances?

Purpose: To conclude a fiction unit

71. How important have the United Nations and the Statue of Liberty been to American history and progress? Why do we still support these landmarks and institutions? What do they represent for our society? Then relate this to symbols authors use in literature.

Purpose: To begin or conclude a careers unit

72. Refer to Bill Gates. How might he treat his employees? Do you want to be an employer or employee when you start working? What could be the personality of an employer like Bill Gates?

73. Refer to Harvard University and its national reputation. Then ask: What are the best colleges in the United States? Why those institutions? How can a high school student determine the best college to attend? Use this especially for all students who are interested in attending college.

74. Refer to Charles Atlas, bodybuilder; Luciano Pavarotti, opera singer; and Shel Silverstein, cartoonist, and ask: What makes these important careers for a person? Which seems most important/worthwhile? Which seems interesting? Why?

75. Refer to William O. Douglas, former U.S. Supreme Court justice, and ask: What are the qualifications a person needs to be a judge? What kind of schooling is required? How does someone become a Supreme Court justice?

> A Supreme Court justice needs a law degree, but not necessarily judicial experience. Simply, to become a member of the Supreme Court, an individual needs to be a lawyer, appointed by the President, and approved by the Senate.

AUDIO/VISUAL ACTIVITIES

Purpose: To promote critical thinking skills

76. Consider John Lennon and the impact his music (and tragic death) had on people. Ask: What themes emerge from his song lyrics? What were his messages to listeners? How do his lyrics compare to other songs? Play some of his songs to prompt the discussion.

77. Use the comics section of the newspaper for students to study. What is the humor? How are people illustrated in the various cartoons? How do these illustrations compare to those of Shel Silverstein?

> **Shel Silverstein's illustrated books for children, like *The Giving Tree* and *Where the Sidewalk Ends*, are simply drawn and teach simple lessons.**

78. Show selected scenes from the movie *War of the Worlds* starring Gene Barry. Ask: What makes this science fiction? How does it compare to H.G. Wells' novel? Why do many film makers seem to focus on our fear of extra-terrestrials?

79. Play a recording of Don McLean's "American Pie" and then *discuss* its poetic quality, symbolism and meaning.

> **MacLean's classic hit song was inspired by the deaths of Buddy Holly, Martin Luther King, John F. Kennedy, and Robert Kennedy.**

Purpose: To practice writing description

80. Wear a tuxedo or show a picture of a tuxedo. Have students describe it in a paragraph using sensory language.

81. Refer to Henry Ford and show pictures of cars taken from magazine advertisements. Then ask: How are the cars visually presented? How are they described? What are some common expressions used in the advertisements?

82. Refer to the first World Series played between Pittsburgh and Boston and either show pictures (from *Sports Illustrated* or other magazines) or a videotape of a baseball game for students to describe. Have them focus on the field, a player, or the action in a single paragraph. Or assign students to watch the World Series games played this month and have students evaluate and report on the commentary of the broadcasters—their diction, vocabulary, clarity of expression.

83. Refer to Thomas A. Edison demonstrating the electric light bulb for the first time in 1879 and ask students to describe "light" *without* using that word in their explanation. Encourage them to examine the light sources in the room.

84. Play a recording of Luciano Pavarotti, opera singer, and have students list the emotions, images, or movements the music arouses in listeners. Challenge them to use descriptive terms.

85. Distribute travel brochures about Nevada, especially Las Vegas, and have students either write or discuss the adjectives they would use to describe the state and city.

Purpose: *To promote an appreciation and an understanding of other nationalities and cultures*

86. Clip five to eight newspaper and/or magazine articles that deal directly or indirectly with different ethnic or cultural heritages and have students read them. Then ask: What did you learn? How are the lives of the people mentioned in the article different from or similar to yours? What do you find most interesting? Refer to the United Nations.

87. Play recordings associated with various nationalities or cultures (see your school music director or use your local library for tapes or CDs) and challenge students to identify the various selections. Refer to the United Nations.

88. Show selected scenes from the movie "Gandhi" starring Ben Kingsley. Have students either write or discuss the traits and characteristics of this famous Indian leader. Use this to develop students' skills at characterization and improve their knowledge of Gandhi's time period.

89. Refer to the Statue of Liberty, the sculpture constructed by Frederic Bartholdi, on Bedloe's Island in New York's harbor in 1886 and show selected scenes from the movie *Coming to America* starring Eddie Murphy. Use this to initiate a discussion on immigration and to improve students' awareness of the difficulties foreigners might have coming to the United States.

90. Show a picture of the Statue of Liberty and prompt students to interview someone who immigrated to the United States to learn why and how this immigrant accomplished this.

Purpose: *To encourage the reading of biographies*

91. Show selected scenes from the movie *Houdini* starring Tony Curtis. Have students either write or discuss the traits and characteristics of this famous magician/illusionist.

Purpose: *To conclude the reading of* Death of a Salesman

92. Show the movie *Death of a Salesman* starring Dustin Hoffman after reading Arthur Miller's classic modern tragedy.

Purpose: *To identify speech skills*

93. Ask students to view news or interview programs on television involving Jesse Jackson to identify his skills as an effective public speaker.

　　　　　　　　Name _____

The Statue of Liberty

Directions:　　Emma Lazarus of New York is responsible for the poetic lines that appear on the base of the Statue of Liberty, which was dedicated by Frederic Bartholdi as "Liberty Enlightening the World" on Bedloe's Island in New York's harbor in 1886. The final lines state:

"Give me your tired, your poor, your huddled masses yearning to breathe free, the wretched refuse of your teeming shore. Send these, the homeless, tempest-tost to me, I lift my lamp beside the golden door."

Now answer in detail the questions that follow.

1. Why did Lazarus choose to appeal only to the poor instead of the wealthy?

2. How do you think immigrants to our country reacted to these sentences?

3. What Europeans in 1886 might have been "yearning to breathe free"?

4. Paraphrase: "the wretched refuse of your teeming shore"

5. What is the "golden door"?

6. What makes these sentences inspirational?

Skill Sheet 10–2   Name _____

Rod Serling's "Twilight Zone"

Read: The "Twilight Zone" premiered in 1959 on television with the following mono-
             logue by Rod Serling:

             "There is a fifth dimension, beyond that which is known to man. It is a dimen-
             sion as vast as space and as timeless as infinity. It is the middle ground between
             light and shadow, between science and superstition, and it lies between the pit
             of man's fear and the summit of his knowledge. This is the dimension of imag-
             ination. It is an area we call the Twilight Zone."

Explain: How does Serling catch the viewer's attention with this monologue and why
             does he connect imagination with "an area we call the Twilight Zone"?

Name _____

The Words of Mahatma Gandhi

Directions: Analyze each of the following quotes from Mahatma Gandhi. Answer the questions that follow.

1. "They may torture my body, break my bones, even kill me. Then they will have my dead body—not my obedience."

   Who are the "they"?

   What risks is Gandhi willing to take to make his point?

   How is freedom truly achieved, according to Gandhi?

2. "An eye for an eye only ends up making the whole world blind."

   Where does the phrase "an eye for an eye" originate?

   What figurative language is used by Gandhi?

   What is his attitude toward violence as a means to achieve freedom?

Name _____

"Do Not Go Gentle into That Good Night"

by Dylan Thomas

Do not go gentle into that good night.
Rage, rage against the dying of the light.

Questions

1. What emotions does Thomas appeal to in these lines?

2. In what ways does Thomas use words unconventionally?

3. What *image* is used here?

4. What does the "dying of the light" mean to you?

5. How do you interpret these lines overall?

Samuel Taylor Coleridge and John Keats

Coleridge

- 1772–1834

- Grew up in an urban environment, but inspired by nature

- Prized intelligence and a reliance on fixed principles, not emotions

- Used the imagination to reach sublime revelations

- Poet = Artist, Magician, Dreamer

- Poetry emphasized symbolism, the supernatural at times, beauty

- Sought comfort and insight in solitude, daydreaming, nature

- In poetry, all things have beauty, including sea snakes, weeds, and yellow leaves

- Influenced by John Milton and William Wordsworth

- Often critical of his own work—much self-criticism

- Noted for "Rime of the Ancient Mariner" and "Kubla Khan"

Keats

- 1795–1821

- Believed the "highest bliss is writing poems in nature, not just observing nature

- wrote: "I am certain of nothing but the holiness of the heart's affections, and the truth of imagination."

- Saw the imagination as his muse (his inspiration)

- Poet = Explorer, Teacher

- Poetry emphasized contrasts between the goodness and darkness in man's soul and death and immortality

- Sought insight in an urn, a nightingale, the seasons, walking

- Purpose of poetry is to "To soothe the cares, and lift the thoughts of man"

- Influenced by Percy Bysshe Shelley

- Often feared failing to reach his potential as a poet

- Noted for "Ode on a Grecian Urn" and "Ode to a Nightingale"

Name _____

R.L. Stine

Directions: Read the following excerpts from R.L. Stine's books. For each, explain how he introduces suspense/mystery into the narrative.

1. *I Saw You That Night*

   He stood above her on a jutting rock, hands at the waist of his jeans. His navy blue T-shirt fluttered in the wind. He glared down at her with narrowed eyes, his black hair over his forehead. The sunlight caught the small silver ring in his ear, making it glow like a diamond.

   Roxie gasped. Why wasn't he locked up? Why did the police let him go?

2. *Bad Dreams*

   Maggie turned a corner and slammed into a wall. Her hand touched something wet and slimy. And then she heard a dry fluttering overhead, like hundreds of tiny umbrellas opening all at once. Something brushed her face. Something furry. She screamed.

3. *Bad Moonlight*

   She couldn't slow down. The moonlight. Something about the moonlight. A shape loomed in front of her. A wall. Big stones with wrought-iron bars sunk into the top.

4. *Dead End*

   Randee jammed her foot down on the brakes. We started to slide. The lights bounced crazily off the fog. I felt myself thrown hard against Carlo. The car skidded harder.

5. *Dance of Death*

   Terry took Niki's hands and twirled her. All around him everyone was laughing, dancing, shouting, and changing partners. In the eerie light it was hard to see who was dancing with whom.

   It was fun, but it went on and on. Whenever Terry started to slow down, the music went faster. Then suddenly the lights went out. The tape player died down with a sad groan. For a moment there was dead silence. Except for the faint glow from the fireplace the room was in total darkness.

Name _____

Ezra Pound: A Traitor?

Background: American poet Ezra Pound moved in 1924 to Italy which had a Fascist government. In 1941 Pound started to broadcast criticism of the American government by short wave radio from Rome. As a result of his pro-Fascist radio broadcasts from Italy, he was indicted for treason in 1943 and arrested near Genoa by the U.S. Army, becoming the only American poet in history charged with treason.

He was brought to Washington where psychiatrists determined he was mentally incompetent so he never appeared in court. In fact, these doctors concluded his broadcasts may have resulted from his apparent insanity. Also, none of his poetry was believed to reflect anti-American views.

After twelve years of captivity in a mental institution, Pound was released, and he left immediately for Italy. Upon arrival there he declared the United States itself was an "insane asylum."

Analyze: Was Ezra Pound a traitor? Why/why not?

Name _____

A Survey: Fiction vs. Reality

Directions: Answer each of the following in detail.

1. What are the differences between fiction and nonfiction?

2. How can readers tell when the person in the story is a character and not an actual individual?

3. What fictional stories are based on an actual historical event? Give some examples.

4. How could an actual news event become the subject of a fictional story?

5. What are some ways to determine if a story is fiction or nonfiction?

Name _____

What Would You Do If You Were President?

John Quincy Adams (Republican) 1825–1829

Accomplishments: Proposed funding for transportation, a national university, and an observatory.

Rutherford B. Hayes (Republican) 1877–1881

Accomplishments: Initiated legislation to make paper money redeemable in gold; first President to visit the West Coast.

Chester A. Arthur (Republican) 1881–1885

Accomplishments: Supported increased funding for the U.S. Navy, transforming the Navy into a major military force; promoted civil service reform.

Theodore Roosevelt (Republican) 1901–1909

Accomplishments: Established U.S. Forest Service to preserve millions of acres of American forests; the first President to travel abroad (Panama) while in office; first to ride in a car and fly in an airplane; earned the Nobel Peace Prize for ending the Russo-Japanese War.

Dwight D. Eisenhower (Republican) 1953–1961

Accomplishments: Ended Korean War in 1953; enforced school integration in Little Rock, Arkansas with federal troops; established interstate highway system nationwide.

Your name _____ Years in office _____

What would be your accomplishments?

_____

_____

_____

_____

© 2001 by The Center for Applied Research in Education

Name _____

Emily Post: The Etiquette Test

Directions: Answer YES or NO to each of the following questions and compare your knowledge of etiquette to the social manners of Emily Post.

1. Does the "ladies first" rule still apply for teenagers?

    A. YES   B. NO

2. Are men still expected to give up their seats for women?

    A. YES   B. NO

3. Is it rude to point out to others when they do not share in doing work (ex) when decorating for a dance?

    A. YES   B. NO

4. Is it permissible to arrive early for a social event?

    A. YES   B. NO

5. Should a teen introduce his or her parents by their first names to another teenager?

    A. YES   B. NO

6. Can personal letters from one teen to another be typed?

    A. YES   B. NO

7. It is rude to inform someone when he or she has offensive body odor?

    A. YES   B. NO

8. Reservations at a restaurant should always be made in the man's name.

    A. YES   B. NO

9. Complaints about a meal at the restaurant should be made first to the waiter.

    A. YES   B. NO

10. When a friend moves away you should bring gifts to his/her farewell party.

    A. YES   B. NO

Name _____

Contributions/Firsts of African Americans

Granville T. Woods (1856–1910)   inventor of the railway telegraph system

Madam C.J. Walker (1867–1919)   first African-American millionaire (hair products, cosmetics)

George Washington Carver (1860–1943)   introduced crop rotation and the many uses of the peanut

Frederick Jones (1892–1961)   invented a refrigeration system for trucks, ships, and railways

Benjamin Banneker (1731–1806)   wrote the first scientific book by an African American

Charles Richard Drew (1904–1950)   set up the first blood bank

Shirley Chisholm (1924–)   first African-American woman to be elected to House of Representatives

Daniel Williams (1856–1931)   performed the first heart operation

Arthur Ashe (1943–1993)   first African-American named to the U.S. Davis Cup team (tennis)

William Harvey Carney (1840–1908)   first African-American to win the Medal of Honor

Mae C. Jamison (1956–)   first African-American woman to be an astronaut

Jack Johnson (1878–1946)   first African-American to become world heavyweight boxing champion

Alice Walker (1944–)   first African-American woman to win the Pulitzer Prize (for her novel *The Color Purple*)

Ralph Bunche (1904–1971)   first African-American to win the Nobel Peace Prize

Matthew Henson (1866–1955)   first person to reach the North Pole (in 1909)

W.E.B. Du Bois (1868–1963)   first African-American to graduate from Harvard with a Ph.D.

Crispus Attucks (1723–1770)   first African-American to die in the war for American independence

OCTOBER
Answer Key

#1 SKILL SHEET 10-1—THE STATUE OF LIBERTY

1. Possibly Lazarus appealed to the poor only because America was seen as a land of opportunity for those who had experienced poverty in other countries. She was sensitive to the needs of the oppressed.

2. Immigrants undoubtedly were inspired and eager to enter the United States. The Statue of Liberty was a symbol of welcome.

3. In many countries, some citizens were persecuted for their religious or political beliefs, especially in countries ruled by corrupt dictators. They also may have been seeking freedom from poverty or overcrowding.

4. "Wretched refuse" can refer to the poor, uneducated, and desperate people from other countries across the Atlantic ("the teeming shore").

5. Typically, the "golden door" can refer to America as the land of opportunity and prosperity.

6. Answers will vary.

#2 SKILL SHEET 10-2—ROD SERLING'S "TWILIGHT ZONE"

Most people are familiar with the first four dimensions—height, width, length, and time—so Serling's reference to the fifth dimension (imagination) certainly catches our attention. His terms to describe this dimension are also interesting and creative, like the reference to the Twilight Zone, which combines the mystery of darkness with an allusion to science.

#3 SKILL SHEET 10-3—THE WORDS OF MAHATMA GANDHI

1. The "they" more than likely refers to the British authorities who still controlled India as part of their colonial empire.

   Gandhi was willing to risk to make his point verbal and physical abuse, a hunger strike, even death.

   Freedom is truly achieved, according to Gandhi, by not submitting to any authority that suppresses individual rights and freedom.

2. The phrase "an eye for an eye" originates from the Bible.

   The figurative language used by Gandhi is personification—as if the world, like a human being, could become blind.

   He rejects violence as a means to achieve freedom; it does not bring an effective resolution to any matter.

#4 SKILL SHEET 10-4—"DO NOT GO GENTLE INTO THAT GOOD NIGHT" BY DYLAN THOMAS

1. anger, rage, frustration

2. gentle, instead of gently, the appropriate adverb

3. darkness, dusk, evening time

4. Answers will vary, but many students might point to death, growing older, the end of the day

5. Answers will vary.

#20 SKILL SHEET 10-8—A SURVEY: FICTION VS. REALITY

1. Fiction claims no reliance on fact or real events; it is imaginative writing; while nonfiction is presented as accurate and based on reality.

2. Typically, readers can tell a character is not an actual person when there is no official record of this person having lived or whose description and behavior seems too unrealistic.

3. Some fictional stories based on actual historical events include *Johnny Tremain, Gone With the Wind, All Quiet on the Western Front, The Grapes of Wrath*, etc.

4. Many news events have been fictionalized; consider Tom Clancy's *The Hunt for Red October, Primary Colors* by Joe Klein, or *In Cold Blood* by Truman Capote.

5. To determine if a story is fiction or nonfiction, simply check the details with other sources. Most often, authors simply identify it on the cover (novel).

#62 SKILL SHEET 10-10—EMILY POST: THE ETIQUETTE TEST

1. Males and females should walk side by side. However, males can proceed in front of females when exiting a car, stepping down a steep slope or stairway, or stepping onto a boat.

2. No, unless the woman is disabled, pregnant, or elderly.

3. Yes, because it would serve no purpose. You will seem to be whining. Just don't work with those people in the future.

4. No, arrive on time or no more than fifteen minutes late.

5. Only if that is how the person to whom they are being introduced are to address them: "Joe, this is my father, John Jones (or Mr. Jones)."

6. Yes.

7. No, just do so kindly, discreetly, and tactfully.

8. No.

9. Yes, but quietly so other diners aren't disturbed, then to the headwaiter or manager.

10. Yes, and it is wise to coordinate yourself with the other guests.

© 2001 by The Center for Applied Research in Education

62

NOVEMBER

INTRODUCTORY PAGE

LEARNING ACTIVITIES

REPRODUCIBLES

QUICK LOCATOR FOR NOVEMBER LEARNING ACTIVITIES

Speech/Oral Presentations   *25, 53, 55, 56, 57, 89, 98, 99, 100, 101*

Composition Skills

Research *13, 14, 22, 27, 28, 29, 39, 52* • Prewriting *76* • Organization *32, 33, 37, 38, 39, 75, 77, 78, 79, 105* • Description *41, 42, 43, 44, 93, 94* • Reflection *48, 49* • Comparison/Contrast *26, 27, 40, 101* • Persuasion *53, 54, 58, 102, 103* • Narratives *50, 51, 52* • Dialogue *5, 45* • Character Sketch *6, 34, 35, 36, 96, 97*

News Unit   *46, 47, 86, 87, 88*

Careers Unit   *17, 21, 90*

Media Unit   *18, 19, 54, 69, 73, 86, 87, 88, 101*

Fine Arts   *91, 95*

Social Skills/Understanding Ethnic Diversity   *21, 29, 45, 51, 80, 81, 82*

NOVEMBER

Origin: November takes its name from the Latin word *novem*, which means nine. In the original Roman calendar November was the ninth month, and later, when the Romans revised their calendar, November became the eleventh month. At first, the Roman Senate offered to name the eleventh month after Tiberius Caesar, much like July was named for Julius Caesar, but he modestly refused the honor.

Holidays: Election Day in the United States is in November as are Veteran's Day and Thanksgiving.

Italy celebrates Victory Day for its victories in WW I, and Russia and the Ukraine commemorate the Great Socialist Revolution of 1917 with a national holiday this month.

Albania, Angola, Barbados, Cambodia, Latvia, Lebanon, Panama, and Poland all celebrate their Independence Days.

Gemstone: Topaz

Flower: Chrysanthemum

Poetry: November's sky is chill and drear,
November's leaf is red and sear.

   by Sir Walter Scott

The wild November comes at last
Beneath a veil of rain;
The night wind blows its folds aside,
Her face is full of pain.

   by Richard Henry Stoddard

BIRTHDAYS

Nov. 1   Stephen Crane, author of *Red Badge of Courage* (1871) [#5, 8, 13, 27, 64, 92]

Nov. 2   Warren G. Harding, 29th President (1865) [#23, 56, 72, 88]; James Polk, 11th President (1795) [#23, 56, 72]

Nov. 4   Will Rogers, writer/humorist/actor (1879) [#1, 55, 68, 74]

Nov. 7   Albert Camus, winner 1957 Nobel Prize for Literature (1913) [#3, 13, 63]; Marie Curie, winner Nobel Prize for Physics for discovery of radium (1867) [#22]; Billy Graham, evangelist (1918) [#55, 98, 101]

Nov. 8   Christian Barnard, South African surgeon who performed in 1967 the first known heart transplant (1922) [#20]; Margaret Mitchell, winner of 1937 Pulitzer Prize for her only book *Gone with the Wind* [#13, 62]

Nov. 11   Fyodor Mikhailovich Dostoyevsky, Russian novelist of *The Brothers Karamazov* and *Crime and Punishment* and political revolutionary who served a sentence in a Siberian prison (1821) [#4, 13, 63]; George S. Patton, U.S. Army General during WW II (1885) [#74, 99]; Kurt Vonnegut, Jr., novelist (1922) [#12, 13, 63, 68]

Nov. 13   Robert Louis Stevenson, Scottish author of *Kidnapped* and *Treasure Island* (1850) [#13, 61, 63]

Nov. 18   Margaret Atwood, author (1939) [#13, 28]

Nov. 19   Roy Campanella, one of the first black major league ballplayers and star for the Brooklyn Dodgers who was the National League's Most Valuable Player in 1951, 1953, and 1955 and later an inspirational spokesperson for the handicapped (1921) [#26, 49, 57, 85]; James Garfield, 20th President and first left-handed President (1831) [#23, 56, 72]; Ted Turner, billionaire owner of radio, film, and television companies (1938) [#17, 82]

Nov. 21   George Ken Griffey, Jr., major league baseball player (1969) [#45, 85]

Nov. 22   George Eliot (Mary Ann Evans), English author of *Silas Marner* (1819) [#13, 70, 71]

Nov. 23   Boris Karloff (William Henry Pratt), actor known for his role in the movies *Frankenstein* and *The Mummy* (1887) [#96]

Nov. 24   Zachary Taylor, 12th President, who died in office (1784) [#23, 56, 72]

Nov. 25 Andrew Carnegie, financier/philanthropist (1835) [#17, 82]; Joe DiMaggio, Major League Hall of Famer and husband to Marilyn Monroe (1914) [#26, 85]

Nov. 26 Charles Schulz, cartoonist of "Peanuts" (1922) [#33]; Mary Walker, first female surgeon and only female to receive the Medal of Honor after the Civil War (1832) [#52, 84]

Nov. 28 William Blake, English artist/poet/philosopher—"Songs of Innocence" (1757) [#7]

Nov. 29 Louisa May Alcott, author of *Little Women* (1832) [#13, 28, 63]; Madeline L'Engle, author of *A Wrinkle in Time* (1918) [#13, 28, 62]

Nov. 30 Winston Churchill, British Prime Minister during WW II and first man to be made an honorary citizen of the U.S. (1874) [#53, 55]; Samuel Langhorne Clemens (Mark Twain), author/essayist/lecturer (1835) [#2, 6, 9, 13, 14, 27, 34, 55, 68, 97]; Jonathan Swift, clergyman/author/satirist—*Gulliver's Travels* (1667) [#13, 58, 68]

MEMORABLE EVENTS

Nov. 1   National Authors' Day—established by the U.S. Dept. of Commerce with this resolution: "By celebrating an Author's Day as a nation, we would not only show patriotism, loyalty, and appreciation of the men and women who have made American literature possible, but would also encourage and inspire others to give of themselves in making a better America" [#11, 35, 59, 61, 66, 75, 76, 77].

Nov. 2   North Dakota was admitted to the Union as the 39th state, and South Dakota was admitted as the 40th state in 1889 [#39].

The first television service began in 1936 by the British Broadcasting Corporation [#19, 54, 73, 86].

Nov. 3   Sandwich Day—to honor John Montague's birthday in 1718. Montague, a notorious gambler and inventor of the sandwich, is said to have invented the sandwich to eat during a 24-hour gambling session in 1762. The Sandwich Islands were named for him by Captain James Cook in 1778 [#43].

Nov. 4   King Tut's tomb was discovered in Luxor, Egypt in 1922 by English archaeologist Howard Carter. Some of the most important archaeological discoveries of all time were unearthed from the tomb of the child king/pharaoh Tutankhamen who died at 19 nearly 3000 years ago [#51, 105].

National Children's Goal-Setting Day—to encourage parents to prompt their children to set goals [#90].

Nov. 6   First intercollegiate football game was played in 1869 between Rutgers and Princeton [#46].

Nov. 7   The first black governor, Douglas Wilder, was elected governor of Virginia in 1989 [#72, 100].

The elephant was used in 1874 by Thomas Nast for the first time to represent the Republican Party in a satirical cartoon for *Harper's Weekly* magazine [#40]. (Later, he characterized Democrats with a donkey.)

Jeannette Rankin of Montana became the first female member of Congress in 1916 [#48, 72, 100].

Nov. 8   Montana was admitted into the Union as the 41st state in 1889 [#39, 103].

X-rays were discovered by physicist Wilhelm Conrad Roentgen in 1895 at the University of Wurzburg in Germany [#22, 83].

Edward Brooke of Massachusetts became the first black American Senator in 1966 [#72, 100].

Nov. 10   "Sesame Street" premiered in 1969. Through singing, puppetry, film clips, and skits children are taught letters, numbers, and concepts by the puppets Ernie, Bert, Grover, Kermit the frog, Cookie Monster, Big Bird, and Mr. Snufleapagus [#19, 74].

Explorer Henry M. Stanley found Missionary David Livingstone in 1871 at Ujiji, Africa, declaring the memorable "Dr. Livingstone, I presume." [#50].

Freighter *Edmund Fitzgerald* sank on Lake Superior in 1975 in a heavy storm killing 29 crew members [#47].

Nov. 11   Washington was admitted to the Union as the 42nd state in 1889 [#39, 103].

National Young Readers' Day—to remind Americans of the joys and importance of reading for young people [#11, 59, 60, 61, 66, 67].

"God Bless America" by Irving Berlin was performed for the first time in 1938. The lyrics, especially written for Kate Smith, became the patriotic favorite of the nation [#31, 91].

Nov. 16   Oklahoma was admitted to the Union as the 46th state in 1907 [#94, 95].

Nov. 18   Charles Dowd, a Connecticut teacher, proposed the Uniform Time Zone Plan in 1883 to establish four time zones of 15 degrees [#21].

Mickey Mouse appeared for the first time in 1928 on the screen of the Colony Theater in New York City in Walt Disney's cartoon "Steamboat Willie" [#16, 36, 102].

Nov. 19   President Lincoln delivered the Gettysburg Address in less than two minutes in 1863 [#10, 25, 89].

Nov. 21   Gerard d' Aboville arrived in Ilwaco, Washington after rowing from Choshi, Japan across the Pacific to complete a four month solo journey in 1991 [#38].

Jean Pilatra de Rozier and Marquis Laurent d' Arlandes became the first men to fly when they ascended three hundred feet in a hot air balloon and traveled 6 miles in 25 minutes over Paris in 1783 [#41].

World Hello Day—to encourage people to greet others and advance peace through personal communication [#81].

Nov. 22   President John F. Kennedy was assassinated at 12:30 P.M. in Dallas, Texas while riding in a motorcade in 1963 [#23, 87].

Nov. 26   *Casablanca* premiered in 1942 in New York City [#69, 104].

Thanksgiving was proclaimed the first U.S. holiday in 1789 by President George Washington after both houses of Congress requested a day of public thanksgiving [#37, 44, 93].

"The Price is Right" premiered in 1956 and continues as America's longest running daily game show [#18, 19, 103].

LEARNING ACTIVITIES FOR NOVEMBER

READING ACTIVITIES

Purpose: To improve critical thinking skills

1. Have students read the humorous quotes from Will Rogers and then ask: What are his views about politicians? Society? Why do we classify these quotes as witty? Which is your favorite? Why? Use **Form 11-1.**

2. Have students read the quotes from Mark Twain to study his views on reading, writing, and living. Use **Form 11-2.**

Purpose: To study characterization in fiction

3. Have students read the excerpt from Albert Camus' novel *The Stranger*. Use **Skill Sheet 11-3** to study Camus' writing style, type of characterization, and narrative effect.

4. Distribute **Skill Sheet 11-4** and have students read the excerpt from Fyodor Mikhailovich Dostoyevsky's novel *The Idiot* to study his writing style, type of characterization, and narrative effect.

5. Have students read the dialogue taken from Stephen Crane's *Red Badge of Courage* to study dialect and characterization. Use **Skill Sheet 11-5.**

> **Stephen Crane had no first-hand experience of war so he based his novel** *Red Badge of Courage* **on history books and the writing of Leo Tolstoy. Crane was a naturalist and his work, especially** *Red Badge of Courage*, **reflected the stark and chaotic atmosphere of war.**

6. Ask students to locate and describe in a paragraph any character from a story or novel by Mark Twain.

> **Mark Twain was the originator of the American "tall tale." He combined much rough humor, exaggeration, and common language in his work as he created some of the most famous fictional characters of American literature—Pudd'nhead Wilson, Tom Sawyer, and Huckleberry Finn.**

Purpose: To improve analysis of poetry

7. Have students read any poems by William Blake that may appear in their literature text or an available anthology. Ask: What topics does he favor? What kind of imagery is evident? Where has he used figurative language? What are some themes?

> William Blake's poems typically dealt with his direct observations of the human condition, especially the contrasts between innocence and experience. He condemned 18th century political and social tyranny as he developed a new mythological vision of life in a fresh lyric style.

8. Have students read any poems by Stephen Crane that appear in their literature text or another available anthology. Ask: What is the *tone* of the poem? Where does Crane use colloquial or conversational language? What are his themes?

> Stephen Crane wrote experimental free verse that often expressed a pessimistic viewpoint, especially about man's fate. Irony, paradoxes, and stark images are commonly found in his verse, which has very simple language.

Purpose: To identify various writing styles

9. Have students study the three responses to Mark Twain's novel *The Adventures of Huckleberry Finn* in **Skill Sheet 11-6**.

10. Distribute **Skill Sheet 11-7A** and **Skill Sheet 11-7B**—Abraham Lincoln's "Gettysburg Address" and his letter to the mother of five soldiers who died in the Civil War. Have students analyze each for the clarity in expression, the economy in word choice, and his emotional appeal to each audience.

Purpose: To promote independent reading of novels

11. Refer to National Young Readers' Day, National Authors' Day, and any interesting narratives or novels students have read to celebrate these days. Then ask: What are the benefits of daily reading? What is the next novel you plan to read? Why that one?

12. Assign students to read a book by Kurt Vonnegut and then use **Form 11-8**—the Novel Study Project form—to evaluate the book.

Purpose: To practice research skills

13. Have students locate and read encyclopedia articles about one or several authors who have birthdays this month. Then students could report on what they find most interesting about those authors.

14. Have students locate stories by Mark Twain that appear in their literature text or another available anthology and also read encyclopedia articles about his life. Ask: What settings, character types, and events seem related?

DEBATING ACTIVITIES

Purpose: To promote critical thinking

15. What is the most important problem facing today's schools? How did these problems originate? What are some solutions?

16. Refer to Mickey Mouse and ask: Who is the most interesting cartoon character today? Which one is the most influential on young children? Are there any benefits to watching cartoons? If so, what are they?

17. Explain that Ted Turner is one of the wealthiest men in America and ask: Is it possible for any one person to become *too* wealthy or have a job that pays too much money? Does Turner's wealth suggest he is greedy? Why/why not? Also refer to Andrew Carnegie.

18. Consider the popular television show "The Price is Right." Do the contestants demonstrate more greed or insight? Why is the public so fascinated with game shows in general? What is the best game show on television? Why?

19. Refer to the first television broadcast by the BBC in 1936 and ask: How valuable is television? What if television had never been invented? Would people read more, learn more, be more creative? What about "Sesame Street" and "The Price is Right"?

20. Refer to Christian Barnard and the transplanting of one person's organs into another person. If parents have a child who needs an organ, should they have another child just to create a donor and a safe match? Why/why not?

21. Is punctuality truly important? How does anyone learn punctuality? Do we need to be punctual all the time—at school, at home, at our jobs? Refer to Charles Dowd, the teacher who created the Uniform Time Zone Plan, and to positive social skills.

22. Which scientific discovery was more beneficial to humanity—the X-ray, which was discovered by physicist Wilhelm Conrad Roentgen in 1895, or Marie Curie's discovery of radium which won her the Nobel Prize for Physics? Use this also to practice research skills.

23. Consider Presidents James Polk, #11; Zachary Taylor, #12; James Garfield, #20; Warren G. Harding, #29; and John F. Kennedy, #35. Examine their records (Use **Form 11-9**) and debate who accomplished the most as President. Also refer to November as a typical election month.

24. Who is the best candidate for (choose any elected position or political office) on the current ballot? Also explain the background of the term *candidate*.

> In ancient Rome a man who wished to gain public office wore a white robe or toga while canvassing for votes so he would be more easily identified. Since the Latin word for white is *candidus*, the would-be official was called *candidatus*, or "one clothed in white." Now we use the term candidate.

Purpose: *To review speech skills*

25. How important is humor in a speech? It is absent entirely from Abraham Lincoln's "Gettysburg Address." How much should speakers use humor? Why?

Purpose: *To practice comparison/contrast*

26. Compare Roy Campanella and Joe DiMaggio. Who was the better professional baseball player? Distribute **Form 11-10** and have students write a paragraph explaining their choice.

27. Who contributed more to American literature: Stephen Crane or Mark Twain? Students could read excerpts from their literature or research the backgrounds of these two important authors.

28. Which of the following writers has the most interesting writing style? Louisa May Alcott, author of *Little Women*; Margaret Atwood; or Madeline L'Engle, author of *A Wrinkle in Time*? Students could read excerpts from their books or research the backgrounds of these important authors.

29. Which country—Albania, Angola, Barbados, Cambodia, Latvia, Lebanon, Panama, or Poland—would you want to visit? Why? What do you know about the people who live there? Students could research the backgrounds of these countries or interview persons who either visited or lived there.

Purpose: *To introduce a grammar lesson*

30. Consider: Is it fair that the majority determines what is and is not standard English in our society? And if not, who should determine standard English today?

Purpose: *To begin a poetry unit*

31. Refer to Irving Berlin and ask: Should song lyrics be considered poetry? Why or why not?

WRITING ACTIVITIES

Purpose: To begin a composition unit

32. Consider the many famous writers whose birthdays are this month. Have students list five or six goals they have for themselves as writers (for example, improve my word choice).

33. Refer to Charles Schulz's dramatic success with his cartoon "Peanuts" and direct students to list criteria for judging/evaluating a cartoon. Then relate this to the rubrics used to evaluate writing.

Purpose: To practice writing characterizations

34. Refer to Twain and have students write a one-page description of the most unusual or interesting character they've ever read (for example, Huckleberry Finn).

35. Consider the famous writers whose birthdays are this month, and National Authors Day. Have students write a one-page essay describing a person they know who is very creative.

36. Refer to Mickey Mouse and have students write a one-page character sketch about their favorite cartoon character.

Purpose: To improve skills at organizing writing

37. Consider Thanksgiving and the ingredients of favorite dishes such as stuffing, apple pie, and pumpkin pie. Prompt students to describe themselves as if they were a recipe. For example: I am half cup of politeness, twenty-nine pounds of muscle, ten tons of courage, a teaspoon of quickness, etc.

38. Have each student write a different log entry by Gerard d' Aboville who rowed across the Pacific Ocean from Choshi, Japan to Ilwaco, Washington to complete a four-month solo journey in 1991. Then collate the finished copies into a single manuscript.

39. Either by personal experience or through the use of any resource, students can write travelogues about Montana, North Dakota, South Dakota, and/or Washington. Be sure they focus on terrain, cities, and bodies of water of the northwestern states. Use **Form 11-11** as a model.

Purpose: To practice comparison/contrast

40. Have students compose a one-page essay comparing and contrasting the Democrat's donkey with the Republican's elephant as political symbols.

Purpose: To practice writing description

41. Have students write a brief descriptive essay using sensory language to describe the observations of Jean Pilatra de Rozier and Marquis Laurent d' Arlandes as they flew in a hot air balloon 6 miles and 25 minutes over Paris in 1783.

42. Have students list sensory language related to the month of November. Ask: What does November smell like? Taste like? Its sights? Sounds? Challenge their creativity.

43. Ask: What is your favorite sandwich? Refer to Sandwich Day and John Montague, who is said to have invented the sandwich to eat during a 24-hour gambling session in 1762. The Sandwich Islands were named for him by Captain James Cook in 1778. Have students describe the sight, smell, taste, and feel of their favorite sandwich in a single paragraph.

44. Consider typical Thanksgiving meals. Have students compare and contrast the tastes of ham and turkey, peas and carrots, cherry pie and apple pie. Introduce terms like *bland*, *sapid*, *palatable*, *soporific*, *sweet*, *minty*, *spicy*, and *refreshing*.

Purpose: To practice writing dialogue

45. Ask: What kind of a relationship do you think major league baseball player Ken Griffey, Jr. has with his father, who is his coach on the Cincinnati Reds? How do you think his father contributed to his development as a professional baseball player? Then have students write one to two pages of dialogue between Ken Griffey, Jr. and his father that could have taken place when he was a child, a teenager, or now as a major leaguer.

Purpose: To teach news writing style

46. Have students construct a news lead about the first inter-collegiate football game played in 1869 between Rutgers and Princeton. Permit them to decide the winner, the score, names of players, etc. Students should include the five W's.

> **Traditional news articles are organized based on Who (Who is involved?); What (What happened to make this a newsworthy event?); Where (Where did this event happen?); When (When did this news event happen?); and Why (Why did this happen?).**

47. Have students construct a news lead about the sinking of the freighter *Edmund Fitzgerald* which went down in Lake Superior in 1975 during a heavy storm.

> **Example: Twenty-nine crew members died when the freighter *Edmund Fitzgerald* sank into Lake Superior during a heavy storm yesterday.**

Purpose: To practice reflective writing

48. Have students write the diary entry of Jeannette Rankin of Montana who became the first female member of Congress in 1916. Use this to focus on the insights and feelings of the first woman congressperson in Washington, DC.

49. Have students write Roy Campanella's diary entry after his first game as a Brooklyn Dodger in 1946.

Purpose: To practice writing narratives

50. Have students create a narrative describing the actions and reactions of explorer Henry M. Stanley and Missionary David Livingstone after Stanley finally found him in 1871 at Ujiji, Africa, after a two year search. Have students begin their narratives with Stanley's famous declaration "Dr. Livingstone, I presume."

51. Prompt students to pretend to be English archaeologist Howard Carter and, using sensory language, they should write a description of the discovery of King Tut's tomb in Luxor, Egypt in 1922, where the greatest archaeological discoveries of all time were unearthed from the tomb. Have them begin the narrative: *When we opened the tomb . . .*

52. Refer to Mary Walker, the only female during the Civil War to receive the Medal of Honor, which is given to those who have risked their lives above and beyond the call of duty and is our nation's highest military award. Instruct students to create a brief narrative that is historically accurate about Mary Walker and her heroic acts.

Purpose: To review persuasive writing

53. Refer to Winston Churchill and his effective leadership of England during WW II. Much of his effectiveness was due to his ability to speak persuasively and eloquently to English citizens. Study an example of his effective style. Use **Skill Sheet 11-12.**

54. Have students write a one-page editorial on the influence of television (Use **Skill Sheet 11-13**). Other options include having students write a letter to parents, lawmakers, or television executives.

Purpose: To introduce speech skills

55. Refer to noted speakers Will Rogers, Billy Graham, Winston Churchill, and Mark Twain and have students complete a survey on speech-making. Use **Skill Sheet 11-14.**

56. Have students write the acceptance speech of a politician who has just been voted into office. Refer to the Presidents who have birthdays this month and the inauguration speech they must make in January after the election. Then if possible, show a videotape of actual acceptance speeches by candidates who have just been elected.

57. Refer to Roy Campanella, who went from playing in the major leagues to being handicapped, and direct students to write his speech to today's rookie professional ballplayers.

Purpose: To introduce the term satire

58. Jonathan Swift wrote "A Modest Proposal" to satirize the English government's failure to address the problems of poverty and overcrowding in Ireland. Have students write their own "modest proposals" that satirize or criticize a current social dilemma such as homelessness.

DISCUSSION ACTIVITIES

Purpose: To encourage independent reading

59. Who is your favorite author? Why? What is your criteria for a great book? How do you think your criteria differs from a student from 1930–40? How do you think it will differ from a student in the future? Use this to introduce the reading of any book and refer to National Authors' Day and National Young Readers' Day.

60. Refer to National Young Readers' Day and ask: What was the first book you read? Why that book? How do you select the books you read now? What makes reading a beneficial and enjoyable activity?

61. What questions would you ask any of the authors who have birthdays this month? Refer to National Authors' Day and National Young Readers' Day.

62. Refer to Margaret Mitchell who wrote only one book in her life: *Gone with the Wind*. Her novel was based on the stories she heard about the Civil War from family and friends while she was growing up in Georgia. *Gone with the Wind* won the Pulitzer Prize and made her very wealthy. Why were those family stories so compelling? What are some interesting stories you have heard from older family members? What parts could you fictionalize?

Purpose: To begin or conclude a fiction unit

63. Distribute **Form 11-15** and ask students to explain how each of these novel titles suggests a book of suspense or mystery. Also ask: What makes these titles interesting and engaging? What are some creative titles for fiction you can offer?

64. Refer to Stephen Crane's *Red Badge of Courage* and the main character, a young soldier in the Civil War named Henry Fleming. The main conflict of the story is Protagonist vs. Self. What kind of an inner conflict might a soldier have? (In the novel, Henry Fleming struggles with his fear of being a coward in battle. In fact, he does run away during a battle but later returns to fight.)

65. Refer to the *Protagonist*, the main character in fiction; the character who occupies the majority of the story and whose struggle is the most important element of the conflict and plot. Examples include Huckleberry Finn, Robinson Crusoe, and Silas Marner. Will all protagonists be heroic figures? Who are some examples of protagonists you've read so far?

    Refer to *Foils*, the minor characters opposite the main characters who do not serve as obstacles but who do influence the plot. Tom Sawyer is a foil in *The Adventures of Huckleberry Finn*, Huckleberry Finn in *The Adventures of Tom Sawyer*. Who are some foils or minor characters from other works of fiction?

66. Refer to National Authors Day and National Young Readers' Day and ask: How do these "e" terms relate to our reading of literature: explain, expand, expound?

> A reader asked to *explain* literature often summarizes its content. A reader asked to *expand* on literature typically seeks a greater depth of understanding—themes, tone, and style. A reader asked to *expound* on literature usually interprets it or makes a point-by-point argument about an interpretation of the content.

67. How do the following "c" terms relate to our understanding of fiction: comprehend, contemplate, construe? Refer to National Young Readers' Day.

> If we *comprehend* literature we can apply the appropriate literary terms to our understanding of the content; if we *contemplate* literature, typically we seek the positive and negative points about the work and its effect on us; and if we *construe* we seek to interpret or make an inference about the literature—its deeper meaning.

Purpose: To review satire in literature

68. Consider Jonathan Swift, Mark Twain, Will Rogers, Kurt Vonnegut, and other satirists who ridicule or make fun of current politics, people's vices, and society's standards, often with the intent to correct or change the behavior or policy. How effective is satire as a literary device? What makes it entertaining to read?

Purpose: To improve critical thinking skills

69. Consider the critical success and popularity enjoyed even to this day of the movie *Casablanca*. What are your favorite movies? What makes them interesting or enjoyable to view? How important are the screenwriters to the success of a movie?

70. Consider Mary Ann Evans who used the name George Eliot as the author of her books. Why did she do this? Use this to introduce the lack of respect some women writers received in the 19th century. Also ask: If you could change your name, what would it be? Why that name?

71. What are your reactions to the George Eliot's quote: "You may try, but you cannot imagine what it is to have a man's force of genius in you, but to suffer the slavery of being a girl"?

72. Refer to the various Presidents who have birthdays this month, Edward Brooke, Jeannette Rankin, Douglas Wilder, the school's class officers and ask: For any upcoming election what is expected of candidates? How should students decide on the best candidate? What are the important qualifications a voter should consider?

73. Refer to television, which was first broadcast by the BBC in 1936 and ask: How has television influenced you? What would you say to television executives about the kind of programming that would benefit young people? Why?

74. What would class be like if any one of the following was the teacher: Will Rogers, George Patton, or Big Bird?

Purpose: To introduce a composition unit

75. Refer to National Authors' Day. Why are we often compelled to write? How can working at writing benefit us? What motivates writers to become published?

76. Consider National Authors' Day and the famous writers whose birthdays are this month and ask: When did you first have a real personal urge to write? When was the first time it was truly important to you to be a writer? What are your feelings now about writing? Why?

77. Refer to National Authors' Day. Do professional writers write multiple drafts? Why write first drafts? What are the benefits of doing multiple drafts of our writing?

> **Professional writers certainly do write multiple drafts because they generally lead to more polished work. This is a key part of the editing stage of the writing process.**

78. Why is capitalization necessary in our writing? What are some rules of capitalization? What makes them necessary?

79. Why is punctuation necessary in our writing? What are some punctuation rules? How can punctuation influence meaning? Use **Skill Sheet 11-16.**

Purpose: To promote an awareness and appreciation of cultures and nationalities

80. How do you think citizens in Albania, Angola, Barbados, Cambodia, Latvia, Lebanon, Panama, and Poland celebrate their Independence Day festivals?

81. Refer to World Hello Day and ask: How important is a greeting when two people meet? How many different ways can a person say hello? What are some ways of greeting in other cultures or languages?

Purpose: To promote community service

82. Explain how Andrew Carnegie and Ted Turner gained great wealth and how they contributed to charity. Then ask: Why do people donate to charities? Why is this important? How much should people contribute?

Andrew Carnegie started work in a cotton mill in 1848 at $1.20 a week. By 1899 he had formed the Carnegie Steel Company, which he eventually sold to the U.S. Steel Corp. for $250 million. Through his life he donated $350 million to educational, cultural, and peace organizations. Carnegie was the personal benefactor to nearly 2800 libraries. He said: "The man who dies rich . . . dies disgraced."

Ted Turner developed a multibillion dollar media company which included television, film, and radio. He sold the parent company TBS for $7.6 billion and then pledged one billion dollars to the United Nations.

© 2001 by The Center for Applied Research in Education

Purpose: To improve skills at word selection/vocabulary

83. How would you explain X-rays, which were discovered by physicist Wilhelm Conrad Roentgen in 1895, to someone who knew nothing about them?

84. Refer to Mary Walker, who won the Medal of Honor which is given to those who have risked their lives above and beyond the call of duty, and instruct students to devise their own award along with a definition.

85. Review jargon and refer to Ken Griffey Jr., Roy Campanella and Joe DiMaggio. Then ask: What are the terms associated with baseball that are personal (jargon) to that sport?

Jargon: speech or writing that is full of unfamiliar or technical terms which are incomprehensible to most persons and expected to impress more than inform.

Examples: ameliorate (improve), peruse (read), epistaxis (nosebleed)

Typical terms for baseball: homerun, bunt, ERA, RBI, no-hitter, slider, fastball, change up, forkball, knuckleball, shortstop, outfielder, squeeze-play, double play, inning, strike, pitcher, on deck, etc.

Purpose: To analyze the news media

86. Refer to the BBC and the first television broadcast. Poll students: Who thinks broadcasters—whether from radio or television stations—should never express opinions during a broadcast? Why?/why not? How should we evaluate news broadcasters' opinions?

87. Refer to the assassination of John F. Kennedy or any of the current front page headlines and ask: Why do news broadcasts and newspapers focus so much on tragedies? What are the current news items that reflect tragedy? Why are positive news stories rarely offered?

88. Explain that President Warren G. Harding was first the publisher of the *Marion Star*, a regional newspaper, then ask: How could his training and work in the newspaper business influence his work in politics? How closely connected are the two professions? Other examples of journalist/politicians?

Purpose: To improve speech skills

89. Refer to Lincoln and his "Gettysburg Address." What would you do to make sure your audience remembered the key points of your speech?

Purpose: To begin a careers unit

90. Refer to National Children's Goal-Setting Day and ask: Is it too early to begin making career goals? What goals do you have for a career? If not, who or what can help you create goals? Why is goal-setting important?

AUDIO/VISUAL ACTIVITIES

Purpose: To improve skills at word selection/vocabulary

91. Play a recording of "God Bless America" by Irving Berlin which was first performed in 1938. How do the lyrics reflect a patriotic message?

92. Show a video of a battle scene from the movie *Red Badge of Courage*. Students can *write* or *discuss* how the soldiers react in a battle. Use this as a lesson in modifiers—scared, angrily, savagely.

93. Show a scene from a movie that portrays people eating (*Tom Jones*, for example) and prompt students to describe the taste of the meal. Use this to increase students' knowledge of sensory modifiers. Refer also to Thanksgiving, which typically is a large meal.

94. Refer to Oklahoma gaining statehood in 1907 and play a recording or show videotape of Gordon McRae singing "Oklahoma" in the musical "Oklahoma." As students listen to the lyrics they should identify the descriptive language used to portray this southwestern state.

Purpose: To highlight a major historical event

95. Show selected scenes from the movie *Cimarron* starring Glenn Ford, which describes Oklahoma during and after the 1889 land rush, and discuss students' reactions.

Purpose: To practice writing character sketches

96. Show a clip(s) from a Boris Karloff movie. Students can either write descriptions or discuss the particulars of his characterizations and roles.

97. Show selected scenes from the movie *The Adventures of Mark Twain* starring Frederic March or a videotape of Hal Holbrook portraying Mark Twain. Use this to have students write a character sketch about Twain's humor, views on society, and appearance.

Purpose: To review speech skills

98. Play a recording or videotape of Billy Graham giving a speech and evaluate his skill and effectiveness as a public speaker. Students should note his sincerity, enthusiasm, and tone.

99. Show the opening scene (Patton's speech to the soldiers) from the movie *Patton* starring George C. Scott. Use this as a lesson in diction, speech skills, or characterization.

100. Refer to Edward Brooke, Jeannette Rankin, and Douglas Wilder and show selected scenes, especially the speechmaking or the debate scenes, from the *The Candidate* starring Robert Redford. Use this to study political language and the traits of effective speakers.

101. Perform charades of various physical gestures—include finger pointing, stomping around the room, and waving arms—that are typical of some television evangelists and public speakers. Compare these actions to Billy Graham or other evangelists.

Purpose: To practice writing persuasion

102. Show a videotape of a cartoon that displays a character—human or animal—being injured or harmed in some way, such as "Inspector Gadget," Tom and Jerry," and "Bugs Bunny and Pals." Then students could write one paragraph explaining why cartoons like this (that show violence) should or should not be seen by children. Have students also make reference to Mickey Mouse.

103. Distribute travel brochures (available from most travel agencies) for Montana and Washington and direct students to cite the persuasive language used to encourage tourists.

Purpose: To teach hyperbole and melodrama

104. Show scenes from *Casablanca*, a television soap opera, or "The Price is Right" and have students study the behavior of the actors and contestants. Then explain how their actions and behaviors are examples of hyperbole and melodrama and how these terms are used in literature.

> **Hyperbole: an exaggeration; overstating the real truth**
>
> **Melodrama: an exaggerated form of drama characterized by heavy emotions and/or suspense**

Purpose: To improve critical thinking skills

105. Refer to King Tut and English archaeologist Howard Carter and assign students to list and categorize the furniture, shelf items (bric-a-brac), and appliances in their homes. Then discuss their lists. Ask: What would archaeologists of the future say about the artifacts and furniture they would find in your house? How much do the possessions we own say about our personalities? What is the most important item in your house?

Name _____

The Philosophy of Will Rogers

Background: Will Rogers was first an Indian, then a cowboy, and finally a legendary American personality. After learning various tricks with a lasso as a tool to work cattle on the family ranch in Oklahoma he dropped out of high school to join wild west shows and vaudeville groups traveling the country. Soon, he was also telling jokes and philosophizing on stage. Audiences loved his folksy commentary as much as his roping skills.

During the 1920s and 1930s Rogers became the star of Broadway, radio, and film (71 movies). He wrote six books and over 4000 syndicated newspaper columns. He also raised thousands of dollars for the Red Cross and Salvation Army.

He died in a plane crash in Alaska in 1935.

Directions: Read and analyze the following quotes from famous humorist and actor Will Rogers.

1. "People talk peace. But men give their life's work to war. It won't stop 'til there is as much brains and scientific study put to aid peace as there is to promote war."

2. "Nowadays it is about as big a crime to be dumb as it is to be dishonest."

3. "Diplomats are just as essential to starting a war as soldiers are for finishing it."

4. "Live your life so that whenever you lose, you are ahead."

5. "My ancestors didn't come over on the Mayflower, but they met the boat."

6. "No man is great if he thinks he is."

7. "It's great to be great, but it's greater to be human."

8. "We will never have true civilization until we have learned to recognize the rights of others."

9. "Don't gamble. Take all your savings and buy some good stock and hold it til it goes up then sell it. If it don't go up, don't buy it."

10. "I never met a man I didn't like."

Name _____

Mark Twain Said . . .

Directions: Read and analyze the following quotes from famous humorist and writer Mark Twain.

1. "A classic [book] is something that everybody wants to have read and nobody wants to read."

2. "Adam was the only man, who, when he said a good thing, knew that nobody had said it before him."

3. "Thunder is good, thunder is impressive, but it is the lightning that does the work."

4. "The man who does not read good books has no advantage over the man who can't read them."

5. "The difference between the almost right word and the right word is really a large matter—'tis the difference between the lightning bug and the lightning."

6. "Let us endeavor so to live that when we come to die even the undertaker will be sorry."

The Stranger

by Albert Camus

[Background: The narrator has just been convicted of murder. He sits in his jail cell, awaiting his punishment, which could be death. The following paragraph is taken from a chapter near the end of the novel.]

It was at one such moment that I once again refused to see the chaplain. I was lying down, and I could tell from the golden glow in the sky that evening was coming on. I had just denied my appeal and I could feel the steady pulse of my blood circulating inside me. I didn't need to see the chaplain. For the first time in a long time I thought about Marie. The days had been long since she'd stopped writing. That evening I thought about it and told myself that maybe she had gotten tired of being the girlfriend of a condemned man. It also occurred to me that maybe she was sick. or dead . . . Anyway, after that, Marie meant nothing to me. I wasn't interested in her dead. That seemed perfectly normal to me, since I understood very well that people would forget me when I was dead. They wouldn't have anything more to do with me. I wasn't even able to tell myself that it was hard to think those things.

1. What is the narrator's attitude?

2. Why do you think he refused to see the chaplain?

3. What are his feelings now for Marie?

4. What suggests he's confused or feeling uncertain?

5. What are your reactions to this narrator?

Name _____

The Idiot

by Fyodor Mikhailovich Dostoyevsky

Varvara Ardalionovna was a girl of twenty-three, of middle height, rather thin. Her face, though not beautiful, possessed the secret of charm without beauty and was extraordinarily attractive. She was very like her mother and was dressed in almost the same way, showing absolutely no desire to be smart. Her gray eyes might have been at times very merry and caressing, if they had not as a rule looked grave and thoughtful; too much so, especially of late. Her face too showed firmness and decision; in fact it suggested an even more vigorous and enterprising determination than her mother's. Varvara Ardalionovna was rather hot-tempered, and her brother was sometimes positively afraid of her temper.

Questions

1. How would you describe the appearance of Varvara Ardalionovna?

2. What are her positive traits?

3. What are her negative traits?

4. How would you respond to her at a first meeting?

5. What kind of diction does Dostoyevsky use here?

Dialogue and Dialect
in the *Red Badge of Courage*

by Stephen Crane

Directions: Read the following quotes from characters in Stephen Crane's war novel the *Red Badge of Courage* and then translate them into modern language and summarize their meaning.

1. "The army makes 'em wild and they like nothing better than . . . leading off a younger feller."

2. "There may be a few of 'em run, but there's them kind in every regiment."

3. "We're goin' t' move t'morrah—sure. We're goin' 'way up the river, cut across, an' come in behint 'em."

4. "An' take good care of yerself in this here fightin' business—you watch out, an' take good care of yerself. Don't go a-thinkin' you can lick the hull rebel army at the start because yeh can't."

5. "That's all true, I s'pose, but I'm not going to skeddaddle."

6. "You jest wait 'till to-morrow, and you'll see one of the biggest battles ever was. You jest wait."

7. "Of course it might happen that the hull kit-and-boodle might start and run."

8. "Billie—keep off m' feet. Yeh run like a cow."

Name _____

What Is the Writing Style?

Directions: Read each passage below that is a response to the book *The Adventures of Huckleberry Finn* by Mark Twain and then answer the questions.

A. Anyway you look at it, "Huck Finn" is a cool book. The way Huck sees things makes the book funny. This Twain may be an old writer, but he sure digs what it's like to be young. You won't find many dudes who can scratch it out like he can. He's got this way of making you wonder what's next, like I kept wondering if Huck and Jim would make it. Even kids who hate reading would dig "Huck Finn."

B. *The Adventures of Huckleberry Finn,* by Mark Twain, is a literary triumph that is terrific in its combination of folk lore and the Southern experience.

The author's background as a river boat pilot obviously helped him select the details related to Huck and Jim's adventures on the Mississippi River, the book's setting, and the characters they encounter with great clarity. The reader is introduced to the human drama of Huck and Jim's journey to freedom down the Mississippi River.

This novel is truly a wonderful and educational read for any student who is interested in both an exciting adventure and excellent descriptions of the Mississippi River.

C. Viewed educationally and literarily, Mark Twain's *The Adventures of Huckleberry Finn* is a major triumph. Poetic in its perception, lucid in its phrasing, and dramatically original in its scope, this novel both delights and educates the reader. This outstanding narrative deserves to be ranked among the exceptional literary works of the 20th century. Possibly the most noteworthy evidence of Twain's talent lies in his capacity to describe the grand Mississippi River as both commonplace and exotic, to elicit the reader's compassion for the runaways Huck and Jim, and to create a breathless tale of suspense and adventure. All students should peruse this classic narrative.

Questions

1. How would you characterize the writing style of each passage?

2. Which passage appeals to you? Why?

Abraham Lincoln's "Gettysburg Address"

Four score and seven years ago, our fathers brought forth on this continent, a new nation, conceived in Liberty, and dedicated to the proposition that all men are created equal.

Now we are engaged in a great civil war, testing whether that nation, or any nation so conceived and so dedicated can long endure. We are met on a great battlefield of that war. We have come to dedicate a portion of that field, as a final resting place for those who here gave their lives that that nation might live. It is altogether fitting and proper that we should do this.

But, in a larger sense, we can not dedicate—we can not consecrate—we can not hallow—this ground. The brave men, living and dead, who struggled here, have consecrated it, far above our poor power to add or detract. The world will little note, nor long remember what we say here, but it can never forget what they did here. It is for us the living, rather, to be dedicated here to the unfinished work which they who fought here have thus far so nobly advanced. It is rather for us to be here dedicated to the great task remaining before us—that from these honored dead we take increased devotion to that cause for which they gave the last full measure of devotion—that we here highly resolve that these dead shall not have died in vain—that this nation, under God, shall have a new birth of freedom—and that government of the people, by the people, for the people, shall not perish from the earth.

Questions

1. Why did Lincoln give this speech (his purpose)?

2. What sentences in the speech establish a sense of rhythm?

3. What specific theme does Lincoln's speech express?

4. How does Lincoln attempt to connect with his audience (establish rapport)?

5. How does Lincoln conclude in order to make an impact on his audience (a lasting impression)?

A Letter from President Abraham Lincoln to the Mother of Five Dead Soldiers

Washington

Nov. 21, 1864

Dear Madam,

I have been shown in the files of the War Department a statement that you are the mother of five sons who have died gloriously on the field of battle. I feel how weak and fruitless must be any word of mine which should attempt to beguile you from the grief of a loss so overwhelming. But I cannot refrain from tendering you the consolation that may be found in the thanks of the republic they died to serve. I pray that our Heavenly Father may assuage the anguish of your bereavement, and leave you only the cherished memory of the loved and lost, and the solemn pride that must be yours to have laid so costly a sacrifice upon the altar of freedom.

Yours very sincerely and respectfully,

A. Lincoln

Questions

1. Why did Lincoln write this letter (his purpose)?

2. What sentences in the letter establish a sense of rhythm?

3. What specific theme does Lincoln's letter express?

4. How does Lincoln attempt to connect with this mother (establish rapport)?

5. How does Lincoln conclude in order to make an impact on the mother (a lasting impression)?

Name _____

Novel Study Project

Select one of the following assignments after completing the reading of your novel.

Key Points

1. When writing a novel title, put it in quotation marks (Ex) John Steinbeck wrote "Of Mice and Men." In fact, use quotation marks when copying any passages from the novel.

2. Use a title page where you center the following:

> Book Title
> by (Name of Author)
> Date of Publication
>
> Your Name
> the class period
> the Date

3. Do not summarize the plot of your novel. Follow the directions below.

The Projects

1. Make a three to four minute **oral presentation** ("Book Talk") where you describe briefly the importance of the title and the conflict, climax, and resolution in the novel. Explain what makes this novel better or worse than other novels that you have read. Be sure to include an **audio/visual** aide to highlight your presentation.

2. A novel's setting is often crucial to our understanding of the theme. In a detailed essay, describe all places/locales used by the author of the novel. You are expected to copy passages from the novel to highlight your essay. Explain why you think the story is set where it is.

3. Make a list of all important characters. At least six to ten characters should be included in this list, and be sure to write their full names and describe each in detail. If the novel lacks this many characters or does not include their full names, be sure to tell the teacher before turning in your project.

   For each character, explain his/her physical traits, background, emotional tendencies, and importance to the novel.

© 2001 by The Center for Applied Research in Education

4. In a detailed essay, explain the main climax in the novel. What characters are involved? What makes it interesting? What is revealed in the final resolution? Keep in mind the climax and resolution occur near the end of the novel.

5. Make a chart. On the left, list details associated with the novel's *protagonist*. On the right, list details associated with the novel's *antagonist*. Be thorough and accurate as you deal with items such as their backgrounds, jobs, appearance, relationships, ambitions, etc.

6. Create an advertising campaign to promote the sale of the novel. Create on a *videotape* a television commercial that promotes the book much like movie trailers promote a movie; a magazine advertisement about the characters, setting, and conflict of the novel, and a 30-second radio *script* that discusses the characters and plot of the novel.

7. Write three descriptive scenes that could have happened in the book, but didn't. After you have written these scenes, explain how they would have changed the novel's climax and resolution.

8. Complete the following statements (three to four sentence responses for each):

   1. The novel made me wish that _____

   2. The novel made me realize that _____

   3. The novel made me decide that _____

   4. The novel made me wonder about _____

   5. The novel made me believe that _____

   6. The novel made me hope that _____

   7. The novel surprised me when _____

   8. My favorite characters in the novel were _____

   9. After reading the novel I felt _____

   10. Some interesting phrases in the novel were _____

Name _____

President vs. President

Directions: Examine the brief biographies of the following Presidents; James Polk, #11; Zachary Taylor, #12; James Garfield, #20; Warren G. Harding, #29; and John F. Kennedy, #35. Then explain your choice for the best President.

James K. Polk (Democrat) 1845–1849

Achievements: Lowered tariff on imported goods by signing the Walker Tariff; added Oregon Territory to the U.S.; defeated Mexico and gained territory in the Mexican War.

Zachary Taylor (Whig) 1849–1850

Achievements: Supported admission of California as a free state; guaranteed neutrality for any canal built in Central America connecting the Atlantic and Pacific Oceans; died in office.

James A. Garfield (Republican) 1881–1881

Achievements: Could write Greek with one hand while writing Latin with the other; strengthened U.S. Customs Service; assassinated in office.

Warren G. Harding (Republican) 1921–1923

Achievements: First President to speak on the radio; approved Immigration Restriction Act which placed quotas on immigration; first President to visit Alaska and Canada.

John F. Kennedy (Democrat) 1960–1963

Achievements: Created the Peace Corps; ordered the Bay of Pigs invasion of Cuba which failed to overthrow Cuban leader Fidel Castro; authorized federal troops to enforce integration in schools in Mississippi and Alabama; assassinated in office; first Roman Catholic President; won the Pulitzer Prize for his book *Profiles in Courage*.

Who's the best?

Name _____

Roy Campanella vs. Joe DiMaggio

Campanella	*DiMaggio*

Campanella

(1921–1993)

- Strong leadership skills as a catcher for Brooklyn Dodgers

- MVP awards in 1951, 1953, & 1955

- Played on five All-Star teams

- Helped team win two World Series titles

- Played 10 seasons

- 1161 total hits

- 242 total homeruns

- 856 total RBIs

- Led National League in 1953 with 142 RBIs

- .325 best hitting year

- "Campy"

- Enshrined in Major League Baseball's Hall of Fame

- Paralyzed in automobile accident but wrote book *It's Good to be Alive* that reveals how a positive attitude can prompt success for anyone.

DiMaggio

(1914–1999)

- Outstanding performances as New York Yankee centerfielder

- MVP awards in 1939, 1941, & 1946

- Played on six All-Star teams

- Helped team win nine World Series titles

- Played 13 seasons

- 2214 total hits

- 361 total homeruns

- 1537 total RBIs

- 56 game hitting streak a major league record

- .381 best hitting year

- "Yankee Clipper"/"Joltin' Joe"

- Enshrined in Major League Baseball's Hall of Fame

- Married Marilyn Monroe but divorced after nine months becoming a cultural icon expressed in the Simon and Garfunkel song "Mrs. Robinson."

Name _____

A Travelogue

Thursday, June 10: We awoke in our campground near Mesa, Arizona to 105-degree heat and a cloudless sky, packed the tent and gear in the back of the Ford van, and drove north along AZ 88 to the Superstition Mountains, where legends can be heard about lost mines and miners. We saw exotic plants, like the suguaro cacti, and took a dip in the chilly water of one of the nearby lakes.

Back in the van, we drove a 25 mile road known as Apache Trail that had many sharp bends and narrow stretches. The road ended at the impressive Roosevelt Dam, which is one hundred feet thick at its widest point, and we camped in a busy campground near Roosevelt Lake beneath a clear sky of bright stars and a full moon.

Friday, June 11: Another hot sunny day began. We drove 70 miles east along I-40 to Albuquerque, NM and wandered around the historic center of town. We shopped in brown, adobe-style stores—one was a chili market where we bought chili jam. It became windy so we drove north into the mountains of the Sante Fe National Forest where we set camp on the edge of a sandstone cliff overlooking the valley below. It was another cool—about 55 degrees—quiet and clear night, and we could see the flickering campfires miles beneath us in the Jemez valley.

Saturday, June 12: This day we headed off towards Arizona on I-10, via a short-cut along a steep new road across the Franklin Mountains, which are just north of El Paso. The highway to Las Cruces was lined with huge dairy cattle markets and an even greater smell of manure. We drove on, passing gray billboards inviting the tourists into ghost towns and nearly lifeless desert, until we finally reached Dragoon, crossed the highway, and headed up a dusty track into the Rincon Mountains. We found a shady camping area with a wide view of the valley below and many empty cartridges and broken bottles suggesting this was a popular shooting area. A forest fire in the distance, with its hazy smoke rising into the dusky sky, had a peculiar orange light. As darkness came, so did an eerie silence, which seemed to remind us of how far away we were from civilization.

Name _____

More on Writing Style

Background: Repetition can be effective at times in our writing—essays, poems, speeches. It can add a sense of drama or emphasis. Read the following famous statement from Winston Churchill, British Prime Minister during WW II, and then explain how it is both an inspirational and political message to the English people.

Statement: "We shall fight on the beaches, we shall fight on the landing grounds, we shall fight in the fields and in the streets, we shall fight in the hills; we shall never surrender."

Questions:

1. What is repeated?

2. Why do you think Churchill chose to repeat that phrase?

3. What is his intent here?

4. How effective is his message? Why?

5. How would you react if you lived in England at the time?

Name _____

Violence on TV

Background: According to the American Psychological Association, the typical American child spends 27 hours a week watching television. In a lifetime he/she will witness 100,000 acts of violence, including 8000 murders.

Directions: Write a one-page editorial on this issue where you effectively persuade the reader of your opinions on the quality of current television programming. Your audience is parents and lawmakers.

Name _____

When You Have to Give a Speech

Directions: Answer in two or three complete and coherent sentences.

1. How would you lessen your anxiety before giving a speech?

2. What two things would you be certain to check fifteen minutes before giving your speech?

3. How can you establish your credibility as a speaker at the beginning of your speech?

4. How can you make your audience feel comfortable at the beginning of your speech?

5. Why is body language important during a speech?

6. How would you deal with possible distractions?

7. How can visual aids assist you as a speaker?

8. How could an outline assist you as a speaker?

Name _____

Titles and Suspense

Directions: Examine each of the titles below and be prepared to explain how it creates a sense of suspense or interest for the reader.

Red Badge of Courage by Stephen Crane

The Stranger by Albert Camus

The Plague by Albert Camus

Gone with the Wind by Margaret Mitchell

Crime and Punishment by Fyodor Dostoyevsky

A Wrinkle in Time by Madeline L'Engle

A Wind in the Door by Madeline L'Engle

A Ring of Endless Light by Madeline L'Engle

Treasure Island by Robert Louis Stevenson

Kidnapped by Robert Louis Stevenson

The Strange Case of Dr. Jekyll and Mr. Hyde by Robert Louis Stevenson

The Wrecker by Robert Louis Stevenson

Slaughterhouse Five by Kurt Vonnegut

Jailbird by Kurt Vonnegut

Hocus Pocus by Kurt Vonnegut

Name _____

The Importance of Punctuation

1. How could the use of an exclamation point change the meaning of a sentence?

2. Examine the following line of poetry from William Wordsworth and analyze its punctuation. Why is each mark used in the place it is? Are there errors? Explain:

    "Up! Up! my friend, and clear your looks; Why all this toil and trouble?"

3. How do you punctuate a sentence that is a question vs. a sentence that is an indirect question?

4. Although both marks are used to "separate" items in sentences, the comma and semi-colon are quite different. What are the differences?

5. What is a comma splice, or a comma fault?

6. When should a writer use parentheses and brackets?

7. Hyphens are used in a variety of ways. One example is in a compound word like self-esteem. Why does the compound word self-esteem require a hyphen but the compound word football does not?

8. What are the rules related to the use of the apostrophe?

9. The sentence *Please bring the following to class: a pen, notebook, and folder* requires a colon but the sentence *Please bring a pen, notebook, and folder to class* doesn't. Why not?

NOVEMBER
Answer Key

#3 SKILL SHEET 11-3—THE STRANGER BY ALBERT CAMUS

1. The narrator is only a little depressed. He is comfortable with his fate, apathetic toward any assistance from his lawyer (he had denied his appeal), the chaplain, or Marie. He has resigned himself to die.

2. Answers will vary, but he probably refused to see the chaplain because he either doesn't believe in religion or sees no need for spiritual comfort.

3. He has no feelings for Marie.

4. The excerpt suggests he's confused or feeling uncertain by the fact that he's doing nothing except feeling his pulse.

5. Answers will vary.

#4 SKILL SHEET 11-4—THE IDIOT BY FYODOR MIKHAILOVICH DOSTOYEVSKY

1. Varvara Ardalionovna is average or middle height, thin, and attractive in the face with gray eyes.

2. She seems to be a determined, thoughtful person.

3. She is hot-tempered and caused fear in her brother.

4. Answers will vary

5. The diction Dostoyevsky uses here is a mix of informal (girl, like her mother) and formal (caressing, enterprising) words.

#5 SKILL SHEET 11-5—DIALOGUE AND DIALECT IN THE RED BADGE OF COURAGE BY STEPHEN CRANE

1. The army causes men to act wild and older soldiers like nothing better than to lead a younger soldier in that direction.

2. There may be a few soldiers who run, but there are those like that in every regiment.

3. We're going to move tomorrow. That's for sure. We're going away up the river, cut across, and come in behind them.

4. And take good care of yourself in this here war (battles). You watch out and take good care of yourself. Don't start thinking you can defeat the whole rebel army at the start because you can't.

5. That's all true, I suppose, but I'm not going to run away.

6. You just wait until tomorrow, and you'll see one of the biggest battles there ever was. You just wait.

7. Of course it might happen that everyone might start and run.

8. Billy, keep off of my feet. You run like a cow.

#9 SKILL SHEET 11-6—WHAT IS WRITING STYLE?

1. Response A to Mark Twain's *The Adventures of Huckleberry Finn* is characterized by the use of slang and a very personalized, almost conversational writing style. Response B is a well-structured essay characterized by informal word choice. C is very formal, almost technical with its literary jargon.

2. Answers will vary.

#10 SKILL SHEET 11-7A—ABRAHAM LINCOLN'S "GETTYSBURG ADDRESS"

1. Lincoln delivered this speech to recognize and honor the soldiers who died on the battlefield at Gettysburg, which had the highest casualties and wounded of any battle to date.

2. The sentences in the speech that establish a sense of rhythm are:

    Four score and seven years ago, our fathers brought forth on this continent, a new nation, conceived in Liberty, and dedicated to the proposition that all men are created equal [Note the use of prepositional phrases here].

    But, in a larger sense, we can not dedicate—we can not consecrate—we can not hallow—this ground. The brave men, living and dead, who struggled here, have consecrated it, far above our poor power to add or detract. (Note here the repetition of *we can* and parallel constructions of *living and dead* and *add or detract.*)

    And, *that we here highly resolve that these dead shall not have died in vain—that this nation, under God, shall have a new birth of freedom—and that government of the people, by the people, for the people, shall not perish from the earth.* (Note the parallel clauses beginning with *that* and the final prepositional phrases.)

3. The theme expressed by Lincoln is that the country must stay committed to preserving the Union and the ideals for which it stands.

4. Lincoln establishes rapport with his audience by saying "our fathers," "that all men are created equal," and "Now *we* are engaged in a great civil war."

5. Lincoln concludes forcefully by making an indirect reference to the Declaration of Independence.

#10 SKILL SHEET 11-7B—A LETTER FROM PRESIDENT ABRAHAM LINCOLN TO THE MOTHER OF FIVE DEAD SOLDIERS.

1. Lincoln wrote this letter to thank and appease a mother whose five sons died in the Civil War.

2. The sentence in the letter that establishes a sense of rhythm is: *I pray that our Heavenly Father may assuage the anguish of your bereavement, and leave you only the cherished memory of the loved and lost, and the solemn pride that must be yours to have laid so costly a sacrifice upon the altar of freedom.* (Note the conjunctions that connect each parallel clause.)

3. The theme of Lincoln's letter is his understanding of the mother's grief and his appreciation of her sacrifice.

4. Lincoln establishes rapport with the mother by admitting to his feelings of weakness and consolation. His sympathy is very evident with such references as *cherished memory, solemn pride,* and *died gloriously.*

5. Lincoln mentions the *altar of freedom* at his conclusion to affirm the mother's sons' contribution to preserving the ideals of the American nation.

#53 SKILL SHEET 11-12—MORE ON WRITING STYLE

1. *We shall fight* is repeated.

2. Churchill probably chose to repeat that phrase in order to affirm the commitment the English people needed to maintain to win the war against the Nazis.

3. Churchill's intent here is to encourage the English people not to lose hope during WW II.

4. Answers will vary.

5. Answers will vary.

#55 SKILL SHEET 11-14—WHEN YOU HAVE TO GIVE A SPEECH

1. To lessen anxiety, you could sit in a comfortable chair, take deep breaths, and review the speech outline.

2. Possible things to check would be note cards, any audio/visual materials, mechanical devices (microphones), seating arrangement of the audience, etc.

3. Speakers can establish credibility by explaining their background and experience with the speech subject, or by asking the person who does the introductions to do that.

4. Humor, an amusing anecdote, or a compliment can make the audience feel comfortable at the beginning of a speech.

5. Body language can suggest the speaker's attitude and enthusiasm for the speech subject. Speakers shouldn't slouch or make wild gestures.

6. Distractions could be ignored or addressed with humor.

7. Visual aids can clarify information or help the audience to understand complex points.

8. An outline can be an effective organizational tool.

#79 SKILL SHEET 11-16—THE IMPORTANCE OF PUNCTUATION

1. An exclamation point changes the meaning of a sentence from declarative to exclamatory.

2. William Wordsworth's poem can be analyzed as follows: The exclamation points come after the strong commands of *Up, Up*. The comma follows *my friend* because it is a form of direct address. The semicolon separates the two clauses, and the question mark is used to form the interrogative sentence.

   Students may argue that the two exclamation points should be eliminated and replaced with commas and possibly inserted where the semi-colon is, or the semicolon should be replaced with a period.

3. A sentence that is a question has a question mark while a sentence that is an indirect question—*I wonder who is going to the party.*—ends with a period.

4. The comma separates words, phrases, and clauses, while the semicolon can only be used to separate independent clauses that are closely related in meaning or have equal grammatical rank.

5. A comma splice, or a comma fault, is the use of a comma where no mark or another mark of punctuation is needed.

6. Parentheses should be used for enclosing supplemental information while brackets are used to enclose words that replace other words in a word-for-word quotation. They are not similar punctuation marks at all.

7. The compound word self-esteem requires a hyphen because each word retains its singular meaning but the compound word football does not require a hyphen because each word combines to make a brand new word.

8. The rules related to the use of the apostrophe are to indicate that a noun is possessive and in contractions.

9. The sentence *Please bring a pen, notebook, and folder to class* doesn't require a colon because colons are unnecessary before a list that begins with a verb.

DECEMBER

DECEMBER

Origin: This month takes its name from the Latin word *decem* which means ten and originally had only 29 days. It became the twelfth and last month of the year according to the Gregorian calendar.

Holidays: Christians celebrate Christmas, the birth of Jesus Christ, on December 25. In some European countries people celebrate St. Nicholas Day on December 6.

Some people in New England observe Forefathers Day to recognize the landing of the Pilgrims on December 21.

Bahrain, Finland, Kazakhstan, Kenya, Libya, Portugal, Tanzania, and the United Arab Emirates celebrate their Independence Days in December.

Jewish people celebrate Chanukah, their "Feast of Lights," and black Americans observe Kwanzaa, meaning "first fruit" in Swahili, which was created in 1966 by Dr. Maulana Karenga to honor traditional African harvest festivals.

Gemstone: Turquoise

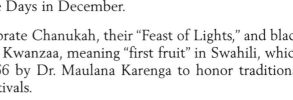

Flower: Poinsettia

Poetry: The sun that brief December day
Rose cheerless over hills of gray,
And, darkly circled, gave at noon
A sadder sight than waning moon.

   by John Greenleaf Whittier

BIRTHDAYS

Dec. 1   Woody Allen (born Allan Stewart Konigsberg), comedian/actor/director (1935) [#3, 28, 89]

Dec. 3   Joseph Conrad, author of *Heart of Darkness and Lord Jim* (1857) [#44, 63]

Dec. 5   Martin Van Buren, 8th President (1782) [#51, 65, 76]; Walt Disney, cartoonist and creator of Disneyland (1901) [#10, 82, 98]

Dec. 7   Willa Cather, winner 1922 Pulitzer Prize for literature (1873) [#8, 19, 44, 63]; Larry Bird, professional basketball player/coach/NBA Most Valuable Player (1956) [#46, 53, 54, 78, 98]

Dec. 8   Jim Morrison, poet and singer for the Doors (1943) [#41, 43, 46, 69, 87, 91, 92, 98]; James Thurber, humorist/story writer (1894) [#9, 74, 75]

Dec. 9   John Milton, English poet—*Paradise Lost* (1608) [#41, 43, 69, 91]

Dec. 10   Emily Dickinson, one of America's greatest poets who published only 7 poems during her lifetime. Over 2000 poems written on the backs of envelopes and scraps of paper were discovered after her death (1830) [#7, 19, 20, 41, 43, 69, 70, 71, 72, 91, 92]

Dec. 16   Jane Austen, author (1775) [#19, 44]; Ludwig van Beethoven, composer (1770) [#80, 96, 97]; Arthur C. Clarke, author (1917) [#44, 63]

Dec. 17   John Greenleaf Whittier, poet (1807) [#7, 41, 43, 69, 91]

Dec. 18   Tyrus (Ty) Raymond Cobb, one of the greatest major league baseball players with a .367 lifetime batting average (1886) [#53, 54, 78, 88, 98]; Steven Spielberg, Academy Award winning director of *Jaws, ET, Raiders of the Lost Ark*, and *Schindler's List* (1947) [#3, 11, 28]

Dec. 22   Edwin Arlington Robinson, Pulitzer Prize winning poet (1869) [#7, 20, 41, 43, 69, 91]

Dec. 27   Louis Pasteur, scientist who originated the process of pasteurization (1822) [#26, 34, 67]

Dec. 28   Woodrow Wilson, 28th President (1856) [#55, 56, 57, 65, 74, 75, 76]

Dec. 29   Andrew Johnson, 17th President (1808) [#51, 65, 76, 98]

Dec. 30   Rudyard Kipling, English writer, winner of Nobel Prize for Literature in 1907, the first English author to win it (1865) [#5, 41, 43, 44, 69, 91]

MEMORABLE EVENTS

Dec. 1   Rosa Parks was arrested in 1955 in Montgomery, AL for refusing to give up her seat on a bus, which initiated a year long boycott of the city bus system and the birth of the civil rights movement [#15, 36, 45].

Dec. 2   John Brown, leader of Abolitionists, was executed by hanging in Charles Town, WV, for his raid on the U.S. arsenal at Harper's Ferry (1859) [#13].

Barney C. Clark, 61, became the first recipient of a permanent artificial heart at the University of Utah Medical Center in Salt Lake City in 1982 [#31, 50, 52, 94, 98].

Dec. 3   Dr. Christian Barnard performed the first transplant of a human heart in Capetown, South Africa on 55-year-old Louis Washkansky in 1967 [#16, 27, 31, 34, 52, 94].

Illinois was admitted to the Union as the 21st state in 1818 [#23, 47, 95].

Dec. 7   Pearl Harbor was attacked by Japanese war planes in 1941: "A date that will live in infamy" (The United States declared war on Japan and Germany on Dec. 8) [#79].

Dec. 10   University of Chicago Professor and scientist Albert Michelson was named winner of the Nobel Prize in 1907 for his research on the speed of light and optics, the first U.S. scientist to receive the award [#58, 67, 98].

Dr. Ralph Bunche became the first black man awarded the Nobel Prize (for Peace) in 1950 for his work as a mediator between Israel and the Arab States in 1949 [#49, 98].

> **The Nobel Prizes are awarded in Stockholm, Sweden each year on this date for achievements in physics, chemistry, medicine, literature, economics, and peace. The Nobel Prizes were founded by Alfred Nobel, Swedish chemist and inventor of dynamite whose $9 million estate funds the awards.**

Mississippi was admitted to the Union as the 20th state in 1817 [#23, 47, 95].

Dec. 11   Indiana was admitted to the Union as the 19th state in 1816 [#23, 47, 95].

Dec. 14 Alabama was admitted to the Union as the 22nd state in 1819 [#23, 47, 95].

Dec. 16 Boston Tea Party took place in 1773 when a group of Boston patriots boarded a British vessel at anchor in Boston harbor and dumped 350 chests of tea into the water [#14, 17].

Dec. 17 *A Christmas Carol* was published by Charles Dickens in 1843 [#64, 86].

Orville Wright made the first powered flight at Kitty Hawk, North Carolina in 1903 [#16, 30, 38].

Dec. 18 Thirteenth Amendment was ratified by Congress in 1865, abolishing slavery: "Neither slavery or involuntary servitude, save as punishment for crime whereof the party shall have been duly convicted, shall exist within the United States, or any place subject to their jurisdiction." [#17, 37].

"To Tell the Truth" premiered on television in 1956 with a celebrity panel and home audience trying to determine which of three guests who all claimed to be the same person was telling the truth. The panelists took turns asking questions, and the actual person's identity was revealed at the end. [#22].

Dec. 19 Ben Franklin published *Poor Richard's Almanack* in 1732 to become the colonies' first best-selling book [#4].

Dec. 21 Pilgrims landed at Plymouth, Massachusetts in 1620 [#25].

Dec. 28 Chewing gum was patented by William F. Semple, an Ohio dentist, in 1869 [#24, 85].

Iowa was admitted to the Union as the 29th state in 1846 [#23, 47, 95].

Dec. 29 Texas was admitted to the Union as the 28th state in 1845 [#23, 47, 84, 95].

LEARNING ACTIVITIES FOR DECEMBER

READING ACTIVITIES

Purpose: To introduce the reading of a biography

1. Ask: Why might a biographer choose to write about that person? What could be the relationship between the biographer and his/her subject? Then allow students time in the library to select a biography for independent reading and use **Form 12-1** to evaluate them.

> Generally, the subject of any biography is well-known or a historical figure who has significant achievements. This person might have an unusual or extraordinary background.
>
> The biographer could be a relative, a close friend, or an accomplished writer whom the subject has asked to write his/her story. Sometimes, the biography could be unauthorized.

Purpose: To improve research skills

2. Help students locate encyclopedia articles about authors who have birthdays this month. Use this to introduce any of these authors and to teach research skills.

Purpose: To improve skills at analysis

3. Have students locate movie reviews in the local newspaper. Then ask: How do the critics describe the movie, the actors, the plot, and the setting? What kind of recommendations are offered? How do they rate the film(s)? Refer to Steven Spielberg and Woody Allen.

4. Have students study the quotes from Benjamin Franklin's *Poor Richard's Almanac*, which was published in 1732. Use **Skill Sheet 12-2** to analyze his word choice, philosophy, and wit.

Purpose: To improve skills at analyzing poetry

5. Have students examine any poems by Rudyard Kipling that may appear in their literature text or an available anthology for their verse, imagery, and themes.

> Rudyard Kipling's rhymed verse was typically written in the slang of a British soldier and often conveyed images that displayed appreciation for the land and people of India. His themes reflected patriotism, imperialism, and duty.

6. Have students read poems commonly associated with winter months found in their literature text or an anthology. Ask: How do these poems reflect the weather, mood, or events of winter?

7. Have students read any poems by American poets Emily Dickinson, John Greenleaf Whittier, and/or Edward Arlington Robinson that appear in their literature text or anthology. Then ask: What type of verse is seen? What are the topics of the poems? How would you describe their writing style? What are their themes?

> **Emily Dickinson** used both rhyme and free verse, but it was her unconventional use of punctuation, especially ellipses and dashes, that separated her work from the traditional poetry of her day. Her use of precise language and intense metaphors helped suggest themes related to the beauty of nature, the power of death, and a reverence for God.
>
> **John Greenleaf Whittier's** narrative poetry focused most often on pastoral themes, especially when he described the rugged farm life of New England. He was also a devout Quaker who was devoted to the abolition of slavery.
>
> **Edward Arlington Robinson** won the Pulitzer Prize for Poetry twice. His narrative poems were most often psychological portraits of unusual people, many from the imaginary Tilbury Town in New England. Some poems also focused on the legend of King Arthur.

Purpose: To review characterization and plot in fiction

8. Distribute **Skill Sheet 12-3,** the excerpt from the Willa Cather story "Neighbour Rosicky," and have students cite the details related to Rosicky they find interesting.

9. Have students read a story, like James Thurber's "The Secret Life of Walter Mitty," that may appear in their literature text or an available anthology. Ask: Where is the humor? Is it seen in the description of a character? In plot events? The resolution? Ask students to cite and compare another writer's humor with Thurber's.

> **James Thurber** was born into a family known for its zaniness and his writing reflected a strong use of understatement, irony, and satire. He often created in his comic fiction characters who typically were beleaguered men living dull lives with domineering women.

DEBATING ACTIVITIES

Purpose: To develop critical thinking skills

10. Refer to the Disney animated movies *Beauty and the Beast, Pinochio, Pocahontas, Cinderella, Aladdin,* and *Little Mermaid,* all of which have either an absent or evil mother. Why has Disney chosen to eliminate the image of a caring and loving mother from these films? Is Disney affecting youngsters' views of the standard two-parent family? Why/why not?

11. Consider the Spielberg movies *Jaws, Raiders of the Lost Ark, Schindler's List,* and *Saving Private Ryan.* Should there be limits on the violence filmmakers should show on screen? Are there some subjects directors, producers, and writers should avoid entirely? Why? Allow students to refer to movies they have seen. Use this also to explore the impact of the media on our lives.

12. Consider December as a chilly, terrible month for the homeless in our country. Do the homeless deserve good housing even if they can't afford it? Why/why not?

13. Consider John Brown's choice to use violence to abolish slavery in the United States. Should we look upon John Brown as a terrorist or a martyr? Do the ends truly justify the means? Should citizens break the law to protest a moral wrong? Why/why not?

> **John Brown began raiding slaveholders in Kansas in the 1850s with the ultimate goal to amass enough arms to invade the South. He and his followers attacked and captured the arsenal at Harper's Ferry but found themselves trapped by federal troops. Brown was captured, turned over to state authorities, and hanged in Charleston.**

14. According to the English government, the Boston Tea Party was an act of vandalism and terrorism when it took place in the Boston Harbor in 1773. American revolutionaries considered it an act of protest for the high taxes placed on the purchase of tea. Were their actions justified? When is vandalism or terrorism an act of protest and not a crime? Use this to review an important historical event and to study our current national concern with terrorism.

15. Consider Rosa Parks who was arrested in 1955 in Montgomery, Alabama for refusing to give up her seat on a bus. Should citizens risk potential imprisonment to make a point on an issue that concerns them? Why/why not?

16. Which is the more important historical event—Orville Wright making the first powered flight at Kitty Hawk in 1903 or Dr. Christian Barnard performing the first human transplant of a human heart in Capetown, South Africa on 55-year-old Louis Washkansky in 1967? Why?

17. Which was the more important historical event—the passage of the 13th Amendment or the Boston Tea Party? Why?

18. What was the most important historical event during the past year? What event will appear most significantly in future history books? Why that one?

19. Which famous writer—Emily Dickinson, Jane Austen, or Willa Cather—contributed most to women's writing in this country? Who achieved most in her field? Use **Form 12-4.**

20. Which poet contributed more to American literature—Emily Dickinson or Edward Arlington Robinson? How? What aspects of each writer's poetry deserve praise? Students could read their poems or research the backgrounds of these two poets.

Purpose: To develop an awareness of other nationalities and cultures

21. Which of the following countries should the United States promote as an ally with funds, aid, or trade—Bahrain, Finland, Kenya, Libya, Portugal, Tanzania, or the United Arab Emirates? In short, which country would be the best ally? Why that country? Have students do research first.

Purpose: To make distinctions between facts and opinions

22. Refer to the television program "To Tell the Truth." Which is more important—facts or opinions? We rarely deal with facts, but express opinions all day in many social and work situations. How can one tell the difference between a fact and an opinion? Between facts and opinions, which are more meaningful?

> **Fact = something that actually happened; reality. These can be proven true or false. Opinion = a belief not based on actual knowledge or certainty.**

WRITING ACTIVITIES

Purpose: To review brainstorming and researching as pre-writing techniques

23. Refer to the states that entered the Union this month and have students list descriptive words and phrases that relate to Illinois, Mississippi, Indiana, Alabama, Iowa, and Texas.

24. Refer to chewing gum, which was patented by William F. Semple, an Ohio dentist, in 1869 and have students list all that they know about it, including brands, costs, tastes.

Purpose: To develop skills at word selection/vocabulary

25. Have students write a one-paragraph newspaper advertisement that might have prompted the English people to travel to the New World and settle in Plymouth in the 1620s. Possibly have students first study some ads from travel agencies.

26. Refer to Louis Pasteur and the pasteurization process used with milk. Ask: Who can list the best adjectives and adverbs to use in a descriptive paragraph about milk?

27. Refer to Dr. Christian Barnard and direct students to write one or two paragraphs that describe the interior of their body when they are sick. Have them follow up by then researching the terms a doctor would use (They should use a dictionary or medical journal).

Purpose: To teach organization in writing

28. Have students write a movie review of a film they have seen recently at a local theater, on video, or on television. Require them to deal in order with the film's characters, dialogue, plot, and special effects, if applicable. Refer to Steven Spielberg and Woody Allen. Distribute a sample movie review from the newspaper, if available.

29. Have students write a travelogue about a journey taken at holiday time.

30. Have students list the events that took place from take off to landing of Orville Wright's first powered flight at Kitty Hawk, North Carolina in 1903.

Purpose: To practice writing description

31. Refer to Dr. Christian Barnard and artificial heart patient Barney C. Clark and have students compose a brief descriptive essay of a hospital experience, focusing especially on sensory language. Then use **Form 12-5** to evaluate it.

32. Have students write a paragraph describing their home during the holiday season (lights, decorations, snow) using sensory language and a combination of simple sentences, compound sentences, and complex sentences. Use **Form 12-5** to evaluate it.

33. Have students write a descriptive essay on the origin, tradition, and creation of any food associated with a culture or nationality, such as Italian pastries. Refer to the countries who celebrate their Independence Day this month and the holiday season. This can also prompt students to appreciate other cultures and ethnicities.

Purpose: To practice writing comparison/contrast

34. Ask: Who contributed more in the area of medical science—Dr. Christian Barnard or Louis Pasteur? Whose contribution was more historically important? Have students write a brief essay comparing/contrasting these two contributors to the field of medicine. Possibly have students research first.

35. Have students write a one-page essay comparing and contrasting Christmas, Chanukah, and Kwanzaa. Use this also to improve cultural awareness and research skills.

Purpose: To practice writing persuasion

36. Have students write an editorial that might have appeared in the Montgomery newspaper the day after Rosa Parks was arrested.

37. Have students write an editorial about the 13th Amendment that could have appeared in any newspaper in 1865.

Purpose: To review news writing style

38. Have students construct a news article about Orville Wright and the first powered flight at Kitty Hawk, North Carolina in 1903. Be sure they follow the format of typical news writing (the five Ws).

> **Example: Orville Wright completed the first powered flight on U.S. soil in a motor-driven aircraft yesterday at Kitty Hawk, North Carolina. He was assisted by his brother Wilbur.**

Purpose: To review letter writing

39. Have students write a letter to a favorite poet (living or dead) telling him/her what they think about his/her poems. They should cite at least one poem to support their points. This also encourages a more critical reading of poetry.

40. Have students write a letter to a teacher, parent, or poet that describes their development as a young poet/writer. In this correspondence they should explain what inspired them to write.

Purpose: To begin or conclude a poetry unit

41. Refer to the poets who have birthdays this month and have students complete a True/False Survey on poetry—**Skill Sheet 12-6.**

42. Have students compose a poem about one of the holidays that take place in December. Challenge their creativity.

43. Have students illustrate, create, and deliver a holiday card that has a brief personal message and a poem by one of the poets who has a birthday this month. Students could also research their backgrounds.

Purpose: To review setting in fiction

44. Refer to the novelists who have birthdays this month and have students select their own favorite author from their literature text or another selected anthology and copy passages that describe setting from a story or novel that they find most interesting.

Purpose: To practice writing reports

45. Consider Rosa Parks. Have students pretend to be the police officer who arrested her and then write a one-page report on the arrest. Use this to develop skills at writing objectively and concisely.

Purpose: To teach the writing of a Decision Essay

46. Consider Jim Morrison and Larry Bird and have students write a Decision Essay. Here, students pretend they have equal interest and talent in both music and basketball but the band director and the basketball coach refuse to let them do both because of the time involved. Ask: What do you do? Students must consider both the advantages and disadvantages in this Decision Essay.

47. Refer to the states that entered the Union this month—Illinois, Mississippi, Indiana, Alabama, Iowa, and Texas—and direct students to decide the one state they would make their home (forced choice). They must explain why they picked that state and describe briefly its attributes. Allow them to research these states first, if necessary.

Purpose: To teach the writing of a personal narrative

48. Have students write a one-page narrative about the most important school event that occurred during the past year. Then use **Form 12-7** to evaluate it.

Purpose: To review reflective writing

49. Have students write a diary entry by Ralph Bunche after he received the Nobel Peace Prize in 1950.

50. Have students write the diary entry of Barney C. Clark, the day after he became the first recipient of an artificial heart.

51. Have students write the diary entry of one of the Presidents who have a birthday this month. The day they select should be during his first official week in office. Instruct them to research the time period, if necessary.

DISCUSSION ACTIVITIES

Purpose: To develop critical thinking skills

52. Consider Barney C. Clark and Dr. Christian Barnard. What kind of relationship should patients have with their doctors? What kind of relationship do you think Barney Clark had with the doctors at the University of Utah Medical Center? Was Clark just an experiment to them? Why/why not?

53. Refer to Ty Cobb and Larry Bird who reached the highest levels of their professions. Both also experienced what some sports psychologists call "burn out." Other terms are "mental fatigue" and "getting stressed out." How would an athlete or person who is experiencing this behave?

54. Refer to Ty Cobb and Larry Bird who reached the highest levels of their professions. What would happen if there were no competitive sports? How important are sports, especially professional sports, to our society?

55. What is your response to Woodrow Wilson's quote: "If you want to make enemies, try to change something." Is he correct? Why/why not?

56. What is Woodrow Wilson suggesting when he advises, "We should not only use the brains we have, but all that we can borrow"? What is he recommending? How might he have followed this advice as President?

57. Woodrow Wilson was the first President to speak on the radio. What impact did that have on the American public? How much influence does the media have on our lives?

58. Refer to Albert Michelson and ask: What has been the most significant technological event in the recent year? Possibly have students research first.

Purpose: *To encourage the reading of biographies*

59. How might biographers obtain the information about their subject?

> **Interviewing the subject, close friends, relatives, and associates; researching records and documents; reading letters written by the subject; reading other books or texts that mention the subject.**

60. What has been the most important/interesting biography that you have read? Why? What person now deserves our attention as the subject of a biography? Why?

Purpose: *To encourage the reading of best-sellers*

61. Refer to Benjamin Franklin's best-seller *Poor Richard's Almanack*. What makes any book a best-seller? What best-sellers have you read?

Purpose: *To preview a fiction unit*

62. How can a reader identify the important characters in a work of fiction? What kind of physical traits, emotional acts, or background details are usually revealed? What makes any character interesting to read about?

63. Refer to novelists Willa Cather, who focused on frontier life, Joseph Conrad, who used a jungle setting, and Arthur C. Clarke, who wrote science fiction, and ask: How is a novel's setting often crucial to our understanding of the theme?

64. Ebeneezer Scrooge, the miserly protagonist in Charles Dicken's story "A Christmas Carol," changes his attitude and feelings completely after a dream involving three ghosts. How can dreams affect us? How could a dream influence the writing of a story or novel? Why do dreams have a profound affect on us? What other works of fiction involve characters who become influenced by their dreams?

Purpose: To develop skills at word selection/vocabulary

65. Refer to the various Presidents who have birthdays this month. What are some of the common words and phrases you've heard or read from politicians, especially Presidents? Which ones are vague or unclear? Which are powerful?

66. What parts of speech are most useful for descriptive writing and which parts of speech are usually less effective?

> **Adjectives, adverbs, prepositional phrases, concrete nouns, and strong verbs are best for descriptive writing while pronouns and conjunctions rarely assist description. One part of editing is replacing words that lack clarity or strength with more descriptive and specific words: replace wind with *breeze*; cold rain with *chilly, December rain*; sound of the horn with *horn's shrill blast*.**

Purpose: To teach organization in writing

67. Refer to Louis Pasteur and Albert Michelson and ask: How do the following scientific methods compare to the writing process: Observe, Hypothesis, Experiment, Data, Analysis, Conclusion?

> **Observe = Select a topic**
>
> **Hypothesis = Prewriting (brainstorming, webbing, cluster)**
>
> **Experiment = Outline**
>
> **Collect data = Research**
>
> **Analyze data = First Draft and Revise/Edit**
>
> **Make a conclusion = Prepare final copy**

Purpose: To teach analogies

68. What is an analogy? What is an example of an analogy? How might analogies appear in our writing?

An analogy is a relationship of similarity between two or more entities. For example, the human heart can be likened to a mechanical pump.

In logic, or inductive reasoning, a reasonable analogy would be that if a high school student who was a champion debater with high test scores was very successful at law school, another high school student who had earned high test scores and championships in debate would also be successful in law school.

Plato used analogies often in his teachings.

We would use analogies in our writing to liken something that was unfamiliar to the reader to something the reader knew well. We would be making an *analogous* or *analogical* relationship. In fact, a writer who chooses to analogize (to show an analogy) would be called an *analogist*.

Purpose: to begin or conclude a poetry unit

69. Refer to the poets who have birthdays this month and ask: What type of verse is more popular—rhyme or free verse? Why? What are some of your favorite poems of each type of verse?

70. Emily Dickinson can be grouped with writers who were considered Naturalists. How would you interpret these lines from one of her poems: "Nature—sometimes sears a Sapling—Sometimes—scalps a tree—Her Green People recollect it when they do not die." What other poets also could be called Naturalists? What aspects of Nature would you write about in a poem?

71. Why do some of Emily Dickinson's poems reflect a sense of gloom or death? How does her poetry differ from that of other poets? What Dickinson poems are your favorites? Why?

72. Emily Dickinson wrote about her poetry: "This is my letter to the world,/That never wrote to me." What did she mean? How could a poem be like a "letter to the world"?

Emily Dickinson wrote many letters to Samuel Bowles of the *Springfield Republican* and to Thomas Wentworth Higginson of the *Atlantic Monthly* pleading with them often to publish her poems, yet they gently refused, claiming most readers would not understand them. Therefore, she withdrew into the personal comforts of her home in Amherst, Massachusetts and continued to write poems, nearly one a day in 1862, some on bits of paper and the backs of envelopes. She left at her death nearly 1500 poems, her "letter to the world."

Purpose: To introduce speech skills

73. What are some famous speeches? What made them so famous? Why improve our speech skills? What speeches or oral presentations might you do in the future?

74. Interpret the following statement: "Writing is a set of marks you make with your fist, whereas speech is a set of marks you make with your face." Refer to Woodrow Wilson and James Thurber who were colorful speakers.

75. Refer to Woodrow Wilson and James Thurber and ask: Who are some speakers you have heard? What made their speeches so effective? Even though Wilson spoke often on the radio, how do speeches also involve nonverbal communication? How should a speech be evaluated? Refer to **Form 12-8.**

Purpose: To begin a careers unit

76. Refer to the various Presidents who have birthdays this month. Martin Van Buren was paid $25,000 a year; Andrew Johnson earned $50,000 and Woodrow Wilson $75,000. Today, the President's salary is $200,000 a year with a $50,000 expense account. Here are some average salaries of other occupations:

    insurance agent—$48,000
    waiter—$14,500
    firefighter—$32,000
    hot dog vendor—$26,000
    bartender—$18,200
    concrete mixer—$33,800
    lawyer—$55,200

    How important is salary to the actual occupation? Do some people get paid too much for their job? How much money do you think you'll earn your first year in a career?

77. What is the difference between a *job* and a *career?* Other than the need for money, why work at all? Why are most people interested in asking, "What do you do for a living?" when they first meet you as an adult?

78. Consider athletes like Larry Bird and Ty Cobb. Of all athletes, which would you like to be? Why? What are the advantages and disadvantages to a career in professional sports?

Purpose: To analyze the news media

79. A 1941 *Chicago Tribune* editorial declared: "Japan cannot attack us. This is a military impossibility. Even our base at Hawaii is beyond the striking power of her fleet." Of course, Japan did attack at Pearl Harbor in 1941. Can we trust the information presented to us in newspapers? How can we determine the accuracy of any news reporting? What other false reporting have you observed?

Usually, we can trust the information provided in newspapers because they have legal and ethical obligations to report the news accurately. We can confirm the accuracy of any news story by checking it with various sources.

AUDIO/VISUAL ACTIVITIES

Purpose: To develop skills at word selection/vocabulary

80. Play a recording or cassette tape of instrumental music and have students list the *action* they recognize (strumming, for example). Refer to Ludwig Van Beethoven and the Doors.

81. Play recordings of holiday songs such as "Jingle Bells" and have students analyze their content and lyrics. Ask: How do the lyrics appeal to our senses? What kind of diction is used? How does it encourage a festive feeling?

82. Show clips from a Disney movie such as *Fantasia*. Students can list descriptive words about their observations.

83. Distribute holiday and greeting cards and have students identify the diction and poetic quality of the message. How effective is it? What type of verse is used? What are the effective phrases?

Purpose: To practice writing description

84. Show selected scenes from the movie *The Southerner* starring Zachary Scott, who portrays a poor farmer in Texas, and have students describe the terrain and climate of Texas.

85. Refer to the patent of chewing gum in 1869 and distribute sticks of bubble gum. Then have students list sensory language to describe the chewing experience.

Purpose: To study characterization

86. Show selected scenes from the movie *Scrooge* and have students list the habits, moods, and traits of the main character as an exercise in characterization.

87. Show selected scenes from the movie *The Doors* starring Val Kilmer and have students list the habits, moods, and traits of the main character as an exercise in characterization or biography.

88. Show selected scenes from the movie *Cobb* starring Tommy Lee Jones and have students list the habits, moods, and traits of the main character as an exercise in characterization or biography.

89. Show selected scenes from any Woody Allen movie and have students list the habits, moods, and traits of the main character as an exercise in characterization. Also study Allen's humor and character types.

Purpose: To begin a poetry unit

90. Play a recording of Jim Morrison's music (the Doors) to analyze his poetic language and themes. Ask: How does rock music at times encourage teenagers to defy authority? Why does rock or rap music prompt a defiance of authority? What words from Morrison's music suggest this?

91. Refer to the poets who have birthdays this month and have students write or locate a poem and attach it to a drawing or illustration they make. Challenge their creativity.

92. Sing Emily Dickinson's poem "Because Death Could Not Stop for Me," if available, to the tune of "Gilligan's Island." Then ask: How did Dickinson accomplish this? How do poets establish rhythm in a poem? What is meter?

> **Meter in poetry is the accent or stress on words in the line of a poem. There are many variations.**

Purpose: To develop research skills

93. Have students create a collage of pictures and headlines from old newspapers and magazines to summarize the important events from the previous year (a.k.a. "The Year in Review"). Use this also to develop organizational skills.

Purpose: To practice writing comparison/contrast

94. Show videotape of a "MASH" episode, the hospital scene from *Gone with the Wind*, or a doctor/patient scene from any other film and have students write descriptions of the medical facilities to contrast them with today's hospitals.

95. Show students travel brochures obtained from a travel agent for Illinois, Mississippi, Indiana, Alabama, Iowa, and Texas. Have students evaluate these states for their attractions and scenery. Ask: Which state would you want to visit? Why? How does it compare to the others?

Purpose: To promote an appreciation of the fine arts

96. Play a recording of the music of Ludwig van Beethoven and have students list the emotions, images, or movements the music arouses in listeners.

Purpose: To improve skills at speech/oral presentations

97. Refer to Jim Morrison and Ludwig van Beethoven and ask students to bring in recordings of their favorite musicians and explain why they admire/enjoy these performers.

98. Ask selected students to pretend to be any of the following individuals (role play) while the rest of the students ask questions:

- Ty Cobb after being named one of the first members inducted into major league baseball's Hall of Fame.

- Larry Bird after being named MVP of the NBA.

- Vice-President Andrew Johnson after learning about the death of Abraham Lincoln.

- Albert Michelson after receiving his Nobel Prize in 1907.

- Dr. Ralph Bunche after receiving his Nobel Prize in 1950.

- Barney C. Clark after recovering from the operation that placed a permanent artificial heart inside of him.

- Walt Disney after announcing the completion of Disneyland.

Name _____

English—Biography Study Projects
(for independent reading)

Select one of the following projects and complete a comprehensive biography study of the book you read independently. Reminder: All written work must be typed on one side of the paper (double-spaced) and approximately 400–500 words. Be sure to include a title page which has . . .

Title of the book middle center;
then double space and put the . . .

Author's name
beneath the book's title.
(Ex) by Keith Manos

Date of the book's publication
beneath the author's name

Name of the person the biography is about
beneath the date.

Your name, class period, and the date
in the middle of the paper at the bottom.

Projects

1. In a detailed and analytical essay, describe each of the persons who had an influence on the subject's life. Be sure to include when, where, and how those persons influenced the subject. Use **direct quotes** from the book to help you explain this influence.

2. Identifying the subject's major experiences are the keys to writing a biography. What are the major experiences, both from childhood and adulthood, that make up your biography? In a **chronological essay,** explain five of these experiences and how they influenced the subject's life.

3. In a detailed and analytical essay, explain why the biographer chose to write about this person. What is the relationship between the biographer and his/her subject? Also, explain how the biographer obtained the information about his/her subject. What about any bias from the biographer?

4. Make a **chart** where you provide the names of each of the places (cities, towns, locales, etc.) important to the subject's life. Then for each, explain the significance of that place. For example . . .

Cleveland, Ohio   Birthplace and home of his parents in childhood years. Father introduced him to all the professional sports teams—the Indians, the Browns

Form 12–1 *(cont.)*

5. In a detailed and analytical essay, explain the **conflicts and obstacles** the person overcame to become famous. Use direct quotes from the book where the subject describes those obstacles/conflicts and how he/she dealt with them. Also, be sure to discover when these difficulties occurred in the person's life and what the subject's attitude was to each circumstance.

6. In a detailed and analytical essay, explain what you found most fascinating about the subject. What aspects of his/her life interested you the most? Why? Go on to explain your opinion of this person as a result of reading the book. Does this person deserve acclaim or criticism? Explain.

7. Create a **resume** for this person. Here, you will need to provide career information, accomplishments, achievements and awards, skills and qualifications. Follow regular resume format and structure.

8. Plot the events of the person's life on a **map.** Make the map large enough to help us understand the locations within a geographical area. Attach a legend to the map, and write a paragraph explaining the importance of each location/event indicated on the map.

9. Make a **test** for the book. Include ten TRUE/FALSE, ten MULTIPLE CHOICE, ten FILL IN THE BLANK, ten MATCHING, and ten SHORT ANSWER ESSAY QUESTIONS. Provide an answer key for the first forty items.

10. Pretend to be a prosecuting attorney and put the subject of the biography on trial for any crime or misdeed. Write a detailed essay that reveals your argument, your evidence, your witnesses, and your expected sentence.

11. Copy 20 to 25 **direct quotes** by the subject that you find through the biography. Create a Question–Answer interview script, as if it were to appear in a magazine.

12. Create a newspaper **front page** detailing the many exploits of your subject. This front page should look as much like a real newspaper page as possible and be based on the events and people associated with the subject's life.

13. Examine the historical time period when the subject of the biography lived. Then write a detailed essay that explains the interesting historical events that probably influenced the subject during his or her life. Make a connection between them.

Benjamin Franklin & Poor Richard's Almanack

Part I

Interpret the following quotes from Benjamin Franklin that appeared in his *Poor Richard's Almanack*. Explain in your own words Franklin's advice to us.

1. "If a man could have half his wishes, he would double his troubles."

2. "Success has ruined many a man."

3. "Keep your eyes wide open before marriage and half-shut afterwards."

4. "Half a truth is often a great lie."

5. "A penny saved is a penny earned."

Part II

Write your own famous quote:

Name _____

"Neighbour Rosicky"

by Willa Cather

Directions: Read the following excerpt from Willa Cather's story "Neighbour Rosicky" and identify the mood of Mr. Rosicky who is 65 and has just learned from a doctor his heart is weak. He's been advised to give up the heavy work he's been doing on his farm. Answer the questions that follow on a separate piece of paper.

It was a nice graveyard, Rosicky reflected, sort of snug and homelike, not cramped or mournful . . . A man could lie down in the long grass and see the complete arch of the sky over him, hear the wagons go by; in summer the mowing-machine rattled right up to the wire fence. And it was so near home. Over there across the cornstalks his own roof and windmill looked so good to him that he promised himself to mind the Doctor and take care of himself. He was awful fond of his place, he admitted. He wasn't anxious to leave it. And it was a comfort to think that he would never have to go farther than the edge of his own hayfield. The snow, falling over his barnyard and the graveyard, seemed to draw things together like. And they were all old neighbors in the graveyard, most of them friends; there was nothing to feel awkward or embarrassed about. Embarrassment was the most disagreeable feeling Rosicky knew.

Questions for discussion:

1. Cather grew up on the prairie lands of Nebraska. How has that experience contributed to this story?

2. What is Rosicky's mood as he journeys home after his visit to the doctor?

3. Why does the graveyard have so much meaning to him?

4. What suggests he is proud of his own farm?

5. Why does he feel "there was nothing to feel awkward or embarrassed about"?

Name _____

Austen vs. Dickinson vs. Cather

Jane Austen (1775–1817)

- Born in Steventon, Hampshire, England and never married, devoting her life to reading and writing novels, especially satires, romances, and parodies.

- Published 3 novels by age 23 (anonymously), and is best known for later works *Sense and Sensibility* and *Pride and Prejudice*. She had little contact with the literary community of London.

- Characters were most often strong female heroines whose morals were tested by forces of heredity, education, economics, and social class.

- Regarded as one of the greatest novelists of the 18th and 19th centuries.

Emily Dickinson (1830–1886)

- Grew up and led a somewhat isolated life in Amherst, Massachusetts.

- Influenced by the poetry of Robert Browning and John Keats.

- Poetry characterized by short lines, intense metaphors, and extensive use of dashes and ellipses.

- Initiated self-publishing by including over 400 poems in letters sent to friends and family but wrote overall nearly 2000 poems, publishing only 7 during her lifetime. She is regarded as America's best known female poet.

- Common themes include God and religious belief, the joy and difficulty of love, the nature of death, the horror of war, and the beauty of nature.

Willa Cather (1873–1947)

- Grew up among pioneering European immigrants in Nebraska whose qualities of courage and perseverance appeared in many of her literary characters. She preferred rural small towns to big cities.

- Worked on a newspaper, as a school teacher, and for a New York magazine.

- Wrote stories, poems, articles, 12 novels (many had strong female characters), editorials, and essays and won the 1922 Pulitzer Prize for Literature (Ranked first among all writers in 1929 for "general literary merit" according to one poll).

- Influenced by the writing of Henry James and Sarah Orne Jewett.

Name _____

Descriptive Essay Evaluation Form

RATING SCALE—1 Weak . . . 3 Average . . . Strong 5

Content & Criteria	Points

1. The essay has a specific focus (topic) and a catchy introduction.   _____

2. The thesis statement which is effectively expressed in the introduction.   _____

3. Sensory language is used (sight, sound, smell, touch, taste).   _____

4. Dull language and clichés are avoided. The writer uses strong verbs and modifiers.   _____

5. Paragraphs are well-structured; they are unified.   _____

6. The writer demonstrates coherence and a clear sense of organization and unity.   _____

7. Includes sentences with a variety of lengths and structures.   _____

8. The essay ends with an effective conclusion.   _____

9. Spelling   _____

10. Grammar and usage   _____

11. * Bonus—The writing style is unique, imaginative, and insightful.   _____

Poetry—True/False Survey

1. _____ Professional poets seldom revise their poems.

2. _____ Poems' themes are usually about love and nature.

3. _____ An epic is longer than an ode.

4. _____ Poets are not eligible to receive the Nobel Prize.

5. _____ Poets are not eligible to receive the Pulitzer Prize.

6. _____ Poems must have a beginning, middle, and end.

7. _____ Some businesses use poems to sell their products or services.

8. _____ Prose can be considered poetic at times.

9. _____ Rhyme is based on syllables and sounds.

10. _____ There are two types of rhyme.

11. _____ Rap music is a type of poetry.

12. _____ A free verse poem has no stanzas.

13. _____ The first winner of the Nobel Prize for literature was a poet.

14. _____ Poetry was a part of the history on every continent.

15. _____ The first poems were songs.

Name _____

Evaluating the Personal Narrative

Points   Criteria

10 _____   **Content**—Was the experience or event dealt with a truly important one? Did the writer apply effective *insight* to the experience? Can it be seen as a turning point?

Comments:

10 _____   **Description**—How descriptive was the writer? Was sensory language used? How effectively did the writer re-create the experience?

Comments:

10 _____   **Organization**—Is there proper paragraphing? Are events arranged in a chronological order? Though there is no established word amount requirement, the thoroughness of the personal narrative will be evaluated here as well. How detailed was the writer?

Comments:

10 _____   **Thematic Purpose**—How effectively did the writer express the theme of the personal narrative? Does the writer apply a lesson or message with the experience?

Comments:

10 _____   **Grammar**—Sentence structure, spelling, usage, capitalization, and punctuation will be evaluated here.

Comments:

50 _____   Total Points

Name _____

Evaluating a Speaker

Speaker's Name: _____

Topic of Speech: _____

Rating System: 1 - - - - - - - - - 2 - - - - - - - - - 3 - - - - - - - - - 4 - - - - - - - 5

                   Poor   Average   Excellent

Criteria	Points
1. Eye contact with entire audience	____
2. Word pronunciation and voice tone	____
3. Evidence of being organized and prepared	____
4. Knowledge of subject	____
5. Delivery of the speech—beginning, middle, and end	____
6. Sincerity of speaker (openness)	____
7. Effective gestures, mannerisms (nonverbal)	____
8. The speech was easily understood and clear overall	____
9. The speaker showed enthusiasm (was dynamic)	____
10. Originality and creativity	____
Total	____

Comments

DECEMBER
Answer Key

#8 SKILL SHEET 12-3—"NEIGHBOUR ROSICKY" BY WILLA CATHER

1. Cather grew up on the prairie lands of Nebraska which is evident in the story by the references to "the long grass," "wire fence," "hayfield," and "cornstalks."

2. Rosicky is feeling comfortable with the knowledge that he is going to die as he journeys home after his visit to the doctor. The graveyard looks like a friendly, serene place. He enjoys his farm.

3. The graveyard has much meaning for him because it is very near his property and friends had been buried there.

4. "He was awful fond of his place" suggests he is proud of his own farm. Also: "He wasn't anxious to leave it."

5. Answers will vary here, but it seems he sees death as a natural outcome of life.

#41 SKILL SHEET 12-6—POETRY TRUE/FALSE SURVEY

1. False—Lines could be revised over and over. Poet Lawrence Ferlinghetti claimed poems were never finished, only abandoned.

2. False—They can cover all subjects.

3. True—Epics are typically book length.

4. False—The work of poetry, fiction, and drama are equally considered under the category of Literature.

5. False—There is a category for Poetry.

6. True—Poems, like stories, have structure.

7. True—Jingles and slogans can be poetic; in fact, one tea bag company puts poems on its packages.

8. True—It is not uncommon to find poetic phrases in prose.

9. True

10. False—Variations include AABB, ABAB, AABBA, etc.

11. True—All lyrics can be considered poetry.

12. False

13. True—French poet Sully Prudhomme (1839–1907) won the first Nobel Prize in 1901.

14. True

15. True—Historians believe the ceremonial chants of ancient man were poetic.

JANUARY

JANUARY

Origin: January is named for Janus, a Roman god who had two faces that looked in opposite directions, and was made the first month of the year (with 31 days) by the ancient Romans.

Holidays: New Year's Day is recognized in most countries.

U.S. citizens celebrate Martin Luther King Day.

Around mid-January Hindus celebrate the festival of Makara Sankranti and possibly bathe in the Ganges River, India's most sacred river.

La Befana Day, a festival in which Befana, a kindly witch, bestows gifts on good children and a lump of coal for the naughty, is celebrated in Italy.

Haiti and Sudan celebrate their Independence Days in January.

Gemstone: Garnet

Flower: Carnation

Poetry: Ring out the old, ring in the new,
Ring, happy bells, across the snow;
The year is going, let him go;
Ring out the false, ring in the true.

by Alfred Lord Tennyson

BIRTHDAYS

Jan. 1	J.D. Salinger, author of *The Catcher in the Rye* (1919) [#3, 16, 68, 79, 80]
Jan. 2	Isaac Asimov, science fiction writer and author of nearly 400 books (1920) [#4, 16, 60, 68, 74, 97]
Jan. 3	John Ronald Reuel Tolkien, author of *Lord of the Rings* trilogy (1892) [#9]
Jan. 4	Jacob Grimm, author of *Grimm's Fairy Tales* (1785) [#9, 67, 98]; Isaac Newton, English scientist who discovered the law of gravitation (1642) [#21, 53, 87]
Jan. 6	Joan of Arc (1412); Carl Sandburg, Pulitzer Prizes for History in 1940 and Poetry in 1951 (1878) [#5, 15, 65, 83]
Jan. 7	Millard Filmore, 13th President (1800) [#14, 20]
Jan. 8	Elvis Presley, singer (1935) [#34, 48, 93]
Jan. 9	Richard M. Nixon, 37th President (1913) [#14, 17, 20, 99]
Jan. 10	Robinson Jeffers, poet (1887) [#5, 65]
Jan. 12	John Hancock, first signer of the Declaration of Independence (1737) [#17, 23]; Jack London, writer (1876) [#1, 13, 15, 95, 97]; Howard Stern, writer/actor/radio personality (1954) [#22, 84]
Jan. 14	Benedict Arnold, traitor during the Revolutionary War (1741) [#19]; Albert Schweitzer, physician/philosopher/musician who won the Nobel Peace Prize in 1952 (1857) [#53, 86]
Jan. 15	Martin Luther King, Jr., minister/civil rights advocate, winner of the Nobel Peace Prize in 1964 (1929) [#23, 61]
Jan. 17	Muhammad Ali (born Cassius Marcellus Clay, Jr.), Olympic and world heavyweight boxing champion (1942) [#44, 48, 100]; Benjamin Franklin, oldest signer of both the Declaration of Independence and the Constitution/diplomat/scientist/author/publisher (1706) [#21, 49]
Jan. 19	Robert E. Lee, General and commander of Confederate troops during Civil War (1807) [#18]; Edgar Allan Poe, poet/story writer (1809) [#2, 7, 15, 41, 65, 72, 78]
Jan. 25	Robert Burns, Scottish poet (1759) [#6, 65, 66]; Somerset Maugham, novelist/playwright (1874) [#68, 73]; Virginia Woolf, English critic/novelist (1882) [#68, 81, 97]

Jan. 27   Lewis Carroll (Charles Dodgson), author of *Alice's Adventures in Wonderland* (1832) [#19]; Wolfgang Amadeus Mozart, regarded as one of the greatest musical geniuses of all time (1756) [#92]

Jan. 29   Anton Chekhov, Russian playwright (1860) [#89]; William McKinley, 25th President (1843) [#14, 20]; Thomas Paine, American Revolutionary leader (1737) [#18, 82]; Oprah Winfrey, television personality/writer/actress (1954) [#48, 62, 94]

Jan. 30   Franklin Delano Roosevelt, 32nd President (1882) [#14, 20, 84, 101]

MEMORABLE EVENTS

Jan. 1   The Emancipation Proclamation was enacted in 1863 by President Abraham Lincoln, freeing the slaves in the rebelling states [#43].

Jan. 3   Alaska was admitted to the Union as the 49th state in 1959 [#13, 27].

Jan. 4   Utah was admitted to the Union as the 45th state in 1896 [#13, 91].

Jan. 6   National Smith Day to honor the commonest surname in the English speaking world. There are an estimated 2.4 million Smiths in the United States [#24].

New Mexico was admitted to the Union as the 47th state in 1912 [#13, 91].

"Wheel of Fortune" premiered in 1975 [#42, 51].

Jan. 7   First commercial transatlantic phone service between New York and London began in 1927. Thirty-one calls were made on the first day [#36].

The first commercial bank in the U.S., the Bank of North America, opened in Philadelphia in 1782 [#35].

Jan. 14   "Simpsons" premiered in 1990 [#33, 54].

Jan. 17   St. Anthony's Day (the patron saint of all domestic animals and patriarch of all monks) [#31, 55].

Jan. 23   Dr. Elizabeth Blackwell became the first woman to receive an MD degree. The Medical Institution of Geneva in New York bestowed this honor in 1849 [#56].

National Pie Day [#25, 37].

Jan. 24   Gold was discovered in Coloma, California in 1848, which prompted the gold rush of 1849 [#38, 57].

Jan. 26   Michigan was admitted to the Union as the 26th state in 1837 [#13].

Jan. 27   National Compliment Day [#47].

Thomas Crapper Day. Crapper is said to be the prime inventor of the flush toilet mechanism [#32].

Jan. 29   Kansas was admitted to the Union as the 34th state [#13, 91].

National Puzzle Day [#37, 96].

Jan. 30   Library of Congress formed with the purchase of Thomas Jefferson's library in 1815 [#71].

Jan. 31   McDonald's opened the first fast food restaurant in the Soviet Union in 1990 [#30].

National Popcorn Day [#37, 90].

LEARNING ACTIVITIES FOR JANUARY

READING ACTIVITIES

Purpose: To improve skills at analyzing fiction

1. Have students read a story by Jack London from their literature text or an available anthology. Students can analyze the short story for its characters and settings.

> **The characters from Jack London's short fiction typically were rugged individuals—prospectors, sailors, hunters—who lived or worked in remote areas of nature, like the Pacific Ocean and the Yukon and Klondike territories of Alaska.**

2. Have students read selected stories by Edgar Allan Poe from their literature text or an available anthology and analyze these works for their characters and settings.

> **The characters from Edgar Allen Poe's short fiction typically were eccentrics, detectives, even murderers—who lived in secluded, gloomy places—dark dungeons, crumbling mansions, dreary cities.**

3. Assign students J.D. Salinger's *Catcher in the Rye* or a novel by Jack London. Have them analyze the novel for its characters, conflict, and theme and then use the Novel Study Project form, **Form 11-8,** to evaluate them.

Purpose: To introduce science fiction

4. Direct students to read a science fiction story from their literature text or available anthology. First ask: How is science fiction different from other types of fiction? Who are some major science fiction writers? What are some science fiction books? Refer to Isaac Asimov.

Purpose: To improve skills at analyzing poetry

5. Have students read selected poems by Carl Sandburg and Robinson Jeffers from their literature text or available anthology. Students can analyze these poems for their language, content, verse, and themes. Use **Form 1-1.**

6. Have students read poems by Robert Burns from their literature text or available anthology and analyze his poems for their language and content.

> **Robert Burns wrote his poetry—ballads and narrative verse—most often in the vernacular of the Scottish dialect. His verse was humorous, satirical, and patriotic, especially when portraying the countryside and farm life of Scotland.**

7. Have students read selected poems by Edgar Allan Poe from their literature text or an available anthology and analyze these poems for their language and content.

> **Edgar Allan Poe's poetry was often melancholy and rhythmic verse about death, isolation, and despair.**

Purpose: To introduce the reading of nonfiction

8. Have students explore the writer's purpose for any nonfiction piece. Ask: Is the writer trying to entertain, inform, persuade, or analyze? What is the writer's theme or message? How interesting is the content and writing style? Use **Skill Sheet 1-2** and **Skill Sheet 1-3**.

> **Nonfiction is writing that focuses on real people, actual places, and historical events. Forms of nonfiction include biography, autobiography, letters, historical narratives, essays, how-to books, and editorials.**

Purpose: To introduce the literary genre of Fantasy

9. Have students locate and read excerpts from Lewis Carroll's *Alice's Adventures in Wonderland* or J.R.R. Tolkien's *The Hobbit* (or another author from the list). Use **Form 1-4**.

Purpose: To analyze a speech

10. Distribute **Skill Sheet 1-5** and have students read orally or silently the excerpts from Martin Luther King's "I Have a Dream" speech to study the content and diction.

Purpose: To study the use of transitional words

11. Have students read and study the essay on New Year's Resolutions **(Form 1-6)**. Use it to review essay unity and coherence. Students should note the use of transitional words in bold face.

Purpose: To improve research skills

12. Have students locate and read encyclopedia articles about the writers who have birthdays this month to introduce the biographical details related to their writing and to review methods of researching.

13. Direct students to investigate encyclopedia articles, any reference books, travel brochures, and websites related to Alaska, Utah, New Mexico, Michigan, and Kansas. Also have students seek interviews with people who either live in or have visited these states.

14. Have students locate the titles of biographies written about the Presidents who have birthdays this month.

DEBATING ACTIVITIES

Purpose: To improve research skills

15. Which poet contributed most to American poetry—Edgar Allan Poe or Carl Sandburg? Students could read their poems or research the backgrounds of these writers.

16. Who contributed most to American fiction—J.D. Salinger, Isaac Asimov, or Jack London? Students could read their literature or research the backgrounds of these writers.

17. Who had a greater influence on American politics—John Hancock or Richard Nixon?

> **John Hancock was a member of the Continental Congress, the first man to sign the Declaration of Independence, and the first governor of Massachusetts. Richard Nixon was a U.S. Representative first and later U.S. Senator from California before becoming Vice President under Eisenhower and a two-term President (1969–1974) until his resignation.**

18. Who had a greater impact on American history—Thomas Paine whose "Common Sense" pamphlet encouraged the creation of the Declaration of Independence and whose "The American Crisis" pamphlet inspired the revolutionary troops; or Robert E. Lee, who turned down a command in the Union Army to fight for his native Virginia before becoming commander-in-chief of the Confederate army and signing the papers of surrender that ended the Civil War?

Purpose: To improve critical thinking skills

19. What makes a citizen a traitor? If an individual's morals are in conflict with the rules of his/her government but not with an enemy government, is this person a traitor? Refer to Benedict Arnold.

20. Refer to the Presidents who have birthdays this month and ask: Who currently is our best world leader? How could we determine this? Who has accomplished the most for his/her people?

21. Which was the more important scientific discovery—Isaac Newton's discovery of gravity or Benjamin Franklin's discovery of electricity?

22. Refer to Howard Stern and ask: Should there be limitations on free speech? When does radio discourse become socially and morally unacceptable/offensive? Should the authorities limit Howard Stern's dialogue during his broadcasts? Use this to introduce or review a unit on censorship and free speech (possibly in speech and literature).

> In ancient Rome, two magistrates held the title of *censor*. Their duties included taking the census of citizens for tax purposes, filling vacancies in the Senate, and supervising the public morals and behavior. The word *censor* has since been passed down to present day where various public officials possess a limited power of censorship on film, television programs, written materials, and radio. Their power to censor is limited in part by the First Amendment which guarantees freedom of expression.

23. Refer to Martin Luther King, Jr., who promoted nonviolence and passive resistance to eliminate Jim Crow laws and to bring about civil rights legislation; and to John Hancock who signed the Declaration of Independence which documented him as a rebel against the British government. Is a passive, nonviolent approach or an open rebellion the most useful method to causing any change in government? Use this to improve students' ability to analyze historical events.

WRITING ACTIVITIES

Purpose: To review brainstorming as a prewriting activity

24. If Smith is the most common name, what are some unusual names that are more interesting? What are some unique names? Challenge students to be creative. Who can offer the most interesting surnames? Have students brainstorm a list.

25. Refer to National Pie Day and have students brainstorm on the board all types of pies along with modifiers.

26. Have students list their New Year's Resolutions. Be sure they consider past events and future expectations, much like the Roman god Janus who could look both ways. Conclude by having them exchange their lists. Use this also to introduce or review the importance of goal setting, as if for a career.

A Resolution is a goal or promise that involves a personal responsibility—for example, to read more books or get better grades; or a relationship with others—to help my father with chores more often.

Purpose: To improve skills at organization of writing

27. Have students write a travelogue about Alaska. Possibly distribute travel brochures that you can pick up from any travel agent, or direct students to an atlas. Use **Form 11-11** as a model

28. Have students construct a step-by-step plan for accomplishing a goal or objective for the coming year. Then relate this to the steps a writer follows to complete a poem, story, essay, or book.

Purpose: To practice writing comparison/contrast

29. Have students write an essay comparing LaBefana, the kindly witch, to Santa Claus. Use this also as a research project to improve students' awareness of other cultures and traditions.

30. Have students write a one-page essay comparing the food, service, and appearance of a local McDonalds to what they imagine the one that opened in 1990 in Moscow had.

Purpose: To improve writing description

31. Refer to St. Anthony's Day (the patron saint of all domestic animals) and to those students who have a pet. First, discuss the benefits of having a pet and then have them use sensory language in a single paragraph to describe the pet they have or would like to have.

32. Have students write a one-page essay about a toilet, using the appropriate technical terms (caution them about words related to the sense of smell). Relate this to Thomas Crapper Day and mail the essays to any toilet manufacturer.

Purpose: To improve writing a character sketch

33. Refer to the "Simpsons" television program and have the students write descriptive character sketches about any character.

34. Elvis Presley was the "King" of rock and roll in the 1950s and 1960s. Ask: Who is the king of rock and roll now? Have students profile the musician/performer who currently can be considered to be the king (or queen).

35. Refer to Janus, the Roman god of gates and doors (openings and beginnings). Have students create a mythological god for January or another month. Use this to challenge their creativity or to initiate a unit on mythology.

Purpose: To work at writing dialogue

36. Have students create the dialogue of any conversation that took place on one of those first commercial transatlantic telephone calls from New York to London in 1927. Thirty-one calls were made on the first day. Challenge their creativity and improve their understanding of dialogue in fiction and drama.

Purpose: To work at writing fictional narratives

37. Challenge students to write a brief narrative that involves popcorn, pie, and a puzzle. Refer to National Popcorn Day, National Pie Day, and National Puzzle Day.

38. Refer to gold being discovered in Coloma, California in 1848 and instruct students to write a narrative about two prospectors who got involved in the gold rush of 1849. Have them begin the narrative with *We arrived in Coloma, gathered supplies, and then headed out to . . .*

39. Have students write a narrative about an event in the coming year. Prompt them to make creative predictions.

Purpose: To practice writing summaries

40. Have students review a story they've read in class before writing a summary of it in one of the following formats: chronology, outline, paragraphs. Use this also to improve their comprehension of a plot.

41. Refer to Edgar Allan Poe's stories which often have gloomy and supernatural settings and have students write a paragraph explaining how those settings influence their understanding of a Poe story.

42. Ask students to consider game shows, like "Wheel of Fortune," and then write a brief explanation/summary of the game's rules, strategies, and prizes.

Purpose: To review speech skills

43. Have students pretend to be Abraham Lincoln and prompt them to write the speech announcing the Emancipation Proclamation which freed the slaves in the South.

Purpose: To improve skills at persuasive writing

44. Refer to Muhammad Ali during and after his career and ask: How much acclaim and recognition should we place on those engaged in the sport of boxing—men (and now women) trying to harm each other? Then have students write a one-page editorial taking a stand on this issue.

45. Have students compose an editorial that evaluates the quality of education in the school system. Students must take a stand for or against the idea that their school provides a quality education.

Purpose: To review letter writing

46. Refer to Dr. Elizabeth Blackwell and ask: What problems do you think she encountered during her school days at the Medical Institution of Geneva in New York? Then have students write her personal letter to an imaginary relative about these difficulties.

47. Refer to National Compliment Day and use this to have students write a letter complimenting another person—a friend, parent, or classmate, for example—for his/her recent performance or contribution.

48. Have students write a letter to a celebrity—sports star, performer, or television personality. Refer to Muhammad Ali, Elvis Presley, and Oprah Winfrey.

Purpose: To improve critical thinking skills

49. Distribute **Skill Sheet 1-7**—Quotes from Benjamin Franklin—and have students analyze and interpret his famous statements.

50. Discuss students' overall expectations for the new year and then have them write a one-page explanation about their personal expectations.

DISCUSSION ACTIVITIES

Purpose: To review skills at word selection/vocabulary

51. Use "Wheel of Fortune" as the format and involve students in a spelling or vocabulary review.

52. Refer to the Bank of North America, the first commercial bank in the United States, and direct students to define terms related only to the banking industry. Use **Skill Sheet 1-8**.

53. Refer to Albert Schweitzer and Isaac Newton, among others, and ask: What are the differences between a concept and a theory? How would these two use a concept and a theory in their work? How would a writer use these terms?

> **A concept is a thought or idea while a theory refers more to a hypothesis, guess, or speculation.**

Purpose: To improve critical thinking skills

54. What makes an event, a situation, or a person funny? Why might some people laugh but not others? Why might some viewers consider Homer Simpson of "The Simpsons" to be humorous, while others feel outraged by his persona?

55. Refer to St. Anthony. Why do people keep pets? How do pets bring enjoyment (or problems) to our lives? What benefits do pets bring to our lives?

56. Consider Dr. Elizabeth Blackwell and her goal to be a physician. What were her dreams/goals? What are your dreams/goals? How can goals benefit our lives? Use this also to introduce the importance of goal setting for a career.

57. Refer to gold being discovered in California and its high value and ask: What is our most valuable commodity? Gold? Jewels? Oxygen (because without it we couldn't live)? What else?

58. Which country would you like to visit: India, Italy, or Haiti? Why? What would you do there on your visit? Have students locate these countries on an atlas and do some research.

59. How effective are New Year's Resolutions? What are yours? What are some resolutions you've made in the past? What resolutions do you have regarding school? Your career?

Purpose: To review speech skills

60. Refer to Isaac Asimov and ask: What do you think he'd talk about at a science fiction convention?

61. Refer to Martin Luther King Jr., and ask: How did he get the attention of all U.S. citizens in his speeches?

62. What makes Oprah Winfrey an effective talk show host? How does she communicate to her audience? How do audiences respond to her? Why?

Purpose: To introduce a poetry unit

63. What are the advantages to memorizing poems? What poems have you memorized? Why are poems more accessible to oral reading than short stories?

64. Is poetry a dying art form or is it more popular today than ever?

> **Poetry, in fact, is more popular today than ever before. More colleges, taverns, coffee shops, and book stores host poetry readings, and more books of poetry have been published in the past decade than were published in the previous four centuries. The U.S. Poet Laureate, among other poets, is given much media exposure, and poems are appearing in more magazines than ever before.**

65. What are the most effective ways for interpreting a poem? Refer to poets Edgar Allan Poe, Robinson Jeffers, Carl Sandburg, Robert Burns, and others. Use **Form 1-1.**

> Interpretation of poetry is both a group and individual activity. Typically, once the reader interprets a poem, he/she seeks agreement from others, usually established literary critics and teachers of poetry. The goal then is to establish a common ground for meaning—for example, Shakespeare's sonnet reflects romantic love. Debates can and do occur, even among the most learned literary critics, yet the evidence for any interpretation must be found in the poem's content. Readers can also explore the poet's background, the historical context, and the type of verse.

66. Consider Robert Burns's famous line "My love is like a red, red rose." Why the repetition of red? Why the connection between the woman he loves and a rose? What type of figurative language is at work here? [simile].

67. Refer to Jacob Grimm, author of *Grimm's Fairy Tales*. What are some famous nursery rhymes? Why do you think some of the earliest poems were in rhyme? What are some other examples of poems that show the use of rhyme? How does rhyme influence the meaning or message of a poem?

> The Grimm brothers' primary intent was to write and publish oral stories. In fact, according to historians, these first stories were not intended for children, as they dealt with plots involving cruelty, sorcery, and betrayal and the themes of love of beauty and the triumph of justice. Their book has become through history second only to the Bible as a best-seller. It was Walt Disney who transformed these tales with their moral, ethical, and psychological over-tones into love dramas and sentimental comedies.

Purpose: To begin or conclude a fiction unit

68. Refer to Isaac Asimov, Virginia Woolf, Somerset Maugham, and J.D. Salinger and their novel titles on **Form 1-9.** Then ask: How can novel titles suggest the main *conflict*, the *climax*, and the *resolution* of the story?

69. What is your favorite novel? What novel would you recommend a classmate read this year? What makes that novel so special?

70. Which novelist in general do you admire most? Why? How would you describe his/her writing style?

71. Refer to the Library of Congress and ask: What book above all others belongs in the Library of Congress? Why?

72. Consider Edgar Allan Poe, who is called the "father of the modern detective story," and his story, "Murders in the Rue Morgue." In a detective/mystery story, what makes for good suspense? Who are some famous literary detectives? What are the traits of good suspects? Who are some current mystery writers?

73. What does Somerset Maugham suggest about reading when he says, "To acquire the habit of reading is to construct for yourself a refuge from almost all the miseries of life."

74. Refer to Isaac Asimov. What science fiction have you read? How would you define science fiction? What are the characteristics of an effective science fiction story? If the the author's science fiction at the time he/she wrote the story becomes fact, does it cease to be classified as science fiction?

75. How does the setting influence our understanding of a story? How does an author create mood such as the gloom and sorrow in a Poe story? How important is the setting to our understanding of the characters and the theme of a story?

76. What have you learned about characterization? What types of characters have you read? How do you identify a positive character? A negative one?

77. For any character from any story we have read in class, insert yourself in his/her place. How would you have acted? What would you have said? Why?

78. Write Edgar Allan Poe's definition, or purpose, of short fiction on the board: "The literary artist . . . invents such incidents and combines such events as may best aid him in establishing the preconceived effect" and "leave in the mind of him who contemplates it . . . a sense of the fullest satisfaction." Then ask: What does Poe mean by "the preconceived effect"? Why does he refer to the reader having "the fullest satisfaction"? Is Poe's definition accurate? Why/why not?

79. A reviewer for the *Christian Science Monitor* said the novel *Catcher in the Rye* "is not fit for children to read." A spokesman for the Detroit Police Department labeled it as "pornographic trash." Should the book be read by teens? Why/why not?

80. J.D. Salinger disappeared to his New Hampshire home and stopped publishing his writing in 1962, claiming that publication was "a terrible invasion of . . . privacy." He became a Zen Buddhist and refuses all requests for interviews. How should we interpret these decisions? Why do you think Salinger refuses to publish his writing, although he continues to write daily? How does this type of behavior add to his status as an author?

81. Explain that Virginia Woolf wrote essays, reviews, some 4000 letters, novels, 30 diary volumes, and sketches. She wrote fiction in the early morning, standing at a tall desk for periods of up to two and a half hours, then used the early afternoon to revise. She enjoyed solitude: "I must be private, secret, as anonymous and submerged as possible in order to write." What are your responses to her routine as a fiction writer? Why was she so productive? Would you adopt this procedure for writing fiction? Why/why not?

Purpose: To identify an effective essay introduction

82. Refer to Thomas Paine's opening line to his famous essay "The American Crisis": "These are the times that try men's souls." How effective is this as an introduction? Why is a reader eager to learn more? To what does this sentence refer?

Purpose: To review an understanding of slang

83. What does Carl Sandburg mean with his definition of slang: "Slang is a language that rolls up its sleeves, spits on its hands, and goes to work"?

Purpose: To explore the influence of the media

84. Franklin Delano Roosevelt was the first President to appear on television. What impact did that have on the public? How have Presidents used television since then? When do Presidents typically use television time?

85. Refer to Howard Stern. If you could broadcast over the radio for an entire day, what would you talk about? What would you say to other teenagers? How would you plan your topics?

Purpose: To introduce a careers unit

86. Refer to Albert Schweitzer, who won the Nobel Peace Prize in 1952. How would you describe the personality of a person who was an accomplished physician, philosopher, musician, and humanitarian?

87. Refer to Isaac Newton. What careers are available in the field of science? What kind of skills and background would a person need to succeed in this field? What high school courses would help a person succeed in science?

88. What are the best jobs for the future?

(1) traveling nurse; **(2)** robotics engineer; **(3)** hotel services; **(4)** environmental engineer; **(5)** lawyers with backgrounds in international law or toxic waste regulations; **(6)** computer services and technology; **(7)** nursing home management (According to the U.S. Dept. of Labor)

Purpose: To begin or conclude a drama unit (Chekhov)

89. Why are Anton Chekhov's plays said to be somber and sad? What kind of subjects and characters does he deal with? How do these characters behave?

Anton Chehkov didn't base his plays on a central character, and the conflict typically dealt with feelings of despair, suicide, and bitter relationships.

Audio/Visual Activities

Purpose: To improve writing description

90. Distribute popcorn and have students touch, smell, study, and taste it before *writing* a complete, coherent, and descriptive paragraph about it.

91. Refer to an atlas and compare the geography and terrain of Utah, New Mexico, and Kansas. Use this to introduce the importance of accuracy in the setting of any story, novel, or drama, especially those that deal with the American frontier of the old West and have students write descriptive paragraphs about a location.

92. Play recordings of Wolfgang Amadeus Mozart, regarded as one of the greatest musical geniuses of all time. Have students list the emotions, images, or movements the music arouses in listeners. Use this also to improve their creativity and culture. See if they can identify the various instruments.

93. Play recordings of Elvis Presley and have students list the emotions, images, or movements the music arouses in the listeners. Use this also to improve their creativity and self-expression.

Purpose: To explore the influence of the media

94. Show a videotape of a brief segment of any Oprah Winfrey show and have students evaluate the actual content of the show (i.e., its originality, the guests' comments, her insights).

Purpose: To conclude a fiction/nonfiction unit

95. Show selected scenes from the movie *Call of the Wild* to review the novel by Jack London.

96. Have students create a puzzle reflecting the setting of a novel they have read. Refer to National Puzzle Day.

97. Assign students to visit the library to locate and list some of the comparable *non-fiction* book titles of the following authors: Isaac Asimov, Virginia Woolf, and Jack London.

Isaac Asimov:	*Asimov's Guide to Science, Intelligent Man's Guide to Science, In Memory Yet Green, In Joy Still Felt, Biographical Encyclopedia of Science and Technology, etc.*
Virginia Woolf:	*Orlando, Moments of Being, Beginning Again,* etc.
Jack London:	*War of the Classes, John Barleycorn, The Road,* etc.

Purpose: To practice writing characterizations

98. Have selected students role-play or dramatize one of Jacob Grimm's fairy tales while the other students write brief characterizations.

99. Show selected scenes from the movie *Nixon* starring Anthony Hopkins and have students list the habits, moods, and traits of Richard Nixon as an exercise in characterization or biography.

> **President Richard Nixon hired two reporters to spy on the Democratic Presidential candidates to discover "who was sleeping with who, what the Secret Service men were doing with stewardesses, who was smoking pot . . ." What does this suggest about Nixon's personality? How should we judge him as President?**

100. Show selected scenes from the movie *The Greatest* which is about the life of Muhammad Ali and have students list his habits, moods, and traits. Use this also to encourage the reading of the biographies of Ali.

> **Titles include *King of the World* by David Remnick, *Muhammad Ali in Fighter's Heaven* by Victor Bockris, *Muhammad Ali: His Life and Times* by Thomas Hauser, *Muhammad Ali: The Greatest of All Time* by Robert Cassidy, among others.**

101. Show selected scenes from the movie *Sunrise at Campobello* starring Ralph Bellamy and have students list the habits, moods, and traits of Franklin Delano Roosevelt as he fights against polio and enters politics. Use this as an exercise in biography or characterization.

Interpreting Poetry—A Checklist

1. _____   What does the poem mean to me?

2. _____   What do my peers say about the poem?

3. _____   How have noted literary critics analyzed the poem?

4. _____   What is the background of the poet?

5. _____   Who is narrating the poem?

6. _____   What type of verse is it (i.e., rhyme, free verse)?

7. _____   What type of poem is it (i.e., ballad, limerick, sonnet, etc.)?

8. _____   Is there special imagery in the poem?

9. _____   Are there any historical, Biblical, or mythological allusions?

10. _____   What is the tone or mood of the poem?

11. _____   What are the key phrases or lines in the poem?

12. _____   How does the title relate to the poem overall?

13. _____   Any unusual use of punctuation or capitalization?

14. _____   Any figurative language?

15. _____   What other inferences can I make after reading the poem again?

16. _____   What, if any, is the historical context of the poem?

17. _____   How would I paraphrase this poem?

18. _____   How does this poem compare to other poems by this poet?

19. _____   How does the poem make me feel (what emotions does it arouse?)?

20. _____   After reading it again, how would I interpret this poem?

Name _____

What Do You Know About Nonfiction Books?

I   TRUE or FALSE

1. _____ Nonfiction books belong in the genre of fantasy.

2. _____ Nonfiction books seldom have themes.

3. _____ Nonfiction books must have titles.

4. _____ Nonfiction books must have a beginning, a middle, and an end.

5. _____ Nonfiction books are generally longer than fictional books.

6. _____ Nonfiction books, since they are based on actual events or people, need not be revised.

7. _____ Nonfiction originated in this century.

8. _____ A biography is a nonfiction book.

9. _____ Nonfiction books can tell a story.

10. _____ A published speech can be classified as nonfiction.

11. _____ Nonfiction books will not have dialogue.

12. _____ An autobiography is a nonfiction book.

13. _____ Persuasive writing is seldom seen in a work of nonfiction.

14. _____ Reference books are nonfiction.

15. _____ Nonfiction books are listed on the *New York Times* bestseller list.

II **Listing**—List all the nonfiction books you read in the last year:

Name _____

Nonfiction Book Study

Title of the book _____

Author _____

Publisher _____ Date _____

1. How would you classify this book?

2. Who is the intended audience for this book?

3. What is the tone of the writing?

4. What quotations from the book illustrate this tone?

5. What message or theme is expressed by the book?

6. How would you describe the writing style—vocabulary, sentence structure, anecdotes?

7. What interesting details are revealed in the book?

8. What special insights does the writer share about the subject?

9. Is the subject presented in an objective way, or is it subjective? Explain.

© 2001 by The Center for Applied Research in Education

Form 1–4 Name _____

The History of Fantasy Writing

The literary genre of fantasy focuses on characters, settings, and events that are wildly imaginative or highly unreal. Below are some of the major works that can be classified in this genre.

Date	Title	Author
1100s	King Arthur	?
1469	*The Death of Arthur*	Sir Thomas Mallory
1726	*Gulliver's Travels*	Jonathan Swift
1729	*Red Riding Hood, Cinderella*	Charles Perault
1819	*Rip Van Winkle*	Washington Irving
1865	*Alice's Adventures in Wonderland*	Lewis Carroll
1872	*Through the Looking Glass*	Lewis Carroll
1894	*The Jungle Book*	Rudyard Kipling
1900	*The Wizard of Oz*	Frank Baum
1904	*Peter Pan*	Sir James Barrie
1908	*The Wind in the Willows*	Kenneth Grahame
1915	*Metamorphosis*	Franz Kafka
1937	*The Hobbit*	J.R.R. Tolkien
1942	*Paul Bunyan*	Carl Carmer
1969	*Slaughterhouse-Five*	Kurt Vonnegut
1972	*Watership Down*	Richard Adams
1977	*Silmarillion*	J.R.R. Tolkien
1977	*Kingdom of Elfin*	Sylvia T. Warner
1996	*The Green Mile*	Stephen King
1998	*Harry Potter*	J.K. Rowling

Name _____

"I Have a Dream"

by Martin Luther King, Jr.

I say to you today, my friends, even though we face the difficulties of today and tomorrow, I still have a dream. It is a dream deeply rooted in the American dream.

I have a dream that one day this nation will rise up and live out the true meaning of its creed: "We hold these truths to be self-evident; that all men are created equal."

I have a dream that one day on the red hills of Georgia the sons of former slaves and the sons of former slave owners will be able to sit down together at the table of brotherhood.

I have a dream that one day even the state of Mississippi, a state sweltering with the heat of injustice, sweltering with the heat of oppression, will be transformed into an oasis of freedom and justice.

I have a dream that my four little children will one day live in a nation where they will not be judged by the color of their skin but by the content of their character. I have a dream today.

I have a dream that one day down in Alabama . . . one day right there in Alabama little black boys and black girls will be able to join hands with little white boys and white girls as sisters and brothers. I have a dream today.

This will be the day when all of God's children will be able to sing with new meaning: My country 'tis of thee, sweet land of liberty, of thee I sing. Land where my fathers died, land of the pilgrim's pride, from every mountainside, let freedom ring!

And if America is to be a great nation, this must become true. And so let freedom ring from the prodigious hilltops of New Hampshire. Let freedom ring from the mighty mountains of New York. Let freedom ring from the heightening Alleghenies of Pennsylvania. Let freedom ring from the snow-capped Rockies of Colorado. Let freedom ring from the curvaceous slopes of California. But not only that, let freedom ring from Stone Mountain of Georgia. Let freedom ring from Lookout Mountain of Tennessee. Let freedom ring from every hill and molehill of Mississippi. From every mountainside, let freedom ring.

And when this happens, when we allow freedom ring, when we let it ring from every village and every hamlet, from every state and every city, we will be able to speed up that day when all of God's children, black men and white men, Jews and Gentiles, Protestants and Catholics, will be able to join hands and sing in the words of the old Negro spiritual:

> Free at last! Free at last!
> Thank God Almighty, we are free at last.

Questions

1. How does King connect to his audience?

2. Where does the sentence "We hold these truths to be self-evident; that all men are created equal" originate?

3. What does "I have a dream" suggest to the listeners?

4. Why does he make so many references to children?

5. What states does he mention in the main body of his speech?

6. Why does he mention those states primarily?

7. How does he want people to be judged?

8. What songs (titles) are mentioned in the speech?

9. How does he conclude forcefully?

10. What elements make this a very dramatic speech?

Name _____

New Year's Resolutions

Each new year almost everyone seeks improvement. Most of us swear, in fact, that we're going to take positive action and eliminate nasty habits. **Indeed,** we promise to lose weight, stop smoking, begin exercising, save money, or make new friends. During those first weeks of January we remain excited about our pledges, but by the middle of February our new year's resolutions are too often abandoned.

Making the resolutions is not the problem. Making the *right* resolution is the challenge. Unfortunately, most people set themselves up for failure because they don't, **for example,** enjoy exercising. If, **however,** your health depends on exercising more, then select an activity you truly enjoy, like bowling, golfing, or dancing. You could, **moreover,** join a group in a volleyball league, or just bike or walk in the park during the spring and summer.

If your new year's resolution is to lose weight, you are not alone. Some recent studies say that over fifty-five percent of the American population is overweight. Instead of just beginning another dreaded diet, increase your level of exercise during the week. **Furthermore,** eat only when you feel hungry and stop when you feel full. Eat healthier by reducing the fat in your diet and the portions at each meal.

In conclusion, resolutions are a wonderful way to begin the new year. Sticking to them can surely improve your mental and physical health. Making them work depends on making them enjoyable. Making them work **also** prevents you from making the same resolution again.

Quotes from Benjamin Franklin

Directions: Interpret each quote below.

1. "We must all hang together, or most assuredly we shall all hang separately." (regarding the signing of the Declaration of Independence).

2. "Without Freedom of Thought, there can be no such thing as Wisdom; and no such thing as publick Liberty, without Freedom of Speech."

3. "If a man empties his purse into his head no one can take it away from him. An investment in knowledge always pays the best interest."

4. "Those who would give up essential Liberty, to purchase a little temporary Safety, deserve neither Liberty nor Safety."

5. "Where liberty is, there is my country."

Name _____

When You Go to the Bank

Directions: Define each of the terms below associated with the banking industry.

1. mortgage:

2. loan:

3. debt/debit:

4. equity:

5. transaction:

6. deposit:

7. withdrawal:

8. credit:

9. overdraft:

10. passbook:

11. accrued:

12. lien:

13. principal:

14. cap:

15. escrow:

Famous English Authors/Famous Titles

Virginia Woolf (1882–1941)

[She suffered from mental illness much of her life and committed suicide by drowning.]

The Voyage Out (1915)

Night and Day (1919)

Jacob's Room (1922)

Mrs. Dalloway (1925)

The Waves (1930)

Somerset Maugham (1874–1965)

[He studied to be a doctor at first before writing full time later in his life.]

Of Human Bondage (1915)

The Moon and Sixpence (1919)

The Painted Veil (1925)

Cakes and Ale (1930)

Christmas Holiday (1939)

The Hour Before Dawn (1942)

The Razor's Edge (1944)

Famous American Authors/Famous Titles

Isaac Asimov (1920–1992)

[He earned his Ph.D. from Columbia in science and taught biochemistry at Boston University Medical School.]

Pebble in the Sky (1950)

I, Robot (1950)

The Naked Sun (1957)

Foundation Trilogy (1951)

Foundation's Edge (1982)

Foundation and Earth (1986)

Prelude to Foundation (1988)

Forward the Foundation (1992)

J.D. Salinger (1919–)

[He has become a reclusive author after writing *Catcher in the Rye*, considered now as America's best coming of age novel.]

Catcher in the Rye (1951)

Franny and Zooey (1961)

Raise High the Roof Beam (1963)

JANUARY
Answer Key

#8 SKILL SHEET 1-3—WHAT DO YOU KNOW ABOUT NONFICTION BOOKS?

1. False	2. False	3. True	4. True	5. False
6. False	7. False	8. True	9. True	10. True
11. False	12. True	13. False	14. True	15. True

#10 SKILL SHEET 1-6—"I HAVE A DREAM" BY MARTIN LUTHER KING

1. King connects to his audience by mentioning the American dream and Jefferson's statement that "all men are created equal." He also cites specific states where members of his audience may have lived.

2. "We hold these truths to be self-evident; that all men are created equal" comes from the Declaration of Independence.

3. "I have a dream" may suggest his vision for a country that is nonracist. It is his objective for the civil rights movement.

4. The many references to children could imply that if they grow up without learning racism then discrimination and bigotry could be eliminated.

5. Georgia, Mississippi, Alabama, Pennsylvania, Colorado, New York, New Hampshire, California, Tennessee

6. He mentions these states to convey the wide scope of his dream and to stress that racism still exists broadly in the South.

7. He wants people to be judged by the content of their character, not the color of their skin.

8. Songs (titles) mentioned in the speech include "My country tis of thee" and some spirituals.

9. He concludes forcefully by inspiring each race, each religion, and all geographical areas to adopt his dream and by repeating the phrase "free at last."

10. Answers will vary.

#49 SKILL SHEET 1-7—QUOTES FROM BENJAMIN FRANKLIN

1. As the delegates to the Continental Congress approached the signing of the Declaration of Independence, Franklin emphasized that it was an act of treason against England, which could be punished by hanging. Therefore, they might as well all sign the document.

2. Franklin proclaims the importance of Freedom of Thought, since that leads to Wisdom. His second reference to Freedom of Speech helped inspire Jefferson when he wrote the Declaration of Independence.

3. Franklin here emphasizes the importance of learning. Education, whatever its cost, must be pursued by all people who wish to succeed in life.

4. This statement refers to those individuals who preferred to remain loyal to England and reject a rebellion. Franklin warns them such a policy will result in greater oppression and little safety. Later, they will be at even greater risk.

5. Franklin wants to live in a country where individuals have individual liberty. That is his hope for America.

#52 SKILL SHEET 1-8—WHEN YOU GO TO THE BANK

1. mortgage: refers to property (typically a home) pledged to a creditor (bank) until a loan is repaid.

2. loan: borrowed money.

3. debt/debit: an obligation or liability to pay a certain amount.

4. equity: the difference between the dollar value of a home and the outstanding mortgage balance; for example, if a home is appraised to be worth $150,000 and the homeowner owes $100,000 the equity is $50,000.

5. transaction: the business negotiation between the lender (bank) and the borrower (home buyer).

6. deposit: money put in the bank.

7. withdrawal: money taken from the bank.

8. credit: the amount of money remaining in a person's bank account.

9. overdraft: the act of withdrawing from the bank a sum of money that exceeds the amount in a person's bank account.

10. passbook: the record of funds kept in the bank.

11. accrued: the increase in value ($) of an account or property.

12. lien: a claim on a property (home) as security against the payment of a debt.

13. principal: the amount of debt.

14. cap: the limit on the interest rate the bank can apply to a loan.

15. escrow: an account set up by the bank to pay taxes and other fees assessed to the home buyer.

FEBRUARY

INTRODUCTORY PAGE

LEARNING ACTIVITIES

REPRODUCIBLES

QUICK LOCATOR FOR FEBRUARY LEARNING ACTIVITIES

Composition Skills

Research *17, 27, 30, 31, 32, 35, 36, 46, 51, 52, 53, 54, 73, 76, 100, 101* • Prewriting *17, 50, 79, 118* • Organization *43, 45, 46, 47* • Description *39, 40, 41, 42, 46, 116* • Reflection *48, 49, 50, 117, 118* • Comparison/Contrast *33, 34, 35, 36* • Persuasion *62, 63* • Dialogue *67, 68, 69* • Character Sketch *64, 65, 66, 110, 111, 112, 113, 114, 115* • Letters *10, 11, 55, 56, 57, 58, 59, 60, 61, 62, 63, 104, 105*

News Unit   *12, 72, 73*

Careers Unit   *74, 102*

Media Unit   *21, 32, 37, 38, 61*

Fine Arts   *118, 119, 120*

Social Skills/Understanding Ethnic Diversity   *15, 57, 58, 60, 64, 70, 73, 77, 86, 99*

FEBRUARY

Origin: February takes its name from the Latin word *februare*, which means "to purify." The ancient Romans would purify themselves during this month to prepare for festivals at the start of the new year. February is the shortest month because, according to legend, the Roman emperor Augustus took a day from February to add to August, the month named for him.

Holidays: Western countries celebrate Valentine's Day on February 14, and the custom of exchanging greetings goes back hundreds of years.

In the U.S., President's Day, in honor of George Washington and Abraham Lincoln's birthdays, is a national holiday.

Ground Hog Day is also in February. According to myth, if the ground hog (or woodchuck) comes out of its burrow, especially in Punxsutawney, Pennsylvania and sees its shadow, winter weather continues.

Dominican Republic, Estonia, Gambia, Grenada, Lithuania, and Sri Lanka all celebrate their Independence Days in February.

Gemstone: Amethyst

Flower: Primrose

Poetry: The February sunshine steeps your boughs,
And tints the buds and swells the leaves within.
by William Cullen Bryant

BIRTHDAYS

Feb. 1   Clark Gable, actor/Academy Award winner (1901) [#32, 54, 109]; Langston Hughes, writer (1902) [#2, 8, 44, 69]

Feb. 2   James Joyce, Irish writer (1882) [#1]

Feb. 3   James Michener, novelist (1907) [#3, 91, 93]; Gertrude Stein, writer (1874) [#27, 85]

Feb. 6   Ronald Reagan, 40th President and the first divorced person and the oldest person to become President [#19, 54]; Babe Ruth (George Herman), baseball player—the "Sultan of Swat"—who was one of the first players elected to the baseball Hall of Fame (1895) [#17, 47, 52, 67]

Feb. 7   Charles Dickens, novelist (1812) [#4, 88, 93, 120]; Sinclair Lewis, novelist and the first American Nobel Prize winner for literature in 1930 (1885) [#28]; Sir Thomas More, scholar, author, martyr, Saint, Lord Chancellor of England who was imprisoned in the Tower of London for refusing to grant the divorce of King Henry VIII from Queen Catherine (1478) [#16, 72]; Laura Ingalls Wilder, novelist (1867) [#27]

Feb. 8   James Dean, actor (1931) [#32, 104, 110]; John Grisham novelist (1955) [#79, 96]; Jack Lemmon, actor (1925) [#54, 115]; Jules Verne, author of *Twenty Thousand Leagues Under the Sea* and *Around the World in Eighty Days* who is sometimes called "the father of science fiction" (1828) [#6, 92, 95]

Feb. 9   William Henry Harrison, 9th President and the one who had the shortest term in office—one month (1773) [#19]; Amy Lowell, poet (1874) [#7, 30, 31]; Alice Walker, 1983 Pulitzer Prize winner for fiction and author of *The Color Purple* (1944) [#29]

Feb. 10   Boris Pasternak, Russian author of *Dr. Zhivago* (1890) [#93, 111]; Mark Spitz, winner of seven gold medals at the 1972 Olympics (1950) [#17, 24]

Feb. 11   Thomas Alva Edison, inventor and holder of 1200 patents (1847) [#21, 83]; Sidney Sheldon, writer (1917) [#69, 91]

Feb. 12   Judy Blume, author (1938) [#29]; Charles Darwin, scientist/philosopher (1809) [#35, 78]; Abraham Lincoln, 16th President (1809) [#36, 39, 40, 98, 113]

Feb. 13   Jerry Springer, television personality (1944) [#37, 103]

Feb. 15 Susan B. Anthony, American suffragette leader (1820) [#22, 60, 70, 98, 107]; Galileo Galilei, Italian physicist/astronomer who proved the theory that the planets revolved around the sun (1564) [#34, 78]

Feb. 17 Jim Brown, professional football player/activist/ actor (1936) [#17, 47, 51, 67]; Michael Jordan, actor/former professional basketball player/ businessman (1963) [#17, 33, 47, 51, 67]

Feb. 18 Toni Morrison, writer (1931) [#29]

Feb. 19 Nicolaus Copernicus, astronomer who revolutionized scientific thought by declaring the sun was at the center of the planetary system (1473) [#34, 78]

Feb. 20 Ansel Adams, photographer (1902) [#23, 116]; Kurt Cobaine, singer for rock band Nirvana (1967) [#76, 103, 118; Sidney Poitier, Academy Award winning actor (1927) [#33, 65]; Carl Stotz, founder of Little League Baseball (1910) [#33, 65]

Feb. 22 James Russell Lowell, poet/essayist (1819) [#9, 31, 87]; Edna St. Vincent Millay, poet (1892) [#7, 30, 89]; Robert Wadlow, who grew to be the tallest man in recorded history at 8'11" (1918) [#48, 50]; George Washington, General of Revolutionary Army and our first President (1732) [#36, 108, 114]

Feb. 23 W.E.B. (William Edward Burghardt) Du Bois, educator/ activist for racial equality (1868) [#35, 84]

Feb. 24 Honus Wagner (born John Peter Wagner), baseball player—the "Flying Dutchman"—and one of the first players elected to the baseball Hall of Fame (1874) [#17, 47, 52, 67, 81]

Feb. 26 Levi Strauss, creator of the world's first pair of jeans in 1850—Levi's 501 jeans, designed for miners (1829) [#53, 117]

Feb. 27 Marian Anderson, singer (1897) [#22]; Henry Wadsworth Longfellow, poet (1807) [#9, 20]; Ralph Nader, consumer advocate (1934) [#59, 82]; John Steinbeck, writer (1902) [#5, 28, 93]; Elizabeth Taylor, actress (1932) [#38, 54, 103]

MEMORABLE EVENTS

Feb. 1   Traveler's Insurance Company issued the first car insurance against accidents with horses in 1898 [#45].

Supreme Court of the United States convened for the first time in 1790 [#42, 79].

Thomas Edison completed the first motion picture studio, located in New Jersey, in 1893 at a cost of $637 [#21].

Feb. 8   "Flora" by Colley Cibber was the first opera performed in the colonies at the Courtroom in Charleston, South Carolina in 1735 [#119].

Boy Scouts of America were founded by William Boyce in Washington D.C. in 1910 [#106].

Feb. 13   First American public school, the Boston Latin School, opened in 1635 [#18, 80].

First magazine in America—*The American Magazine*—was published by Andrew Bradford in 1741 [#61, 101, 102].

Get a Different Name Day [#88, 97].

Feb. 14   Arizona was admitted to the Union as the 48th state in 1912 [#46].

Ferris Wheel Day [#41].

Oregon was admitted to the Union as the 33rd state in 1859 [#46].

Valentine's Day [#56, 75, 77, 112].

Feb. 15   Susan B. Anthony Day [#22].

Feb. 20   Student Volunteer Day [#57, 64, 86].

John Glenn in Friendship 7 became the first American to orbit the Earth, in 1962 [#14, 68].

President George Washington signed the Postal Act, which established the U.S. Post Office in 1792 [#10, 11, 55, 57, 62, 63, 104, 105].

Frederick Douglass, escaped slave, journalist, orator, and anti-slavery activist died in 1895 [#60, 70, 98].

Feb. 21   Lucy Hobbs became the first woman to graduate from a dental college in 1866 [#49].

Feb. 22   Martin Luther King and Rosa Parks, along with 80 others, were arrested in Montgomery, Alabama in 1956 for refusing to encourage the end of the bus boycott [#15, 58, 73].

Feb. 23   The first cloning of an adult animal (a sheep) was announced by researchers in Scotland in 1997 [#13].

Feb. 24   General Motors announced a $4.5 billion loss on this day in 1991, the largest recorded financial loss by a U.S. company [#12].

LEARNING ACTIVITIES FOR FEBRUARY

READING ACTIVITIES

Purpose: To improve skills at analyzing fiction

1. Have students read any stories by James Joyce that may appear in their literature textbook or available anthology and study them in terms of characters, settings, and themes.

> James Joyce's characters typically were the blue collar citizens of 20th century Dublin. He used much symbolism, especially in regard to the Catholic church, in stories that portrayed common people experiencing *epiphanies*, or dramatic realizations.

2. Have students read any stories by Langston Hughes that may appear in their literature textbook or available anthology and study them in terms of characters and language.

> The characters of Langston Hughes's fiction were most often the underdogs, like Jesse B. Simple, who, though ignorant and downtrodden, still approach their circumstances in a clear-headed and gallant way. Plain speech and black dialect were common in his narratives.

Purpose: To improve an understanding of novels

3. Introduce the definition of a *tome*. Relate this to James Michener and his books.

> Tome = an especially large book, typically 600-plus pages

4. Distribute **Form 2-1** and have students analyze the opening paragraphs of several Charles Dickens' novels. Ask: What makes these books interesting to read?

5. Assign students to read a novel by John Steinbeck and study its characters, settings, and theme. Then use the Novel Study Project—**Form 11-8**—to evaluate them when they finish reading.

> John Steinbeck had tremendous sympathy for the poor, and his characters were usually laborers and farmers who were drawn to the movement westward, to California, a land of potential opportunity. Their conflicts were with rich landowners, society's moral confusion, and the painful disappointment of unfulfilled dreams during the great Depression.

6. Assign students to read a book by Jules Verne and then ask: When was it published? What makes it science fiction? Why is the plot interesting? Use the Novel Study Project form (**Form 11-8**) to evaluate students when they have finished reading.

Purpose: To improve an understanding of poetry

7. Have students read any poems by Amy Lowell and Edna St. Vincent Millay that may appear in their literature text or available anthology and compare their types of verse, the poetic language, and topics/themes.

> Amy Lowell displayed colorful imagery in a free verse style known for its tight precision of language. She was part of a group of poets known as Imagists and won the Pulitzer Prize in 1926.
>
> Edna St. Vincent Millay favored traditional verse forms, like the sonnet, and her poetry had a lyrical quality. She won the Pulitzer Prize in 1923.

8. Direct students to read any poems by Langston Hughes that may appear in their literature text or available anthology and study his topics, poetic language, and themes.

> The verse of Langston Hughes reflected the language of the black culture and jazz rhythms. His poetry served as a means of social protest against the injustice experienced by African Americans.

9. Have students read poems by James Russell Lowell and Henry Wadsworth Longfellow that may appear in their literature text or available anthology to compare their types of verse, poetic language, and topics/themes.

James Russell Lowell followed Longfellow as professor of languages at Harvard University and joined him in a group of poets called the Fireside Poets, whose poems often made reference to the warmth and comfort of the hearth. His poetry, at times written in Yankee dialect, was political in scope—opposing the Mexican War and slavery.

Henry Wadsworth Longfellow, another Fireside Poet and Harvard professor, reestablished in America a public audience for poetry. His poetry had sentimental themes about colonial America and human relationships and was written in a melodious language known for its simplicity and clarity.

Purpose: To identify letter writing formats

10. Refer to the Postal Act, which established the U.S. Post Office in 1792 and have students read any pages in their textbook about business and personal letters.

11. Refer to the Postal Act and have students read letters they bring from home. Then ask: Who is the writer? Is this a formal or friendly letter? What kind of language is used? What is revealed about the personality of the writer? Is the letter special? Why/why not?

Purpose: To analyze newspaper articles

12. Collect and then distribute any newspaper's business pages and have students study the articles and stock listings on selected companies. Refer to the largest recorded financial loss by a U.S. company—General Motors announced a $4.5 billion loss in 1991—and then direct students to evaluate companies or compare stock listings.

DEBATING ACTIVITIES

Purpose: To encourage critical thinking

13. Should science alter a person's genetics? Refer to the cloning of an adult animal (a sheep) which was announced by researchers in Scotland in 1997. What if it meant eliminating a potential disease that has been passed down in a family? Should we permit genetic engineering?

14. Refer to John Glenn who became the first American to orbit the Earth in 1962 in Friendship 7. Is scientific research worth the risks, especially regarding the exploration of space? Why/why not?

15. Refer to Martin Luther King, Jr., and Rosa Parks, who along with 80 others, were arrested in Montgomery, Alabama in 1956 for refusing to encourage the end of the bus boycott. When, if ever, is accepting imprisonment justified? Should moral beliefs take priority over legal responsibilities? Do citizens have the right to disobey laws they don't believe in? Why/why not?

16. Refer to Sir Thomas More, Lord Chancellor of England who was imprisoned in the Tower of London for refusing to grant the divorce of King Henry VIII from Queen Catherine in the 16th century. Was this the correct course of action for Sir Thomas More? Should we disobey authorities if their moral standards are in conflict with our own? Why/why not?

17. Who was the best athlete—Babe Ruth, Honus Wagner, Jim Brown, Mark Spitz, or Michael Jordan? What are the traits of great athletes (athletic ability excluded)? Use this also to review research skills or brainstorming.

18. Refer to the first public school in America, the Boston Latin School which opened in 1635. Should there be compulsory education for all children in the United States? Why/why not?

19. Should the President have age limitations? Currently, the law states no one under 35 can hold the office of President. Should this be changed? Should there be a maximum age limit? Why/why not? Refer to Ronald Reagan, our oldest President, and to William Henry Harrison, the 9th President and the one who had the shortest term in office—one month (1773).

20. Write the following quote from Henry Wadsworth Longfellow on the board: "Music is the universal language of man-kind." Then have students respond—Do you agree? Why/why not?

21. Refer to Thomas Edison's motion picture studio which he constructed in 1893 for $637. Today, a single film may cost $50–150 million on the average. Could this money be spent more wisely? Why/why not?

22. Who made the more dramatic contribution to the social advancement of women—Susan B. Anthony, president of the National American Women Suffrage Association, who worked for the constitutional amendment granting women the right to vote, or Marian Anderson, who was the first African American to perform at the Metropolitan Opera House in New York City, an alternate delegate in 1958 to the United Nations, and a recipient of the Presidential Medal of Freedom in 1963?

23. Write the following quote from Ansel Adams on the board: "A great photograph is a full expression of what one feels about what is being photographed in the deepest sense, and is, thereby, a true expression of what one feels about life in its entirety." Have students respond—Do you agree? Why/why not?

24. Refer to Mark Spitz. Should Olympic teammates inform on fellow teammates who use steroids? It is, of course, very possible that these athletes would be unable to win any medal without using steroids. Should the Olympic authorities be informed? Why/why not?

Purpose: To begin a fiction unit

25. What do you prefer more—oral or written stories? Which is more appealing? Why?

26. Which is a better form of story-telling—a ballad or a short story? Why?

27. Which female writer contributed most to American fiction—Laura Ingalls Wilder or Gertrude Stein? Students could read their works and/or research their backgrounds.

28. Which early 20th century author contributed more to American literature—John Steinbeck (winner of the 1940 Pulitzer Prize and the 1962 Nobel Prize) or Sinclair Lewis (winner of the 1926 Pulitzer and the 1930 Nobel Prize)? Students could use **Form 2-2**.

29. Which female writer of modern American fiction—Alice Walker, Judy Blume, or Toni Morrison—was most controversial in terms of topics, characters, and themes? Distribute **Form 2-3** or have students read their works.

Purpose: To improve research skills

30. Which poet contributed most to American poetry—Edna St. Vincent Millay or Amy Lowell? Students could read their poems and/or research their backgrounds.

31. Which poet contributed most to American poetry—James Russell Lowell or Amy Lowell? Students could read their poems and/or research their backgrounds.

32. Who showed the most skill as an actor—Clark Gable, James Dean, or Sidney Poitier? Students could view clips of these actors' films or research their backgrounds as a means to teach or review research skills. Extend the assignment by having students compare these actors to several current film stars.

Purpose: To work at comparison/contrast

33. Who had the greater impact on youth sports—Michael Jordan, who served as a popular role model in the 1980s and 1990s, or Carl Stotz, who founded Little League of America in 1939?

34. Who had the more important scientific discovery—Nicolaus Copernicus, who revolutionized scientific thought by declaring the sun was at the center of the planetary system or Galileo Galilei, the Italian physicist and astronomer who proved the theory that the planets revolved around the sun?

35. Who had the greater impact on social education—Charles Darwin, who proposed the theory of natural selection and evolution, or W.E.B. Du Bois, who reported his research on the economic and social conditions of urban black Americans? Students could research their backgrounds or simply speculate.

36. Which President had the greater impact on American politics—George Washington or Abraham Lincoln? Students could research their backgrounds or simply speculate.

Purpose: *To evaluate the media*

37. Consider Jerry Springer and the "Jerry Springer Show." Springer claims his shows, which typically involve guests fighting and cursing, are not scripted, that his guests' behaviors are totally unrehearsed. Is this acceptable television viewing, especially for younger viewers? We do have the right not to watch the show, but should there be limitations placed on the shows' topics and guests? Why/why not?

38. Elizabeth Taylor's marriages and divorces have received as much attention from the media as her acting performances. Should there be limitations on the kind of news the media presents to viewers or readers? Why/why not?

WRITING ACTIVITIES

Purpose: *To review writing description*

39. Have students write a descriptive paragraph about the log cabin where Abraham Lincoln was born.

40. Challenge students to write a 200-word paragraph using effective modifiers to describe a *penny*. Refer to Abraham Lincoln.

41. First, discuss the experience of riding on ferris wheels and then have students compose a brief essay describing a ride they took on one. Ask: How would you describe the ride on a ferris wheel to someone who has never been on one? Use **Form 12-7** to evaluate the essays.

42. Refer to the Supreme Court, which convened for the first time in 1790, and direct students to first *map/illustrate* and then write a description of a courtroom, as if for a person who has never seen one.

Purpose: *To begin a composition unit*

43. Distribute **Skill Sheet 2-4** and follow up with a discussion on these terms.

44. Explain that Langston Hughes termed himself a "a writer who wrote mostly because when I felt bad, writing kept me from feeling worse." Then ask students to explain in a detailed paragraph how writing helped Hughes or when *they* felt like this.

Purpose: *To teach organization in writing*

45. Refer to the Traveler's Insurance Company which issued the first car insurance and have students write a step-by-step checklist for avoiding danger or problems while traveling (i.e., safety tips like getting traveler's checks, contacting the Department of Transportation about road conditions, checking the tire pressure of the car, etc.).

46. Have students create travelogues about Arizona or Oregon, who achieved state-hood this month, in the form of chronologs. Refer to **Form 11-11** as a model and direct them to use an atlas or travel brochures, if necessary.

47. Refer to Babe Ruth and Honus Wagner (baseball), Michael Jordan (basketball), and Jim Brown (football) and direct students to construct an outline where each major topic is a professional sport and the subtopics are the best players currently competing.

Purpose: *To review reflective writing*

48. Have students pretend to be Robert Wadlow, the world's tallest man at 8'11", and write his journal/diary entry. Then combine the final copies into a complete manuscript. Be sure each student uses a different date.

49. Have students pretend to be Lucy Hobbs after she graduated from dental college in 1866 as the first woman dentist and write her journal/diary entry. Then combine the finished copies into a complete manuscript. Be sure each student uses a different date.

50. Refer to Robert Wadlow, the tallest man in history, and have students brainstorm a list of advantages to being very tall.

Purpose: *To review research skills*

51. Distribute **Skill Sheet 2-5,** The Chronologs of Jim Brown and Michael Jordan, and ask: What possible obstacles and/or conflicts did Jim Brown and Michael Jordan confront on their way to becoming professional athletes? Use this to review conflict in fiction or to practice researching skills.

> **Potential conflicts could have been with high school, college, and professional opponents in their sports; jealous teammates; stubborn coaches; insensitive fans; the media invading their privacy; maintaining top athletic performances; contract negotiations; etc.**

52. Refer to Babe Ruth and Honus Wagner, two of the original inductees in major league baseball's Hall of Fame. Ask students to identify and profile the other three original inductees.

> **The original inductees in the major league baseball Hall of Fame were Babe Ruth, Honus Wagner, Ty Cobb, Christy Mathewson, and Walter Johnson, which took place in 1936.**

53. Levi Strauss is known, of course, for Levi's 501 jeans. Direct students to identify and describe the types of apparel of other clothes designers (primary research).

54. Have students list at least ten movies that the following actors appeared in: Clark Gable, Ronald Reagan, Jack Lemmon, and Elizabeth Taylor.

Purpose: To introduce or review letter writing

55. Refer to the Postal Act which established the U.S. Post Office in 1792 and distribute any or all of the following surveys on letter writing: **Skill Sheet 2-6—Survey #1**, **Skill Sheet 2-7—Survey #2**, **Skill Sheet 2-8—Survey #3**, or **Skill Sheet 2-9—Survey #4**.

56. Have students write a personal letter or Valentine to a friend or relative living outside the city. Challenge them: Whose message can be the most compelling?

57. Refer to the Postal Act and to Student Volunteer Day. Use this to prompt students to write a personal letter to a classmate or friend that encourages this person to volunteer in a school or community activity. This could promote community service and social skills.

58. Refer to Martin Luther King, Jr., and Rosa Parks and then prompt students to write a letter to a politician who can respond to a genuine concern they might have about a local, state, or federal program or issue (for example, conservation of a local habitat).

59. Refer to Ralph Nader and then direct students to write a consumer letter to a business or company that deserves praise or criticism for one of their products or services.

60. Refer to the controversial (at the time) stands taken by Frederick Douglass and Susan B. Anthony and then direct students to write a letter to the editor of the school newspaper on any school related issue, such as the dress code.

61. Refer to *The American Magazine*, the first magazine in the United States, and encourage students to write a letter to the editor of a magazine they read about a specific teen issue or problem, such as dealing with peer pressure. Students could also respond to an issue in a previously published article.

62. Have students write an editorial offering critical or positive commentary about the U.S. Postal Service.

63. Have students compose essays predicting the future of the postal service (the technology, delivery systems, post offices, etc.). Ask: What do you think the postal service will be like 100 hundred years from now? Challenge them to extrapolate.

Purpose: To introduce character sketch writing

64. Refer to Student Volunteer Day and have students write the profile/character sketch of the classmate they think has made the most valuable contribution to the school or the community and present this essay to that individual.

65. Refer to Carl Stotz and ask students to describe a little league baseball player in terms of appearance, behavior, and skills.

66. Have students write a one-page biography of any famous historical figure—for example, George Washington—that portrays this person's most interesting qualities.

Purpose: To review dialogue

67. Have students create the dialogue between any two professional athletes from different eras who have birthdays this month—Michael Jordan and Babe Ruth or Jim Brown and Honus Wagner. Challenge students' creativity.

68. Have students create the dialogue between John Glenn in Friendship 7 and Mission Control as he orbited the Earth in 1962.

69. Direct students to locate and copy the interesting dialogue they find in a play or story by Langston Hughes or Sidney Sheldon.

Purpose: To improve speech skills

70. Have students create a speech by Susan B. Anthony promoting women's right to vote or by Frederick Douglass criticizing slavery. Students should attempt to use the language of their day.

71. Distribute **Skill Sheet 2-10,** dealing with overcoming problems when giving a speech, and discuss the responses afterwards.

Purpose: To review news article format

72. Have students write a newspaper article (a feature, if necessary) about Sir Thomas More and his defiance of King Henry the VIII's order. Students should provide the five Ws (Who, What, When, Where, Why).

73. Have students write a newspaper article (a feature, if necessary) about Martin Luther King, Jr., and Rosa Parks, who were arrested in Montgomery in 1956. Students should provide the five Ws (Who, What, When, Where, Why).

Purpose: To conclude a careers unit

74. Have students construct a resume for one of the famous individuals who has a birthday this month. Here, students will need to research some career information, accomplishments and achievements, skills and qualifications.

DISCUSSION ACTIVITIES

Purpose: To expand skills at word selection/vocabulary

75. Refer to Valentine's Day. How would you define romance? What words should a writer use to show admiration or affection for another person? Here, are words more important than actions? For background details use **Form 2-11.**

76. Consider Kurt Cobain and his band called Nirvana and ask: What is the meaning of Nirvana? What does this term suggest about Cobain's group? What are some other interesting band names?

> *Nirvana* **means in Hindu an extinguishing of the flame of life while Buddhists use this term to refer to the absorption of the soul into the supreme spirit, a state of perfection and blessedness.**

77. What could be the words of an argument used by a couple who are in a romantic relationship? Refer to Valentine's Day.

78. Refer to Charles Darwin, Galileo Galilei, and Nicolas Copernicus and ask: How much do scientists rely on their senses when making scientific conclusions? What senses are especially important to a scientist? How might sensory language relate to an experiment? Consider expressions like "This doesn't smell right" or "That does not sound right."

79. Refer to John Grisham and the Supreme Court and ask the students to brainstorm legal terms—for example, lawyer, litigation, bailiff, jury, witness, lawsuit, trial, etc.

Purpose: To encourage critical thinking

80. Refer to the first American public school, the Boston Latin School which opened in 1635, and ask: What if there were no more schools? If students don't want to learn, should they be allowed to leave the classroom? What is the attitude about school of the students in your grade?

81. Explain that a Honus Wagner near mint condition baseball card of the Pittsburgh Pirates shortstop sold for $1.1 million. The owner said: "I wanted to know that I had the best card in the world. If you ask people in card collecting, this is the Mona Lisa of our hobby. And now, someone else will be able to have some fun with it." How can a baseball card bring "fun" to a person? What is the fun in collecting anything? What other small items also have great value?

82. Refer to Ralph Nader and then ask: What products do you find to be inferior or dangerous?

83. What is Thomas Edison suggesting with his famous quote: "Genius is one percent inspiration and ninety-nine percent perspiration"? How does this relate to school work? How did Edison demonstrate the accuracy of this statement?

84. How would you paraphrase W.E.B. Du Bois's famous 1909 quote: "The cost of liberty is less than the price of repression"?

85. Write Gertrude Stein's quote on the board: "We are always the same age inside." Then have students respond—Do you agree? Why/why not?

86. How could you contribute to your community? Why is any volunteering important? What are the benefits of volunteering? Refer to Student Volunteer Day.

87. What is James Russell Lowell suggesting to us with his famous quote: "The foolish and the dead alone never change their opinion"?

88. If you could select a new name, what would it be? Why that name? How important is the name given to us? How could it relate to our personality? Refer to Get a Different Name Day and the names from novels by Charles Dickens.

Purpose: To conclude a poetry unit

89. How do you interpret Edna St. Vincent Millay's famous lines of poetry?

   "My candle burns at both ends;
   It will not last the night;"

90. How do you interpret Henry Wadsworth Longfellow's lines of poetry?

   "So when a great man dies for years beyond our ken,
   The light he leaves behind him lies upon the paths of men."

Purpose: To begin a fiction unit

91. What awards are there in being a published writer? How would you feel about being published? Refer to writers James Michener and Sidney Sheldon and distribute **Form 2-12.**

92. Consider Jules Verne who wrote *Twenty Thousand Leagues Under the Sea* about a submarine, which had yet to be invented when he lived. Now they are very common. Ask: How do we know when a story, whether written or verbal, is fiction or nonfiction?

> **Stories could be checked to other sources. Several people might narrate the same story, or several sources might offer the same details. Fiction, however, though it may refer to actual events or people, arrives from a single source, a single narrator whose story cannot be documented in any other official source. There is only one *Gone with the Wind* and only one *The Adventures of Tom Sawyer*.**

© 2001 by The Center for Applied Research in Education

93. Where do writers get their ideas for stories? How do authors make fictional stories seem realistic? What are some examples of very realistic fiction? Refer to Boris Pasternak, who used the Russian Revolution for *Dr. Zhivago*; Charles Dickens, who used the French Revolution for *A Tale of Two Cities*; John Steinbeck, who used the Depression for *The Grapes of Wrath*; and James Michener, who used WW II for *The Bridge at Toyko-Ri*.

94. What is the function and importance of a story's title? What are some interesting titles? How does the title influence your desire to read a book? Use **Form 2-1, Form 2-2, Form 2-12,** and **Form 2-13.**

95. Refer to Jules Verne, the "father of science fiction" and to the titles of some of his novels. What science fiction have you read? How would you define science fiction? What are the characteristics of an effective science fiction story? If the author's science fiction at the time he/she wrote the story becomes fact, does it cease to be classified as science fiction?

96. Distribute **Form 2-13**—books by John Grisham—and then ask: What makes his books so popular (best sellers)? What kind of characters populate his books in general? Why have John Grisham's books become so popular?

97. Refer to Get a Different Name Day and ask students to list interesting names either from their literature text or the book couples may use to find a name for their child. Have them also investigate the meaning behind some names (or nicknames). Also ask: If you were to write a story, what names would you give your characters? Why?

Purpose: *To begin a speech unit*

98. Refer to Abraham Lincoln, Susan B. Anthony, and Frederick Douglass who were known as excellent speakers and ask: What are the characteristics of an *ineffective* speaker?

99. How can speech skills benefit a student in school? An employee with his/her employer? A person in a romantic relationship? A customer in a large department store? Parents with their children?

Purpose: *To improve research skills*

100. When gathering research it is always wise to obtain information from a variety of sources. Why? Also, what makes one source better than another?

Using a variety of resources, especially those that are current and updated, helps any research provide detailed, thorough, and accurate information in the report.

101. Refer to *The American Magazine*, the first magazine published in America, and have students examine several different magazines to compare their content, quality, and diction. Ask: Who are the intended readers of each one? What kind of articles appear in each? Which do you prefer as a source of research, and why?

Purpose: To encourage creating a class magazine

102. Refer to *The American Magazine*, the first magazine in America, distribute **Skill Sheet 2-14,** and ask: Would you like to produce a class magazine? Would you one day like to work for a magazine? Why?

Purpose: To begin a biography unit

103. Refer to celebrities like Elizabeth Taylor, Jerry Springer, and Kurt Cobaine. Why would biographers choose to write about them? How might biographers obtain information about these people? How could readers detect a biographer's bias—either positive or negative—about them?

AUDIO/VISUAL ACTIVITIES

Purpose: To begin a letter writing unit

104. Show various kinds of envelopes and stamps—for example, James Dean's postage stamp. Ask: Why isn't there just one envelope size? Why has the postal service chosen to place so many celebrities' faces on stamps? What postage stamps do you find most interesting?

105. Have students bring in and study various types of junk mail—notice the language, the content, the format. Ask: Which letter stands out from the others? Why?

Purpose: To improve skills at speeches/oral presentations

106. Select a student to role-play William Boyce introducing the Boy Scout creed to a group of young boys.

107. Select a student to role-play Susan B. Anthony speaking on the issue of women's right to vote.

108. Select a student to role-play George Washington in front of his troops announcing the plan to cross the icy waters of the Delaware river at night to attack the Hessian troops at Valley Forge.

109. Show selected scenes from the Clark Gable movie *Gone with the Wind*, especially those when he makes speeches to the Southern aristocrats, and ask students to analyze Gable's skills as a speaker and performer.

Purpose: To improve understanding of characterization

110. Show selected scenes from *Rebel without a Cause* starring James Dean. And ask: What kind of behavior is portrayed? How accurately does he characterize teenagers? How are teens presented in this classic film?

111. Show selected scenes from *Dr. Zhivago* starring Omar Shariff and ask: How is he different from the other characters? What attitudes does he project? How would you describe his persona?

112. Show selected scenes from *Valentine's Day* starring Mario Van Peebles. Ask: How do the characters respond to Valentine's Day? How do they behave? How would you describe their personalities?

113. Show selected scenes from the movie *Abe Lincoln in Illinois* starring Raymond Massey and have students list the habits, moods, and traits of Abraham Lincoln. Use this also to introduce a biography unit.

114. Show selected scenes from the movie *The Crossing* starring Jeff Daniels and have students list the habits, moods, and traits of George Washington. Use this also to introduce a biography unit.

115. Show selected scenes from any movie starring Jack Lemon and have students list the habits, traits, and characteristics of his character.

Purpose: To teach clarity in writing description

116. Refer to Ansel Adams, the famous photographer, and ask students to bring in and exchange favorite photographs. Then have them write paragraphs describing the scene in the picture exactly.

Purpose: To encourage reflective writing

117. Show some jeans. Refer to Levi Strauss and have students write paragraphs explaining how the 501 jeans created in 1850 for miners are now almost exclusively worn by young people.

118. Play a song(s) by Nirvana and Curt Cobain and direct the students to list their feelings and reactions to the music.

Purpose: To prompt an appreciation of the fine arts

119. Refer to "Flora," the first opera performed in America, and play a recording of an opera to improve student's cultural backgrounds and to explore the feelings and reactions the lyrics and music inspire.

120. Show videotape of *Great Expectations, A Tale of Two Cities, Oliver,* or another movie made from a Charles Dickens novel to connect classic literature to film.

The Charm of Charles Dickens

Directions: Examine the opening sentences of various novels by Charles Dickens. Analyze his writing style—the diction, sentence structure, and content—of each passage and then explain how Dickens engages the reader to continue.

From *The Pickwick Papers* (1837)

"The first ray of light which illumines the gloom and converts into dazzling brilliancy that obscurity in which the earlier history of the public career of the immortal Pickwick would appear to be involved, is derived from the perusal of the following entry in the transactions of the Pickwick Club, which the editor of these pages feels the highest pleasure in laying before his readers, as proof of careful attention, indefatigable assiduity, and nice discrimination, with which his search among multifarious documents confided to him has been conducted."

From *Oliver Twist* (1838)

". . . and in this workhouse was born, on a day and date which I need not trouble myself to repeat, inasmuch as it can be of no possible consequence to the reader, in this stage of the business at all events; the item of mortality whose name is prefixed to the head of this chapter."

From *Nicholas Nickleby* (1839)

"There once lived, in a sequestered part of the county of Devonshire, one Mr. Godfrey Nickleby: a worthy gentleman, who, taking it into his head rather late in life that he must get married, and not being young enough or rich enough to aspire to the hand of a lady of fortune, had wedded an old flame out of mere attachment, who in her turn had taken him for the same reason."

From *A Christmas Carol* (1843)

"Marley was dead: to begin with. There is no doubt whatever about that."

From *David Copperfield* (1850)

"Whether I shall turn out to be the hero of my own life, or whether that station will be held by anybody else, these pages must show."

From *A Tale of Two Cities* (1859)

"It was the best of times, it was the worst of times, it was the age of wisdom, it was the age of foolishness, it was the epoch of belief, it was the epoch of incredulity, it was the season of Light, it was the season of Darkness, it was the spring of hope, it was the winter of despair, we had everything before us, we had nothing before us . . ."

Name _____

Sinclair Lewis vs. John Steinbeck

© 2001 by The Center for Applied Research in Education

Sinclair Lewis (1885–1951)

- Educated at Yale University

- Other jobs included working as a newspaper reporter and literary critic.

- The themes of his novels dealt with the monotony, materialism, and conformity of the middle class and their lack of moral, ethical, and spiritual values.

- **Novels**

  Main Street (1920)

  Babbitt (1922)

  Arrowsmith (1925)

  Elmer Gantry (1927)

  Dodsworth (1929)

  It Can't Happen Here (1936)

Pulitzer Prize—1926

Nobel Prize—1930

John Steinbeck (1902–1968)

- Educated at Stanford University

- Other jobs included working as a ranch hand, fruit picker, store clerk, and laborer.

- The themes of his novels dealt with the struggle of the poor to keep their dignity and pursue a dream of a better life during the Depression era.

- Novels

  Cup of Gold (1929)

  To a God Unknown (1933)

  Tortilla Flat (1935)

  In Dubious Battle (1936)

  Of Mice and Men (1937)

  Grapes of Wrath (1939)

  Cannery Row (1945)

  East of Eden (1952)

  The Winter of our Discontent (1961)

Pulitzer Prize—1940

Nobel Prize—1962

Name _____

Toni Morrison vs. Judy Blume vs. Alice Walker

Toni Morrison (1931–)

- Educated at Howard University with an M.A. from Cornell University in 1955.

- Her books include *Bluest Eye* (1970); *Song of Solomon* (1977); *Tar Baby* (1981); *Beloved* (1987), and *Paradise* (1998). These works celebrate in poetic language the black experience and community and deal with issues such as slavery, family history, and romance.

- Pulitzer Prize winner (1988) and Nobel Prize winner (1993)

Judy Blume (1938–)

- Educated at New York University

- Her books include *Are You There God? It's Me, Margaret* (1970); *Then Again, Maybe I Won't* (1971); *It's Not the End of the World* (1972); *Forever . . .* (1975). These works explore in very frank and informal language the difficult world of adolescence—the often emotional, physical, and spiritual problems of growing up. Blume is one of the first young adult writers to portray a young girl's first sexual experience.

- Newberry Award winner several times

Alice Walker (1944–)

- Educated at Spelman and Sarah Lawrence Colleges

- Her books include *The Third Life of Grange Copeland* (1970); *Revolutionary Petunias and Other Poems* (1973); *Meridian* (1976); *The Color Purple* (1982); *Living by the Word* (1988); *Possessing the Secret of Joy* (1992); *Anything We Love Can Be Saved* (1997). Her writing portrays the lives of poor, oppressed African American women in the early 1900's and during the civil rights movement in a style characterized by strong colloquial language.

- American Book Award winner and Pulitzer Prize winner (1982)

Name _____

Chart the Writing Terms

Directions: Make a chart about the various terms associated with writing as either being positive (it can help writers), negative (it can hurt writers), or neutral (neither positive nor negative).

Be prepared to explain your choices.

The Terms

SLANG	THESIS	WEBBING	GENERALIZATION
CLARITY	OUTLINE	SYNONYMS	CLICHÉ
COHERENCE	WORDINESS	REVISION	AMBIGUITY
PARAGRAPH	RUBRIC	EDITING	TRANSITIONS
CLUSTERING	LISTING	RUN ONS	PROOFREAD

The Chart

Positive   **Neutral**   **Negative**

Name _____

Chronologs

	Jim Brown	Michael Jordan
Event:	Attends mostly all white Manhasset High School and earns 13 varsity letters playing five sports.	Attends Laney High School and in 1979 gets cut from the varsity. In 1981 he leads team to the Division II state title.
Obstacle?	_____ _____ _____	_____ _____ _____
Event:	Signs football scholarship to attend Syracuse Univ.	Signs basketball scholarship to attend North Carolina Univ.
Obstacle?	_____ _____ _____	_____ _____ _____
Event:	Named 1st Team All-American in FB and lacrosse in 1956.	Named 1st Team All-American in BK in 1983.
Obstacle?	_____ _____ _____	_____ _____ _____
Event:	Sixth pick in the 1st round of the 1957 NFL draft.	Third pick in the 1st round of the 1984 NBA draft.
Obstacle?	_____ _____ _____	_____ _____ _____
Event:	Named NFL Rookie of the Year in 1957.	Named NBA Rookie of the Year in 1985.
Obstacle?	_____ _____ _____	_____ _____ _____

Event: Sets NFL rushing record (1863 yards) and wins two NFL MVP awards.

Obstacle?   _____

             _____

             _____

Event: Leads Cleveland Browns to 1964 NFL Championship.

Obstacle?   _____

             _____

             _____

Event: Accused of assault and battery by several women through the years.

Obstacle?   _____

             _____

             _____

Event: Retires from FB in 1965 to become a movie actor and continue work helping black Americans (Amer-I-Can program for gang members).

Obstacle?   _____

             _____

             _____

Wins NBA scoring championships and named "Sportsman of the Year" by Sports Illustrated (1991).

_____

_____

_____

Leads Chicago Bulls to first NBA Championship in 1991.

_____

_____

_____

Father James Jordan murdered in August, 1993.

_____

_____

_____

Retires from BK in 1998 to continue work in commercials, business, and acting.

_____

_____

_____

Letter Writing Survey #1
What Do You Know About Letter Writing?

Directions: Fill in the blank for each of the following.

1. One type of a business letter is _____

2. The best diction for a business letter is _____

3. The heading of a business letter refers to _____

4. The purpose of a newsletter is to _____

5. "Junk" mail is _____

6. A letter of application should be sent to the _____ director.

7. A proper closing in a business letter is _____

8. A proper salutation in a business letter (when you don't know the name) is

   _____

9. A signature on a letter proves _____

10. The mark of punctuation most often required for the salutation of a business

    letter is _____

Letter Writing Survey #2

Directions: Answer the following questions in detail.

1. Name the person(s) who last wrote you a letter:

2. Name the person(s) to whom you last wrote a letter:

3. What is a pen pal?

4. What are some types of letters?

5. What separates a letter from other types of writing?

6. What are the differences between a postcard and a letter?

7. How could a letter influence someone's career more than a phone call could?

8. Even though we can communicate faster over long distances with computers (with modems), why do letters still remain important?

9. How many letters do you think are mailed each day across the United States?

10. What would you like to learn about letter writing?

Name _____

Letter Writing Survey #3
What Do You Know About the Business
of Letter Writing?

Directions: Answer the following questions in detail.

1. What is a letter-to-the-editor?

2. What is C.O.D.? Why is it used?

3. What are some other types of closings other than Sincerely?

4. Why is the salutation "Dear Sir or Madam" no longer appropriate in standard business letters?

5. What do you think the post office does with letters that are incorrectly addressed and lack a return address on the envelope?

6. What is junk mail?

7. What do businesses try to accomplish with junk mail if so many of us just throw it away?

8. Why is a date so important on a business letter?

9. Why must a business letter be typed or in ink?

10. What does "enclosure" refer to when written at the bottom of a business letter?

Letter Writing Survey #4
What Do You Know About Personal Letters?

Directions: Answer each question in detail.

1. How can you prompt the receiver to write back?

2. What are some traditional messages in personal letters?

3. What could be some unusual comments on a postcard or in a personal letter?

4. How could a personal letter not be a friendly letter?

5. What are the various types of personal letters?

6. What would you write in the first sentence of a letter where you want to end a relationship?

7. What are several useful closings in a personal letter?

8. What should be the structure and diction of a personal letter?

9. Why should a personal letter be saved?

10. What makes a letter more useful than a phone conversation?

Name _____

Speech Problems

Directions: How would you fix the following problems that typically can be associated
with giving a speech?

1. Anxiety:

2. Going blank:

3. Nerves:

4. Forgetting:

5. Distractions:

Valentine's Day—The History

In ancient Rome, more than 2000 years ago, the Romans celebrated "Lupercalia," or feast of Lupercus who was the god of herds and crops. Roman shepherds believed that praying to him would protect their sheep from wolves and their crops from drought.

The celebration involved women writing their names on pieces of paper and dropping them into a community urn. On Lupercalia Eve, each young man would draw a name, and that girl would become his partner at dances and parties for the coming year. Sometimes, these couples even married.

As Christianity grew and pagan rituals died out, the Romans revised Lupercalia and named it after a legendary priest, St. Valentine. According to legend, the Roman emperor Claudius needed an army in the third century to fight in a border war, and he banned marriages, believing that married men would be too reluctant to enlist. The priest, St. Valentine, disobeyed Claudius and performed secret weddings. His act of treason was discovered, and Claudius first imprisoned and then beheaded him—on February 14.

Valentine's Day became a celebration of this priest who died for love. The custom of exchanging notes and cards (i.e., valentines) spread through Europe, and in the 1700s Americans also began exchanging valentines. Often, these valentines were poems. As more and more Americans became literate, valentines became more and more popular. By the early 1800s, Valentine's Day was one of the postal service's busiest days.

Name _____

James Michener vs. Sidney Sheldon: A History of Excellence in Writing

James Michener	Sidney Sheldon
Tales of the South Pacific (1947)	"Bachelor and the Bobby Soxer" screenplay (1948)
Pulitzer Prize for Fiction (1948)	**Academy Award** (1948)
Return to Paradise (1951)	"Annie Get Your Gun"—a musical (1951)
The Bridges at Tokyo-Ri (1953)	**Screen Writers Guild Award for Best Musical**
Sayanora (1954)	"Redwood"—a musical (1959)
Bridge at Andau (1957)	**Tony Award** (1959)
Hawaii (1959)	Writer for the "Patty Duke Show" and "I Dream of Jeannie" (1963–1964)
Caravans (1963)	**Emmy Award** (1967)
The Source (1965)	*The Naked Face* (1969)
Einstein Award (1967)	**Edgar Allan Poe Award**
Centennial (1974)	*The Other Side of Midnight* (1974)
Sports in America (1976)	*A Stranger in the Mirror* (1975)
Medal of Freedom (1977)	*Bloodline* (1977)
Chesapeake (1978)	*Rage of Angels* (1980)
The Watermen (1979)	*Master of the Game* (1982)
The Covenant (1980)	*If Tomorrow Comes* (1986)
Franklin Award (1980)	*Windmills of the Gods* (1987)
Space (1982)	*The Sands of Time* (1988)
Texas (1985)	**Star on Hollywood Walk of Fame** (1988)
Legacy (1987)	*Memories of Midnight* (1990)

James Michener *(cont.)*

Alaska (1988)

Donates $15 million to Univ. of Texas Graduate Writing Program (1991)

Recessional (1994)

A Miracle in Seville (1995)

Has received more than 30 honorary doctorates in Humane Letters, Law, Theology, and Science

Sidney Sheldon *(cont.)*

The Doomsday Conspiracy (1991)

The Stars Shine Down (1992)

Nothing Lasts Forever (1994)

Morning, Noon & Night (1995)

Most Translated Author in the World according to the Guinness Book of World Records (1997)

Best Laid Plans (1997)

Tell Me Your Dreams (1998)

Name _____

John Grisham
A History of Best Sellers

- Born in Jonesboro, Arkansas in 1955.

- Receives undergraduate degree in accounting from Mississippi State University in 1977.

- Earns law degree from University of Mississippi in 1981.

- Practices both criminal and civil law and elected to the Mississippi House of Representatives in 1983.

- Publishes *A Time to Kill* (Wynwood Publishing) in 1989.

- Publishes *The Firm* (Doubleday) in 1990.

- Paramount Pictures purchases film rights to *The Firm* for $600,000.

- Publishes *The Pelican Brief* (Doubleday) in 1992.

- Warner Brothers releases *The Pelican Brief* movie in 1993.

- Publishes *The Client* (Doubleday) in 1993.

- Publishes *The Chamber* (Doubleday) in 1994.

- Warner Brothers releases *The Client* in 1994.

- Publishes *The Rainmaker* (Doubleday) in 1995.

- Publishes *The Runaway Jury* (Doubleday) in 1996.

- Universal Pictures releases *The Chamber* in 1996.

- Warner Brothers releases *A Time to Kill* in 1996.

- Publishes *The Partner* (Doubleday) in 1997.

- Constellation Films releases *The Rainmaker* in 1997.

- Publishes *The Street Lawyer* (Doubleday) in 1998.

- Publishes *The Testament* (Doubleday) in 1999.

Name _____

Class Magazine Checklist

1. ____   Computer training—typing, publishing, ClipArt

2. ____   What should be the cover and title of the magazine?

3. ____   Approval from administration

4. ____   How will we sell and distribute (lunch periods, study hall, city hall, local stores) the magazine?

5. ____   How can we advertise (posters in hallways, flyers, p.a., etc.) the publication of our magazine?

6. ____   What supplies do we need?

7. ____   How much should each magazine cost? What about a subscription? What kind of order form should be made?

8. ____   Due date for articles?

9. ____   Type, topics, and length of articles?

10. ____   Pictures and graphics—What kind?

11. ____   What is the role of the teacher in this process?

12. ____   Student editors—Who?

13. ____   Who will meet with the principal and school treasurer?

14. ____   How can we market the magazine when it is ready to be published?

15. ____   Who will present the first issue to the principal and Board of Education?

16. ____   Other concerns or questions?

FEBRUARY
Answer Key

#43 SKILL SHEET 2-4—CHART THE WRITING TERMS

The Chart

Positive	Neutral	Negative
THESIS	SYNONYMS	SLANG
CLARITY	PARAGRAPH	GENERALIZATION
WEBBING	RUBRIC	CLICHÉ
OUTLINE	LISTING	WORDINESS
COHERENCE		AMBIGUITY
REVISION		RUN ONS
EDITING		
TRANSITIONS		
CLUSTERING		
PROOFREAD		

#55 SKILL SHEET 2-6—KETTER WRITING SURVEY #1—WHAT DO YOU KNOW ABOUT LETTER WRITING?

1. One type of a business letter is a letter of application or one from one company executive to another.
2. The best diction for a business letter is formal.
3. The heading of a business letter refers to the address of the sender and the date.
4. The purpose of a newsletter is to update members of a city, organization, and business about events, policies, and people.
5. "Junk" mail is advertisements sent to all residents.
6. A letter of application should be sent to the personnel or employment director.
7. A proper closing in a business letter is Sincerely, Cordially, Respectfully.
8. A proper salutation in a business letter (when you don't know the name) is Dear (title of the person): Dear Manager.
9. A signature on a letter proves the authenticity of the writer.
10. The mark of punctuation most often required for the salutation of a business letter is the colon.

SKILL SHEET 2-7—LETTER WRITING SURVEY #2

1. Answers will vary.
2. Answers will vary.

3. A pen pal is someone typically separated by a great distance but corresponds on a regular basis.

4. Business, Personal, Fan Mail, Newsletters, Invitations, Postcards, Holiday Cards, Love letters, etc.

5. A letter follows a certain format with its heading, inside address, salutation, and closing.

6. The postcard is different from a letter in that its message is exposed and brief, it usually shows a picture, and is cheaper to mail than a regular letter.

7. A letter could influence someone's career because it serves as a permanent record of correspondence, unlike a phone call.

8. Letters still remain important and official forms of correspondence in the business world.

9. 500 million approximately

10. Answers will vary.

SKILL SHEET 2-8—LETTER WRITING SURVEY #3—WHAT DO YOU KNOW ABOUT THE BUSINESS OF LETTER WRITING?

1. A letter-to-the-editor is a correspondence sent to the editor of a magazine or newspaper.

2. C.O.D. refers to Cash On Delivery, and it is used to avoid having to send cash in the mail.

3. Respectfully, Cordially, With appreciation

4. "Dear Sir or Madam" is no longer appropriate in standard business letters because it is outdated and demonstrates a lack of certainty about the receiver on the part of the writer.

5. The post office sends letters that are incorrectly addressed and lack a return address on the envelope to the Dead Letter Office where staff members hold and study letters for seven years before destroying them.

6. Junk mail is advertisements sent to all residents.

7. Businesses feel that even a one percent return on junk mail is profitable for them although many of us just throw it away.

8. A date is important on a business letter because it establishes an official date of the correspondence.

9. A business letter must be typed or in ink to prevent alterations being done on it.

10. "Enclosure" at the bottom of a business letter indicates something else is included in the envelope.

ACTIVITY 2-9—LETTER WRITING SURVEY #4—WHAT DO YOU KNOW ABOUT PERSONAL LETTERS?

1. You can prompt the receiver to write back by asking questions or simply requesting he/she does so.

2. Some traditional messages in personal letters are to announce or congratulate an anniversary or birthday, to express love or devotion, to offer sympathy or thanks, etc.

3. Answers will vary.

4. A personal letter may not be a friendly letter if it expresses the writer's desire to end a relationship, to make an accusation, to bring bad news, etc.

5. Love letters, holiday/birthday correspondences, pen pal

6. Answers will vary.

7. Sincerely, Thanks, Love, Your friend, Yours truly

8. The structure and diction of a personal letter should be informal and conversational.

9. A personal letter might be saved in case the writer refutes a statement made in the letter; the letter might also provide a pleasant memory; etc.

10. A letter can be more useful than a phone conversation because it is less expensive, more detailed, a sign the writer put in much time and effort, etc.

#71 SKILL SHEET 2-10—SPEECH PROBLEMS

1. Anxiety could be handled by being thoroughly prepared and receiving a positive introduction.

2. If a speaker goes blank he/she should check notecards or return to the previous point and add to it until memory returns.

3. A speaker should perform relaxation techniques to handle a case of nerves: deep breathing, comfortable chair or couch, exercise, a shoulder/neck massage are all possibilities.

4. Forgetting can slow a speech but should not stop it. The speaker should just get to the next point he/she does remember.

5. Distractions can be ignored, or the speaker could refer to them in a humorous way.

MARCH

INTRODUCTORY PAGE

LEARNING ACTIVITIES

REPRODUCIBLES

QUICK LOCATOR FOR MARCH LEARNING ACTIVITIES

News Unit   *50, 51*
Careers Unit   *88*
Media Unit   *10, 11, 19, 20, 21, 22, 39, 40, 79*
Fine Arts   *95, 96, 97, 98, 105*
Mythology   *52, 53, 98*
Social Skills/Understanding Ethnic Diversity   *28, 29, 31, 34, 36, 37, 41, 42,
72, 73*

MARCH

Origin: The ancient Romans originally termed this month *Martius* to honor Mars, the god of war. Some superstitions about March are that "March comes in like a lion and goes out like a lamb," which implies the first day is stormy and the final days are mild.

Holidays: St. Patrick's Day is celebrated on March 17 to commemorate the patron saint of Ireland, Bishop Patrick (AD 389–461), who introduced Christianity to Ireland. The Jewish festival of Purim usually occurs in March.

Bangladesh, Bosnia, Bulgaria, Ghana, Greece, Korea, Namibia, Pakistan, and Tunisia all celebrate their Independence Days in March.

Gemstone: Bloodstone

Flower: Violet

Poetry:
The stormy March has come at last.
With wind, and cloud, and changing skies;
I hear the rushing of the blast
That through the snowy valley flies.

    by William Cullen Bryant

BIRTHDAYS

March 1	Ralph Ellison, author of *Invisible Man* (1914) [#26, 69]; William Gaines, founder/publisher of *MAD* magazine (1922) [#11]; Ron Howard, actor/director (1954) [#22, 104]
March 2	Theodor Geisel (Dr. Seuss), creator of *The Cat in the Hat* and *How the Grinch Stole Christmas* whose books have sold more than 200 million copies, earning him a Pulitzer Prize in 1984 (1904) [#3, 104]
March 3	Alexander Graham Bell, inventor of the telephone (1847) [#14, 31, 81]; Jackie Joyner-Kersee, Olympic gold medalist (1962) [#17, 104]
March 4	Knute Rockne, legendary Notre Dame football coach (1888) [#32, 71, 104]
March 6	Elizabeth Barrett Browning, English poet (1806) [#4, 76, 87]; Michelangelo, Italian painter/sculptor (1475) [#83, 104]
March 9	Robert Fischer, world chess champion (1943) [#39, 82, 106]; Mickey Spillane (born Frank Morrison), mystery writer (1918) [#24, 60, 64]; Amerigo Vespucci, Italian navigator/explorer whose name was applied to the new world after his two expeditions there (1451) [#45]
March 12	Jack Kerouac, writer of the Beat Generation (1922) [#8, 23, 25, 26, 60, 70]; Liza Minnelli, singer/performer (1946) [#38, 40, 92, 104]
March 14	Billy Crystal, actor/comedian (1947) [#33, 38, 40]; Albert Einstein, physicist (1879) [#13, 27, 75]
March 15	Andrew Jackson, 7th President (1767) [#30, 57, 77]
March 16	James Madison, 4th President (1751) [#15, 57]
March 17	Nat "King" Cole, singer/performer, and first black entertainer to host a national television show [#72]; Rudolph Nureyev, ballet dancer (1938) [#96]
March 18	Grover Cleveland, 22nd and 24th President (1837) [#15, 57]; John Updike, writer (1932) [#24, 25, 60]
March 20	Spike Lee, actor/director (1957) [#22, 104]; Isaac Newton, physicist who discovered laws of gravity (1642) [#27]
March 21	Johann Sebastian Bach, German composer (1685) [#12, 95, 104]
March 22	Marcel Marceau, pantomimist (1923) [#99]; Andrew Lloyd Webber, composer—*Phantom of the Opera* (1948) [#97]

March 24   Harry Houdini, magician/author (1874) [#78, 90, 104]

March 26   Robert Frost, Pulitzer Prizes for Poetry in 1924, 1931, 1937, and 1943 (1874) [#2, 85, 86]; Sandra Day O'Conner, first woman Associate Justice to Supreme Court (1930) [#18, 104]; Diana Ross, singer/performer 1944) [#38, 40, 72, 104]; Tennessee Williams, playwright (1911) [#5, 26, 105]

March 28   Elton John (born Reginald Dwight) (1947) [#12, 38, 40, 57, 93, 104]; Sir David Lean, director and winner of 28 Academy Awards (1908) [#22]; Gloria Steinem, author/feminist (1935) [#18, 104]

March 29   John Tyler, 10th President and the first to marry while in office (1790) [#30]; Cy (Denton) Young, baseball's all-time winningest pitcher with 511 victories (1867) [#39]

March 30   Celine Dion, singer (1968) [#38, 40, 91]; Vincent Van Gogh, Dutch post-impressionist painter (1853) [#83]

March 31   Jack Johnson, first black world heavyweight champion (1878) [#72, 78, 104]

MEMORABLE EVENTS

March 1   Nebraska was admitted to the Union as 37th state in 1867 [#44, 47, 55].

Ohio was admitted to the Union as 17th state in 1803 [#44, 55].

Peace Corps was founded in 1961 and has sent more than 148,000 volunteers to teach nutrition, agriculture, health, and sanitation to 132 developing countries [#73].

March 3   Florida was admitted to the Union as the 27th state in 1845 [#44, 55].

National Anthem Day—"The Star Spangled Banner" was adopted as our national anthem in 1931 by President Herbert Hoover [#94].

March 4   *People* Magazine first published in 1974 and featured Mia Farrow on the cover [#10, 20, 79, 80].

Vermont was admitted to the Union as the 14th state in 1791 [#44, 47, 55].

March 9   The Barbie doll debuted in 1959. Since then more than 800 million have been sold [#88].

Panic Day [#101].

March 10   Alexander Graham Bell transmitted the first phone message in 1876 [#13, 31, 81].

The first paper money in the U.S. was issued in 1862 [#43, 102].

March 11   Johnny Appleseed Day (the anniversary of the death of John Chapman, planter of orchards, in 1845) [#53].

Bureau of Indian Affairs was established under the jurisdiction of the United States War Department in 1824 [#28].

Mary Shelley published *Frankenstein*, which began as a ghost story to entertain guests (1818) [#6, 60].

March 14   Save a Spider Day [#35].

March 15   Maine was admitted to the Union as the 23rd state in 1820 [344, 55].

March 16   Nathaniel Hawthorne published *The Scarlet Letter* in 1850 [358, 60].

March 17   St. Patrick's Day [#34].

March 20   Proposal Day [#42].

Harriet Beecher Stowe published *Uncle Tom's Cabin* in 1852 [#7, 60].

March 22   Laser was patented in 1960. The laser is light amplification by stimulated emission of strong radiation [#84].

A Russian cosmonaut set the record for days in space at 439 aboard the spacecraft Mir in 1995 [#48, 89].

March 26   The "The Young and the Restless" premiered in 1973 [#21, 41, 103].

Dr. Jonas Salk announced his vaccine against polio in 1953 [#56, 74].

March 28   Pecan Day [#100].

March 30   "Jeopardy" premiered in 1964 [#68].

Doctor's Day [#9, 54, 74].

Anesthetic was first used in surgery in 1842 by Dr. Crawford W. Long who used ether on a patient to remove a tumor from his neck. [#51].

Pencil eraser was patented in 1858 by Hyman Lipman [#16].

The 15th Amendment passed in Congress guaranteeing the right to vote to all races in 1870 [#50].

LEARNING ACTIVITIES FOR MARCH

READING ACTIVITIES

Purpose: To encourage independent reading

1. Promote the annual "Read Across America" campaign and invite local celebrities, politicians, and parents into your classroom to read to students, either their favorite books or selections you pick out.

Purpose: To improve skills at analyzing poetry

2. Have students read poems by Robert Frost that may appear in their literature text or an available anthology to study the type of verse, the poetic language, and the topics/themes.

> **Robert Frost used traditional metrical schemes in his poems which often were blank verse (he disliked free verse). He used the language of rural New England, which was also the subject of much of his poetry, along with the beauty and danger of nature.**

3. Ask students to locate and read a Dr. Seuss narrative to study the unconventional use of language, especially the made-up words, the topics, and the humor.

4. Have students read any poems by Elizabeth Barrett Browning that may appear in their literature text or any available anthology to analyze the type of verse, the poetic language, and the topics/themes, especially her focus on romantic relationships.

> **Elizabeth Barrett Browning used classical and lyrical language in her sonnets, which typically reflected themes related to Italy, religion, women's rights, and romantic love, which was influenced by her love for fellow poet and husband Robert Browning.**

Purpose: To improve skills at analyzing drama

5. Have students read orally a play by Tennessee Williams that may appear in their literature text or available anthology to study the characters, conflicts, and topics/themes, especially his emphasis on tragedy.

Purpose: To improve skills at analyzing fiction

6. Read orally excerpts from Mary Shelley's *Frankenstein* and have the students identify the gothic writing style and any elements of characterization.

> Gothic writing style is characterized by mystery and horror where characters routinely occupy isolated castles and face violent extremes of nature and supernatural antagonists.

7. Have students read excerpts from Harriet Beecher Stowe's *Uncle Tom's Cabin* and ask students to identify the historical time period. Also, deal with her description of characters and use this to connect literature with history. Preview this with Abraham Lincoln's statement: "This is the little lady who wrote the book that made this big war."

8. Distribute **Form 3-1**—passages from Jack Kerouac's novels *The Town and the City* (1950) and *On the Road* (1957). Then ask: What problems did you encounter with the passages? Why did Kerouac intentionally use run-on sentences? What is the overall effect of the passages?

> Kerouac's writing is typically characterized by run-ons, improper punctuation, colloquialisms, and slang which he uses for dramatic effect. His restlessness as a person can be seen in his narrative prose, which reflects the "beatnik" subculture. Other books that demonstrate this are *The Dharma Bums* (1958) and *Big Sur* (1962).

Purpose: To expand skills at word selection/vocabulary

9. Refer to Doctor's Day and the Hippocratic Oath—**Form 3-2**—and direct students to define the terms hypochondriac, epidemic, plague, quarantine, and contagious. They should then use these terms in creating a brief narrative.

Purpose: To explore the influence of the media

10. Prompt students to locate and read articles from *People* Magazine. Then ask: What people are profiled? Why were they selected as subjects of articles? What did you learn about them? Use **Skill Sheet 3-3** to expand the lesson.

Purpose: To review satire

11. Ask students to locate and read *MAD* Magazine articles and to define *satire*. Then ask: How do the articles demonstrate satire?

> Bill Gaines founded *MAD* as ten-cent comic book in 1952 to satirize other comics, but soon broadened its satire to include movies, television shows, politicians, songs, and corporations, among other targets. Currently, there are also over 135 MAD paperback books.

DEBATING ACTIVITIES

Purpose: To expand critical thinking skills

12. Who is the more talented musician—Johann Sebastian Bach or Elton John? (or any current rap artist)? Play some of their recordings.

13. Albert Einstein decided to complete his work on nuclear fission, knowing this research would be used to create a nuclear bomb. Should Einstein's work be praised or criticized? Use his letter—**Form 3-4**—to initiate the debate.

14. Are prank phone calls a serious offense? How could a prank call injure a person? How should those persons convicted of making prank phone calls be punished? Refer to Alexander Graham Bell.

15. Which President was the more experienced politician—James Madison who was a delegate to the Continental Congress, Secretary of State under Thomas Jefferson, and President when the United States defeated Great Britain in the War of 1812; or Grover Cleveland who served as mayor of Buffalo, governor of New York, and President for two nonconsecutive terms?

16. Refer to the pencil eraser which was patented in 1858 and ask: Is a pencil eraser still necessary today? Why/why not? Refer to new technology that includes white out, the delete button on computers, and spellcheck on most word processors.

17. Is it more or less challenging for female Olympic athletes than males to compete? Refer to Jackie Joyner-Kersee. Use this also to explore the issue of gender bias.

18. Who contributed more to the social advancement of women—Gloria Steinem who founded the National Women's Political Caucus, published articles and books about women's rights, and lectured across the country; or Sandra Day O'Conner who served as an assistant state's attorney general and a state senator before becoming the first woman on the U.S. Supreme Court?

Purpose: To explore the influence of the media

19. Refer to the many authors, performers, and actors who have birthdays this month and ask: What provides the best type of entertainment—a great book, a great concert, or a great movie? Why?

20. What are the differences between *People* Magazine and the *National Enquirer* (both use articles based on interviews)? Which is more informative? Which is more accurate? Which is more popular? Why?

21. Refer to "The Young and the Restless" and ask: Does this title suggest an unfair image of young people? Why/why not?

22. Who has directed the more entertaining and important films—Sir David Lean, Spike Lee, or Ron Howard? Use **Form 3-5** to explore students' understanding of the motion picture industry and quality cinema.

Purpose: To expand skills at word selection/vocabulary

23. Consider Jack Kerouac who used much slang and/or "street talk" in his writing. Is this appropriate? Should stories read by young adults have such language? Why/why not? Use **Form 3-1**.

Purpose: To begin or conclude a fiction unit

24. In fiction, which is more important—characters or plot? Refer to the novelists who have birthdays this month.

25. Who contributed more to American literature in the 1950s and 1960s—Jack Kerouac or John Updike? Students could read their works or research the backgrounds of these writers.

26. Who contributed more to American literature—Ralph Ellison who won a National Book Award or Tennessee Williams who won two Pulitzer Prizes? Students could read their works and/or research the backgrounds of these writers.

Purpose: To expand research skills

27. Who contributed more to scientific discovery—Isaac Newton or Albert Einstein? Use this also to improve students' work with comparison and contrast.

28. Explain that the Bureau of Indian Affairs was created in 1824 by the War Department and added to the Department of the Interior in 1849. It currently employs about 14,500 people, mostly American Indians, whose mandate is to provide technical assistance to tribal governments. Then ask: Is this department still necessary? Why/why not?

29. Which would be the best country to visit—Greece, Korea, or Pakistan? Why? Use this also to promote students' understanding of other nationalities and cultures.

30. Who did more for America's economic development as President—Andrew Jackson or John Tyler? Jackson served two terms as President and restored positive trade relations with England and France. Tyler was the first President to open up trade with Asia.

WRITING ACTIVITIES

Purpose: To review brainstorming as a prewriting strategy

31. Have students list all the people they have called on the phone in the last one or two months. Students could also explain how any of those phone calls affected their lives. Refer to Alexander Graham Bell.

32. Refer to Knute Rockne and have students list all they know about football. Then have them place their list of items in categories.

33. Refer to Billy Crystal and direct students to first list and then rank from best to worst 10–15 other comedians.

Purpose: *To expand skills at writing description*

34. Refer to St. Patrick's Day and Irish folklore to prompt students to write a descriptive paragraph about an Irish leprechaun.

> **Leprechauns are a mythical race of elves who would bestow their treasure on anyone who could catch them.**

35. Have students write a detailed, one-page essay using sensory language about the appearance, movement, and behavior of spiders. Students possibly could wander the room to look for spider webs. Refer to Save a Spider Day and use **Form 12-5** to evaluate students.

36. Have students write a descriptive, one-page essay about the clothing or fashions of any nationality or culture that is particular to that culture or nationality, such as a turban. Refer to Ghana, Pakistan, or Greece. Use **Form 12-5.**

37. First, explore what students know about the ancient Greek temples and then have them list descriptive phrases and sentences about them. Use this also to improve students' understanding of the ancient Greek culture.

Purpose: *To improve skills at writing characterizations*

38. Refer to Liza Minnelli, Diana Ross, Billy Crystal, Celine Dion, and Elton John and instruct students to select one of these performers to describe in a brief essay.

39. Refer to the backgrounds and accomplishments of Cy Young and Bobby Fischer and instruct students to place their names as the headings to two columns on their papers. Then have them list the traits, skills, and training of both in their respective columns. Allow them to research or simply speculate.

Purpose: *To review the format/diction of letters*

40. Refer to Liza Minnelli, Billy Crystal, Diana Ross, Celine Dion, and Elton John and have students write a fan mail letter to their favorite performer.

Purpose: *To expand skills at word selection/vocabulary*

41. Refer to the "Young and the Restless" and have students select any abstract term associated with human behavior—love, loyalty, kindness, etc.—often exhibited by soap opera characters and write a paragraph that defines that term.

42. Refer to Proposal Day and challenge students to write the most formal and eloquent proposal of marriage, other than the trite "Will you marry me?" Discover who can be the most creative.

43. Refer to paper money, which was first issued in 1862, and to coins and have students list the terms used to identify the bills or coins of other nations, such as the German mark.

Purpose: *To improve organizational skills in writing*

44. Have students write a travelogue about Florida, Nebraska, Maine, Vermont, or Ohio, whichever state they have visited. Use **Form 11-11** as a model.

45. Refer to Amerigo Vespucci and instruct students to compose an itinerary for his voyage to the New World.

46. Distribute **Form 3-6** and have students follow the guidelines to construct their own outlines about any of the following: states that entered the union this month; performers who have birthdays this month; or writers who have birthdays this month.

Purpose: *To practice writing comparison/contrast*

47. Have students write a brief essay comparing the terrain and landscape of Nebraska and Vermont. Use this also to develop research skills. Direct students to an atlas and other reference books.

48. Have students write a brief essay comparing the frontier of the American West with the frontier of deep space. Refer to the Russian cosmonaut who spent 439 days aboard the Mir in 1995. Possibly allow students to do research first.

49. Refer to the various musicians who have birthdays this month and have students write a one-page comparison/contrast essay explaining the similarities and differences between hip/hop and other types of music.

Purpose: *To practice writing news articles*

50. Have students consider the time period (1870) and write a news lead about the passage of the 15th amendment by Congress, which guaranteed the right to vote to all races.

51. Have students write the news lead for an article or a feature about Dr. Crawford W. Long, who used anesthetic in surgery for the first time in 1842.

> **Example: Dr. Crawford W. Long, of Danielsville, Georgia, used an anesthetic, a new technique to lessen pain during surgery, in an operation yesterday to remove a tumor from a patient's neck.**

Purpose: To introduce a mythology unit

52. Refer to Mars, for whom the Romans named this month, and challenge students to list the Greek gods of mythology. Use this also to review listing as a prewriting technique.

53. Refer to Johnny Appleseed Day and the myths about John Chapman, who, legend says, traveled barefoot in shabby clothing with a tin pot on his head through Ohio, Indiana, and Illinois planting apple seeds. Have students create their own myth about a real or imaginary person.

Purpose: To review writing personal narratives

54. Refer to Doctor's Day and have students write a descriptive narrative about a visit to a doctor. They should deal with the doctor's appearance, actions, and attitude. What was the illness or problem? What did the doctor do to help them? How did he/she behave? How would you describe the office or examination room? Use **Form 12-7** to evaluate them.

55. Direct students to write a descriptive personal narrative about a journey or visit to Nebraska, Ohio, Florida, Vermont, or Maine. Use **Form 12-7** to evaluate.

Purpose: To improve research skills

56. Refer to Jonas Salk and polio and ask: What are the major *diseases* affecting humanity today? Have students select any three major diseases and explain in a detailed essay how they affect the human body.

57. Direct students to discover the wars that involved the Presidents who have birthdays this month.

> **Andrew Jackson was a general during the War of 1812, winning the Battle of New Orleans, and later led an army expedition against the Seminole Indians. James Madison first declared war on Great Britain in 1812 and signed the treaty ending the war in 1814. Grover Cleveland paid a Polish immigrant $150 to serve in his place during the Civil War, and as President refused to have U.S. troops get involved in the Cuban War of Independence against Spain. John Tyler headed a peace convention that tried to prevent the Civil War.**

Purpose: To conclude a fiction unit

58. Distribute **Skill Sheet 3-7** and have students respond to the motifs in Nathaniel Hawthorne's *The Scarlet Letter*.

59. Have students construct a chart about the major and minor characters from a story or a novel read for class. Apply headings like Appearance, Habits, Family, Occupation(s), Values, and Speech.

60. Refer to any story or novel students have read and ask them to write a persuasive essay about the story or novel that has the most unusual setting, the most unique characters, or the most dramatic climax. Refer also to Mickey Spillane, John Updike, Nathaniel Hawthorne, Harriet Beecher Stowe, Mary Shelley, and Jack Kerouac.

61. Have students create a different ending to a story read in class or to a story by one of the writers who has a birthday this month. Use this to challenge students' creativity and understanding of resolution. Ask: Is the new ending logical?

DISCUSSION ACTIVITIES

Purpose: To begin or conclude a fiction unit

62. What makes for a successful story beginning? What do most readers expect to see at the beginning of a story? How do many authors begin their stories?

63. Should stories end optimistically or pessimistically? Why?

64. Refer to Mickey Spillane and ask: What makes for a great mystery story?

65. In what stories or novels that you've read is the setting more important than the plot?

66. When reading fiction, are plot events always in chronological order? What novels do not have events in a chronological order?

67. How important is our knowledge of history to understand the setting(s) in a story or novel? What about world geography? How can a reader determine the setting of a story if the narrator doesn't identify it specifically?

68. Refer to "Jeopardy" and direct students to respond to a series of *answers* about literary terms with the appropriate question. Use **Skill Sheet 3-8.**

69. Write the quote from the prologue from Ralph Ellison's classic novel *Invisible Man:* "I am an invisible man . . . I am a man of substance, of flesh and bone, fiber and liquids—and I might even be said to possess a mind. I am invisible, understand, simply because people refuse to see me." Then ask: Why does Ellison use the term *invisible*, rather than one like *ignored*? How does Ellison suggest people are racist? How does the quote also suggest an identity crisis?

70. Explain that Jack Kerouac was the major spokesperson of the "Beat Generation" of writers. He applied the term to identify a group of writers and artists in the 1940s and 1950s who rebelled against social conformity and materialism, using "beat" to portray the *beat*en individual against society, the *beat* of jazz music, and *beat*itude, or the happiness they had with their alternative lifestyle. Beatniks were people who adopted this philosophy and lifestyle. Ask students: What was the 1960s version of beatniks? [hippies] What other writers in history used their

writing to express nonconformity? [Ralph Waldo Emerson, Henry David Thoreau, T.S. Eliot, etc.] What are the characteristics of the writing styles of the Beat Generation? [not following grammar rules, use of slang, rhythmic quality to sentences]

Purpose: To expand critical thinking skills

71. How important is coaching to an athlete's success? Refer to Knute Rockne. Also ask: In what ways do you need coaching as writers? As readers?

72. Explain to students that understanding often improves by asking questions about a subject. Then refer to Jack Johnson, the first black heavyweight champion; Nat "King" Cole, the first black performer to host a national television show; and Diana Ross, one of the most popular black female singers of all time, and ask: What questions would you ask these individuals if you could talk to them?

73. What are the benefits to joining the Peace Corps? What are some disadvantages? Why do many young people join it?

74. What would happen if no doctor would treat people with communicative diseases? What if drug companies didn't try to produce drugs for rare diseases? Why are some doctors willing to spend a lifetime investigating a cure for a single disease? Refer to Jonas Salk and Doctor's Day.

75. Write the following quote from Albert Einstein on the board: "The attempt to combine wisdom and power has only rarely been successful and then only for a short while" and ask: How accurate is Einstein? What examples of this can you cite? Why can't wisdom and power unite cooperatively?

76. Write the following quote from Elizabeth Barrett Browning on the board: "An artist must, I fancy, either find or make a solitude to work in, if it is to be good work at all." Then ask: How accurate is Browning? When do you prefer to work in solitude? Why can this be helpful?

77. Write the following quote from Andrew Jackson on the board: "One man with courage makes a majority" and ask: Do you agree with Andrew Jackson? Why/why not?

78. How would you feel if you were Harry Houdini in his last performance or Jack Johnson after his last fight? What would be their thoughts or emotions?

79. Refer to *People* Magazine. How do some magazines violate peoples' privacy? How would you feel about being the focus of an article in *People* magazine?

80. How could a writer's failure to distinguish between a fact and an opinion cause harm to someone else? How would you react to a statement—either written or oral—that harmed either directly or indirectly your reputation or status? Refer to *People* Magazine, various celebrities, and the definitions of libel and slander.

> **Libel = any written or printed statement that seriously damages a person's reputation or exposes a person to public ridicule. Slander = oral comments that seriously damage a person's reputation or expose a person to public ridicule.**

Purpose: To begin a letter writing unit

81. What is the best form of communication: e-mail, letters, phone calls, or faxes? What are the advantages and disadvantages of each type? Refer to Alexander Graham Bell.

Purpose: To expand skills at word selection/vocabulary

82. Refer to Bobby Fischer and ask: What are some chess terms? What are the connotations of some of them? How could you use these terms in a regular conversation?

> *King* **implies a master, leader, authority;** *queen* **suggests power mixed with grace;** *bishop* **implies spiritual leadership;** *knight* **can be identified with military force and chivalry;** *pawn* **refers to someone easily manipulated;** *checkmate* **means defeat;** *in check* **indicates defeat is near.**

83. Refer to Michelangelo and Vincent Van Gogh and ask: If you were a painter, what would you paint? Why? How would you describe the most beautiful painting you have ever seen?

84. Refer to the laser, which was patented in 1960, and ask: How would you explain the laser to someone who has never seen it before? What terms would you use? What comparisons or analogies could you offer?

Purpose: To begin or conclude a poetry unit

85. Distribute and discuss **Skill Sheet 3-9**—Robert Frost's quotes on poetry.

86. Robert Frost was the first poet to read a poem—"The Gift Outright"—at a Presidential inauguration (for John F. Kennedy in 1961). Why do you think Kennedy requested Frost? What did the reading of a poem add to this prestigious ceremony? What are the benefits to hearing a poem read?

87. How would you interpret these famous lines from Elizabeth Barrett Browning?

   "How do I love thee? Let me count the ways.
   I love thee to the depth and breadth and height my soul can reach . . ."

> **Elizabeth Barrett Browning answers her own question by applying a sense of dimension and spirituality to the intensity of her love. The implication here is that her love is so great it cannot be truly measured.**

Purpose: *To begin or conclude a careers unit*

88. Have students consider the Barbie doll and the fact that over 800 million have been sold since 1959, making millions for its manufacturer. Then ask: Why did this doll become so popular? What other dolls have sold well? If you were to create a doll as an entrepreneur, what would it be?

Purpose: *To teach writing characterizations*

89. Refer to the Russian cosmonaut who spent 439 days alone in space in the spacecraft Mir in 1995 and ask: What were his thoughts as he traveled in space? How did he occupy his time? How did he behave when he returned to earth?

90. Have students consider Harry Houdini and then ask: Who are some other famous magicians? How would you describe their appearance? What is their act (props, devices, actions)?

AUDIO/VISUAL ACTIVITIES

Purpose: *To begin or conclude a poetry unit*

91. Play a recording by Celine Dion and explore the feelings and reactions the lyrics and music inspire. Ask: How poetic are the lyrics? What images does the music provide? What words or phrases describe the music? Use this to connect music, lyrics, and language.

92. Play a recording of Liza Minnelli and explore the feelings and reactions the lyrics and music inspire. Ask: How poetic are the lyrics? What images does the music provide? What words or phrases describe the music? Use this to connect music, lyrics, and language.

93. Play a recording(s) of Elton John and explore the feelings and reactions the lyrics and music inspire. Ask: How poetic are the lyrics? What images does the music provide? What words or phrases describe the music? Use this to connect music, lyrics, and language.

94. Play a recording of the National Anthem and have students identify the words and phrases that demonstrate the poetic quality of the lyrics.

Purpose: To expand appreciation for the fine arts

95. Play a recording of Johann Sebastian Bach and explore the feelings and reactions the music inspires. Ask: What images does the music provide? What words or phrases describe the music?

96. Refer to Rudolph Nureyev, show a videotape of a ballet, and ask: How does the dancing tell a story? What images or moods does the dancing inspire? How would you describe the dancers?

97. Play a recording of Andrew Lloyd Webber's *Phantom of the Opera* and have students list modifiers that describe the music and characters.

Purpose: To begin or conclude a mythology unit

98. Show sellected scenes from the movie *Clash of the Titans* starring Harry Hamlin and refer to Mars. Ask students to identify mythological references.

Purpose: To expand skills at writing description

99. Refer to Marcel Marceau and have students pantomime without words any specific action (for example, exercising). Other students could *write* paragraphs, describing the mime's appearance and gestures.

100. Distribute pecans to students on Pecan Day and ask them to list the appropriate modifiers that describe the taste. If possible, have them compare the taste to other nuts.

101. Refer to Panic Day and ask selected students to role play a person who is experiencing panic. Other students should write descriptive phrases based on their observations, such as "wild eyes."

102. Refer to the first paper money in the U.S. that was issued in 1862 and have students study paper money or use Monopoly money for them to describe using sensory language.

Purpose: To teach writing characterizations

103. Show scenes from a television show like "The Young and the Restless" to identify the values, beliefs, personalities, and habits of the characters.

> **Students need training in how the popular media like radio, television, and films portray social skills and personal values. This type of examination can encourage critical thinking, especially about drug/alcohol references, the violent habits of movie heroes, and the exploitive depiction of females common in so many popular programs.**

104. Ask students to role-play a conversation between any of the following pairs. Ask: What would they say to each other? How would they behave? What would be their attitudes? Reward those students who convey strong theatrical characterizations or dialogue.

    • Johann Sebastian Bach and Elton John about music.

    • Justice Sandra Day O'Connor and Gloria Steinem about women's rights.

    • Diana Ross and Liza Minnelli about performing.

    • Theodor Geisel and Knute Rockne about dealing with young people.

    • Jackie Joyner-Kersee and Jack Johnson about competing as athletes.

    • Spike Lee and Ron Howard about the movie industry.

    • Michelangelo and Harry Houdini about their beliefs.

105. Show selected scenes from any Tennessee Williams play that has been made into a movie, like *The Glass Menagerie*, *A Streetcar Named Desire*, or *Cat on a Hot Tin Roof*, and ask students to identify the backgrounds, traits, and habits of the characters.

Purpose: To review organization in writing

106. Refer to Robert Fischer, world chess champion, and display chess pieces and a board. Then have selected students who are familiar with chess to write a step-by-step sequence of moves as a comparison to the step-by-step way of organizing a composition.

© 2001 by The Center for Applied Research in Education

Form 3–1   Name _____

Jack Kerouac

Directions: Examine the following passages from novels by Jack Kerouac. Why would Kerouac intentionally use run-ons and slang? What is the overall effect of each passage?

Passage #1—*The Town and the Country*

Afternoons in Lowell long ago I'd wondered what the grimy men were doing with big box-cars and blocks of wood in their hands and when far above the ramps and rooftops of the great gray warehouse of eternity I'd see the immortal canal clouds of redbrick time, the drowse so heavy in the whole July city it would hang even in the dank gloom of my father's shop outside where they kept big rolltrucks with little wheels and flat silvery platforms and junk in corners and boards, the ink dyed into the oily wood as deep as a black river folded therein forever, contrasts for the whitepuff cream-clouds outdoors that you just can see standing in the dust moted hall door over the old 1830 Lowell Dickens redbrick floating like an old cartoon with little bird designs floating by too, all of a gray daguerreotype mystery in the whorly spermy waters of the canal.

Thus is the same way the afternoons in the S.P. redbrick alley, remembering my wonder at the slow grinding movement and squeal of gigantic boxcars and flats rolling by with that overpowering steel dust crunching closh and clack of steel on steel, the shudder of the whole steely proposition, a car going by with a brake on and so the whole brakebar—the frightening fog nights in California when you can see thru the mist the monsters slowly passing and hear the whee whee squee, those merciless wheels that one time conductor Ray Miles on my student trips said, "When those wheels go over your leg they don't care about you" the same way with that wood that I sacrifice.

Passage #2—*On the Road*

But then they danced down the streets like dingledodies, and I shambled after them as I've been doing all my life after people who interest me, because the only people for me are the mad ones, the ones who are mad to live, mad to talk, mad to be saved, desirous of everything at the same time, the ones who never yawn or say a commonplace thing, but burn, burn, burn like fabulous yellow roman candles exploding like spiders across the stars and in the middle you see the blue center light pop and everybody goes "Awwwww!"

Name _____

Hippocrates and the Hippocratic Oath

Directions: Study the Hippocratic Oath below and then define the terms hypochondriac, epidemic, plague quarantine, and contagious. Next, use these terms
and the oath somehow in a brief narrative.

I swear by Apollo the physician, by Aesculapius, Hygeia, and Panacea, and I take to witness
all the gods, all the goddesses, to keep according to my ability and my judgment the following Oath:

I will prescribe regimen for the good of my patients according to my ability and my judgment and never do harm to anyone. To please no one will I prescribe a deadly drug, nor give
advice which may cause his death. Nor will I give a woman a pessary to procure abortion.
But I will preserve the purity of my life and my art. I will not cut for stone, even for patients
in whom the disease is manifest; I will leave this operation to be performed by practition-
ers (specialists in this art). In every house where I come I will enter only for the good of my
patients, keeping myself far from all intentional ill-doing and all seduction, and especially
from the pleasures of love with women or with men, be they free or slaves. All that may
come to my knowledge in the exercise of my profession or outside my profession or in daily
commerce with men, which ought not be spread abroad, I will keep secret and will never
reveal. If I keep this oath faithfully, may I enjoy my life and practice my art, respected by
all men and in all times; but if I swerve from it or violate it, may the reverse be my lot.

Your narrative:

Name _____

People **Magazine and Celebrities**

Directions: Answer each of the following questions in detail.

1. Why are celebrities' interviews so popular?

2. Why are we so interested in learning about the personal lives of celebrities?

3. How might writers obtain information about a celebrity other than by an interview?

4. How have criminal acts turned some people into celebrities?

5. Why do we feel inferior, at times, to celebrities?

6. How could reading an interview with a celebrity benefit the reader?

7. How could an interview hurt or help a person's success?

8. How could an interview make an ordinary person famous?

© 2001 by The Center for Applied Research in Education

Form 3–4

Name _____

A Letter from Albert Einstein to President Franklin Delano Roosevelt

Dear Mr. President:

In the course of the last four months it has been made probable that it may become possible to set up a nuclear chain reaction in a large mass of uranium, by which vast amounts of power and large quantities of new radium-like elements would be generated. Now it appears almost certain that this could be achieved in the near future. This new phenomenon would also lead to the construction of bombs, and it is conceivable—though much less certain—that extremely powerful bombs of a new type may thus be constructed. A single bomb of this type, carried by boat and exploded in a port, might very well destroy the whole port together with some of the surrounding territory. However, such bombs may well prove to be too heavy for transportation by air.

In view of this situation, you may think it desirable to have some permanent contact maintained between the Administration and the group of physicists working on chain reactions in America.

Yours very truly,

A. Einstein

Sir David Lean

Directed *Brief Encounter* (1945) a mystery—nominated for an Academy Award.

Directed *The Bridge on the River Kwai* (1957)—which portrayed the lives of British prisoners of war in a Japanese jungle prison camp—Oscar winner for Best Director.

Directed *Lawrence of Arabia* (1962)—the biography of T. E. Lawrence, the British lieutenant who mobilized the Arab revolt against the Ottoman Empire during WW I—Oscar winner for Best Director.

Directed *Doctor Zhivago* (1965)—which portrayed the life of the main character before, during, and after the Russian Revolution of 1917.

Directed *Ryan's Daughter* (1970).

Received D.W. Griffith Award (1973)—highest honor from the Director's Guild of America.

Directed *A Passage to India* (1984)—nominated for an Academy Award.

Spike Lee

Directed *She's Gotta Have It* (1986)—which portrays the lives of young African Americans.

Directed *School Daze* (1988)—a musical about black college students.

Directed *Do the Right Thing* (1988)—which describes race relations in Brooklyn, New York.

Directed *Mo Better Blues* (1990)—a story of black musicians.

Directed *Jungle Fever* (1991)—a story of an interracial affair.

Directed *Malcolm X* (1992)—the biography of the famous civil rights activist.

Directed *Crooklyn* (1994)—which describes a summer in the life of one black family in Brooklyn.

Directed *Clockers* (1995)—a mystery.

Directed *Girl 6* (1996)—a documentary.

Ron Howard

Had acting debut at age 18 months on stage with parents.

Played Opie in the "Andy Griffith Show" (1960–1968) and Richie in "Happy Days" (1974–1984).

Appeared in movies *The Music Man* (1962), *The Courtship of Eddie's Father* (1963), and *American Graffiti* (1973).

Directed *Grand Theft Auto* (1977)—the story of two young car thieves.

© 2001 by The Center for Applied Research in Education

Directed *Night Shift* (1982)—a comedy of two workers in the city morgue who operate a prostitution ring.

Directed *Splash* (1984)—the story of a relationship between a human and a mermaid.

Directed *Cocoon* (1985)—which describes a group of senior citizens rejuvenated by swimming in a pool that contains alien cocoons.

Directed *Parenthood* (1989)—the story of several suburban families.

Directed *Backdraft* (1991)—which portrays the personal and professional lives of firefighters.

Directed *Apollo 13* (1995)—the story of the failed NASA space mission.

Won Best Director Award from the Director's Guild of America and nominated for an Academy Award for *Apollo 13* (1995).

Outlining—Key Points

1. Use Roman numerals—I, II, III, IV, etc.—indicate the major topics of an essay.

   For example, for an essay on Cleveland's ethnic population, a major topic would be

   I   Greek neighborhoods

2. Use capital letters to indicate the subtopics for each major topic.

   I   Greek neighborhoods
      A. hold annual festival every August
      B. strong family backgrounds
      C. speak Greek at local cafes

3. Use Arabic numbers (1, 2, 3, etc.) to show specific examples that relate directly back to the subtopics.

   I   Greek neighborhoods
      A. hold annual festival every August
         1. at Annunciation Greek Orthodox Church
         2. serve pastries like baklava
         3. demonstrate Greek dances
      B. strong family backgrounds
         1. live with grandparents
      C. speak Greek at local cafes
         1. like Athens Cafe

4. For logical organization, an outline is necessary. An effective outline will help you write the composition. Major topics form the topic sentences of paragraphs of an essay. The subtopics and supporting details form the supporting sentences of the essay's paragraphs.

5. When writing an outline, avoid using just single words like the example below:

   I   Population
      A. Italians
      B. Germans
      C. Greeks

6. Review your outline after constructing it. Do not circle any item or use parentheses. Check: Is the form correct with Roman numerals against the left margin and subtopics and supporting details indented properly?

Name _____

Motifs in Nathaniel Hawthorne's
The Scarlet Letter

Motif = a main feature, element, or idea (theme) elaborated on throughout a literary work. The following motifs appear in his novel *The Scarlet Letter*.

- Nathaniel Hawthorne grew up heavily influenced by the values of his Puritan ancestors who were very religious and hard working.

  What are your values?

- Hawthorne examined the idea of moral responsibility. What are some typical morals people might have?

- Hawthorne confronted the notion of good vs. evil. What other books deal with this motif?

- The main character in *The Scarlet Letter* had to wear a large *A* on her chest to label her as an adulterer.

  How does society label people today?

Name _____

Literary Terms and "Jeopardy"

1. Protagonist
   A. What is the main character of a poem?
   B. What is the main character of a fictional story?
   C. What is the enemy or obstacle of the main character?

2. Antagonist
   A. What is the main character of a ballad?
   B. What is the main character of a fictional story?
   C. What is the enemy or obstacle of the main character?

3. Climax
   A. What is the conflict of the story?
   B. What is the end of the story?
   C. What is the highest point of action in a story

4. Resolution
   A. What is the conflict of the story?
   B. What is the end of the story?
   C. What is the highest point of action in a story?

5. Dialogue
   A. What is where and when the story takes place?
   B. What are the spoken words of the characters?
   C. What is the problem or obstacle in the story?

6. Conflict
   A. What is where and when the story takes place?
   B. What are the spoken words of the characters?
   C. What is the problem or obstacle in the story?

7. Plot
   A. What is where and when the story takes place?
   B. What are the events of a story?
   C. What is the mood or feeling of a story?

8. Theme
   A. What is the author's message to the reader?
   B. What is the end of a story?
   C. What is the point-of-view of a story?

Skill Sheet 3–9   Name _____

Robert Frost and His Wisdom

Directions: Respond to each of the following quotes about writing from Robert Frost.

1. "I have never started a poem yet whose end I knew. Writing a poem is discovering."

2. "Writing free verse is like playing tennis with the net down."

3. "A poem begins in delight and ends in wisdom."

4. "You can be a little ungrammatical if you come from the right part of the country."

5. "No tears in the writer, no tears in the reader. No surprise for the writer, no surprise for the reader."

MARCH
Answer Key

#10 SKILL SHEET 3-3—*PEOPLE* MAGAZINE AND CELEBRITIES

1. Celebrities' interviews are popular because we have little contact with them; they have wealth; their lifestyles are so different from ours; they are often interesting and unique people; etc.

2. We are interested in learning about the personal lives of celebrities because of our interest in gossip and to compare their personal lives with our own.

3. Writers obtain information about a celebrity other than by an interview from talking with co-workers and family members, by researching newspaper articles; by receiving a media guide.

4. Criminal acts turned some people into celebrities especially if they are bizarre or terrible acts (e.g. Charles Manson, Jeffrey Dahmer, John Gotti, etc.).

5. We could feel inferior, at times, to celebrities because they have great wealth or positions.

6. Reading a celebrity interview could help a reader decide on a career, make a personal decision, choose a role model, select a movie to see or book to read, etc.

7. An interview could hurt a person if he/she comes off as being arrogant or obnoxious, or help a person in terms of his/her career or celebrity status.

8. An interview could make an ordinary person famous if it appears in a national magazine.

#68 SKILL SHEET 3-8—LITERARY TERMS AND "JEOPARDY"

1. B	2. C	3. C	4. B
5. B	6. C	7. B	8. A

#85 SKILL SHEET 3-9—ROBERT FROST AND HIS WISDOM

1. For Frost, the poem results in a true, spontaneous fashion. Like an explorer, he discovers the poem.

2. There are no limitations or boundaries when writing free verse.

3. A poem begins as an enjoyable and special activity and leads to knowledge for both the poet and the reader.

4. Here, if you live where no one really adheres to grammar rules then your poems don't have to follow the rules either.

5. The writer has to be emotionally involved in the work in order to affect the reader's emotional response, especially regarding sadness and suspense.

APRIL

Speech/Oral Presentations   *34, 108, 109, 110*

Composition Skills

Research *5, 20, 28, 29, 30, 31, 32, 39, 44* • Prewriting *35, 36* • Organization *87, 88* • Description *37, 38, 39, 40, 41, 98, 99, 100, 101, 102, 103, 104, 105* • Reflection *62, 63* • Comparison/Contrast *5, 20, 22, 23, 28, 29, 30, 51, 61, 102* • Persuasion *18, 42, 43, 44, 45, 50, 51, 60, 67, 68* • Narratives *55* • Character Sketch *52, 53, 54, 84, 96, 100, 108* • Letters *457, 58, 59*

News Unit   *17, 18, 64, 65, 90*

Careers Unit   *97*

Media Unit   *21, 25, 58, 90, 100*

Fine Arts   *103, 104, 111, 112, 116, 117*

Social Skills/Understanding Ethnic Diversity   *44, 56, 74, 82, 89*

APRIL

Origin: The ancient Romans called this month *Aprilis*, which may refer to a Latin word meaning "to open" or to the goddess Aphrodite, the goddess of love. It is the fourth month according to the Gregorian calendar.

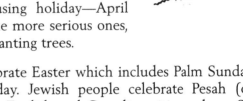

Holidays: April has the most amusing holiday—April Fool's Day—and one of the more serious ones, Arbor Day, which is for planting trees.

Christians celebrate Easter which includes Palm Sunday and Good Friday. Jewish people celebrate Pesah (or Passover) while English and Canadian citizens have St. George's Day to honor the patron saint of England.

Israel, Senagal, Sierra Leone, the Syrian Arab Republic, Togo, and Zimbabwe all celebrate their Independence Day in April.

In the U.S., April is traditionally National Poetry Month.

Gemstone: Diamond

Flower: Daisy

Poetry:
April cold with dropping rain
Willows and lilacs brings again,
The whistle of returning birds
And trumpet-lowing of the herds.
> *by Ralph Waldo Emerson*

When proud-pied April, dressed in all his trim
Has put a spirit of youth in everything.
> *by William Shakespeare*

BIRTHDAYS

April 2	Hans Christian Andersen, writer of 150 fairy tales (1805) [#9, 84]; Dana Carvey, comedian/actor (1955) [#25, 58]; Emmylou Harris, singer/performer (1947) [#40, 58, 107, 111]
April 3	Marlon Brando, Academy Award winning actor (1924) [#20]; Washington Irving, author of *The Legend of Sleepy Hollow* and *Rip Van Winkle* (1783) [#54, 84, 99]; Eddie Murphy, actor/comedian (1961) [#25, 58, 87]
April 4	Maya Angelou, author of *I Know Why the Caged Bird Sings* (1928) [#5, 84]
April 5	Booker T. Washington, educator (1856) [#75]
April 7	Billie Holiday, considered by many jazz critics to be the greatest jazz singer ever (1915) [#40, 111]; William Wordsworth, English poet (1770) [#8, 27, 51, 76, 79]
April 8	Buddha (original name was Siddhartha), founder of Buddhism whose name means "the enlightened one" in Sanskrit (563 BC) [#93]
April 9	Paul Robeson, performer/singer/actor (1898) [#28, 104]
April 12	Beverly Cleary, writer of children's books (1916) [#3, 72, 84]; Scott Turow, best-selling author (1949) [#2, 72, 84]
April 13	Samuel Becket, author/playwright—*Waiting for Godot* (1906) [#11, 12, 53, 80, 84, 85]; Thomas Jefferson, 3rd President (1743) [#15, 30, 32, 34]; Eudora Welty, writer (1909) [#5, 72, 84]
April 14	Anne Sullivan, teacher of Helen Keller (1866) [#94]
April 15	Evelyn Ashford, Olympic Gold medalist (1957) [#43, 44, 61]
April 17	Thornton Wilder, Pulitzer Prize winning playwright—*Our Town* (1897) [#11, 12, 28, 53, 80, 84]
April 21	Charlotte Brontë, author of *Jane Eyre* (1816) [#1, 84]; John Muir, conservationist/naturalist (1838) [#37, 42, 105, 106]
April 23	James Buchanan, 15th President and the only one who never married (1791) [#29, 32, 34]; William Shakespeare, poet/playwright (1564) [#10, 11, 12, 19, 24, 46, 51, 53, 79, 80, 81, 82, 83, 84, 86, 115, 116, 117]
April 25	Ella Fitzgerald, singer/"First Lady of Song" (1917) [#40]; Al Pacino, Oscar winning actor (1940) [#20]

April 27   Ulysses S. Grant, 18th President (1822) [#30, 32, 34]

April 28   Harper Lee, author of *To Kill a Mockingbird* (1960) [#4, 19, 84]; James Monroe, 5th President (1758) [#29, 32, 34]

April 29   Duke Ellington (born Edward Kennedy Ellington) (1899) jazz musician [#40, 103]; William Randolph Hearst, editor/publisher (1863) [#17, 18, 90]; Rod McKuen, poet (1933) [#27, 50, 51, 79]; Jerry Seinfeld, actor/comedian (1954) [325, 87]

MEMORABLE EVENTS

April 1   "General Hospital," ABC's longest-running soap opera, premiered in 1963 [#100].

April 2   Reconciliation Day—A day established by Ann Landers to promote reconciliation between people in conflict [#74].

Ponce de Leon discovered Florida, landing at St. Augustine in 1513 [#36].

April 3   Pony Express mail service began in 1860 [#55].

April 4   The Flag Act was approved by Congress creating the first flag for the United States in 1818 which had thirteen stripes and one star for each state [#85].

Martin Luther King, Jr., was assassinated in Memphis in 1968 by James Earl Ray.

First woman elected mayor in United States in 1887. Susanna Salter was elected mayor of Argonia, Kansas and served a one-year term for a salary of one dollar [#97].

April 6   First modern Olympics were held in Athens, Greece in 1896 after a 1500-year hiatus [#44, 61].

April 7   World Health Day [#43, 92, 113].

April 9   End of the Civil War occurred in 1865 as General Robert E. Lee, who commanded the Army of Northern Virginia, surrendered to General Ulysses S. Grant, Commander-in-Chief of the Union Army, at Appomattox Court House, Virginia [#110].

Civil Rights Bill was passed by Congress over the veto of President Andrew Johnson in 1866, granting blacks the rights and privileges of United States citizens. The bill became the basis of the 14th Amendment [#33].

April 11   Jackie Robinson joined the Brooklyn Dodgers in 1947, becoming the first African-American in major league baseball [#62, 91].

April 12   Yuri Gagarin, a Russian cosmonaut, became in 1961 the first human to orbit the earth in a 108-minute voyage in Vostok 1 [#63].

April 14   Noah Webster published, after 22 years of research, the first dictionary of American English—*American Dictionary of the English Language*—in 1828 [#16].

John Steinbeck's *The Grapes of Wrath* was published in 1939 and won the 1940 Pulitzer Prize [#73, 118].

President William Howard Taft began a sports tradition by throwing out the first baseball at an American League game between Washington and Philadelphia in 1910 [#57].

April 15   The first McDonalds opened in 1955 in Des Plaines, Illinois by Ray Kroc. Currently, 15,000 McDonalds operate in seventy countries [#68].

Income Tax Day [13, 14].

Thank You School Librarians Day [#69, 71].

The Titanic sank in 1912, killing over 1500 people [#65].

April 18   Choco-Mas Day—to recognize the heavenly qualities of chocolate [98].

Paul Revere rode to warn American patriots between Boston and Concord in 1775 about the advance of British troops [#7].

San Francisco earthquake occurred in 1906, killing 4000 people and destroying 10,000 acres of property [#64].

The term "Third World" country was introduced by Indonesia President Sukarno in his opening speech at the Bandung Conference which was attended by nearly 30 African and Asian countries in 1955 [#89].

April 21   Rome was founded in 753 B.C. [#101].

Kindergarten Day (to recognize the importance of play, games, and creativity in children and to celebrate the birthday of Friedrich Froebel, the founder of the first kindergarten in 1837) [#52, 108].

April 22   Earth Day [#42, 45, 105].

April 23   The first motion picture was shown in New York City in 1896 [#21, 67].

April 24   First personal computer was introduced in 1981 by IBM [#22, 23, 95, 114].

April 25   License plates were installed on automobiles for the first time in 1901 in New York [#66].

Hubble Space Telescope was deployed in 1990, allowing viewers to see objects up to 14 billion light years away [#22].

April 29   Moment of Laughter Day (to recognize the physical, emotional, and spiritual benefits of laughter) [#102].

April 30   Hairstylist Appreciation Day [#41].

Louisiana was admitted to the Union as the 18th state in 1812 [#39].

National Honesty Day [#74].

First theatrical performance in North America took place in 1598 on the banks of the Rio Grande River near El Paso, Texas. It was a Spanish comedy performed by soldiers [#81].

The Pulitzer Prize is an annual award given to American authors and other artists each year in April for work done the preceding year. The $1000 award was initiated in 1911 by Joseph Pulitzer, a wealthy newspaper publisher. The prize for literature (poetry, fiction, drama, biography, nonfiction) is selected by the Columbia University Pulitzer Prize Board who consider high literary quality and originality.

LEARNING ACTIVITIES FOR APRIL

READING ACTIVITIES

Purpose: To begin or conclude a fiction unit

1. Have students read the excerpt from Charlotte Brontë's *Jane Eyre*—Use **Skill Sheet 4-1**—and examine her Victorian writing style.

   > It is a little known fact that Charlotte Brontë published many of her works under the masculine name Currer Bell. Her Victorian writing style was known for its formal diction; expansive vocabulary; and complex and lengthy sentence structure, which was typical of many writers from 1830–1900, including Charles Dickens.

2. Assign students to read a Scott Turow novel and ask: What qualifies this as a best-seller? Who are the characters? What makes the story line appealing? Use **Form 11-8** to evaluate them when they finish.

3. Read orally an excerpt from a Beverly Cleary book. Then ask: How does she appeal to young people? What type of characters populate her book? How would you describe her writing style?

4. Assign students to read the book *To Kill a Mockingbird* by Harper Lee and then evaluate them using the **Form 11-8**.

5. Prompt students to read any of the literature of Eudora Welty and Maya Angelou to compare/contrast the writing styles of these two famous women writers who wrote in different time periods. Use this also to improve students' research skills.

Purpose: To improve skills at analyzing poetry

6. Support National Poetry Month by inviting local poets, celebrities, politicians, and parents to read their favorite poem(s) to students.

7. Refer to Paul Revere and have students read the poem "The Midnight Ride of Paul Revere" by Henry Wadsworth Longfellow to connect poetry (a ballad) to a historical event. Distribute **Skill Sheet 4-2**—the opening stanzas of the poem and ask students to analyze its verse and content.

8. Distribute **Form 4-3** and direct students to read any poems by William Wordsworth that appear in their literature text or available anthology and to analyze them for their type of verse, the poetic language, and topics/themes.

Purpose: To introduce the literary genre of Fairy Tales

9. Have students locate and read a fairy tale by Hans Christian Andersen that appears in their literature text or an available anthology. They should investigate the lesson or moral children are to learn from the fairy tale. Ask: How effectively do fairy tales teach these lessons?

Purpose: To introduce the plays of William Shakespeare

10. Distribute **Skill Sheet 4-4**—the famous lines from some of Shakespeare's plays. Have students interpret their meaning.

Purpose: To improve skills at analyzing drama

11. Have students skim a play that appears in their literature text for any *soliloquies*, *asides*, or *stage directions*. Then explain these terms and their function in a play and refer to Samuel Becket, Thornton Wilder, and William Shakespeare.

> **A soliloquy** = Spoken words or thoughts of a character heard by the audience, but not by any other character; as if the character were speaking to himself/herself.
>
> **An aside** = A remark uttered by a character that is meant to be heard by the audience alone.
>
> **Stage directions** = the movements and actions of the characters on stage.

12. Have students read a play by William Shakespeare, Samuel Becket, or Thornton Wilder that appears in their literature text or an available anthology to study its characters, conflicts, setting, and themes. Ask: How many acts does the play have and how are they structured? What dramatic or interesting events take place in the play? How did the play affect you? What did you find most entertaining? What is the turning point of the play?

> **Drama is literature in play form to be performed by actors on stage, in movies, on television, or over the radio. Like fiction, drama has characters, plot, conflict, and themes, but differs in that it relies on dialogue and stage directions to tell the story. When reading a play students need to use their imaginations to hear what the characters say and how they say it.**

Purpose: To expand skills at word selection/vocabulary

13. Refer to Income Tax Day and distribute an income tax form (commonly available in most post offices and banks at this time). Students can study the language and directions.

14. Refer to Income Tax form and explain *gobbledygook*. Then ask: How does this interfere with effective writing? Use **Skill Sheet 4-5**.

> **Gobbledygook commonly refers to inflated and unnecessarily obscure language characteristic of bureaucratic forms and announcements. The word was coined by Maury Maverick, the chairman of the Smaller War Plants Corporation during WW II. As head of this government agency he encountered an endless flow of trite and pompous language, which he named *gobbledygook*.**

15. Distribute **Skill Sheet 4-6**—Phrases taken from Thomas Jefferson's "Declaration of Independence"—for students to analyze the wording/phrasing in this historic document.

16. Refer to Noah Webster and have students skim dictionary pages to list the 10–20 most interesting words they find.

Purpose: *To analyze newspaper feature articles and editorials*

17. Refer to William Randolph Hearst and have students locate and read a feature article for its content and tone. Ask: Is the article meant to inform, persuade, or entertain?

18. Have students locate and read newspaper editorials. Refer to William Randolph Hearst, the famous editor and publisher and ask: What is the writer's purpose? What is the tone of the editorial? What passages truly reveal the tone and purpose? Do you agree with the editorial? Why/why not?

DEBATING ACTIVITIES

Purpose: *To expand critical thinking skills*

19. The term *universal justice* refers simply to the idea that the "good" are always rewarded and the "bad" are always punished. This is a common motif in literature, especially in the works of William Shakespeare and Harper Lee. Ask: What is your attitude toward universal justice? Are the good always rewarded and the bad punished? Why/why not?

20. Who is the better actor—Marlon Brando or Al Pacino? Both won Oscars and, in fact, appeared together in *The Godfather*. Possibly direct students to do research before debating.

21. Refer to the first motion picture shown in New York City in 1896. Which is the best movie released in the past year? Why? Use this to establish a standard criteria to judge movies (much like the criteria used to evaluate essays).

22. Which is the more important technological advancement—the Hubble Space Telescope which allows viewers to see objects up to 14 billion light years away or the personal computer introduced in 1981 by IBM?

23. How has the personal computer helped and hindered learning? Explain interpersonal (communicating and cooperating with others) vs. intrapersonal (working independently on self-paced projects) learning. Deal with advantages of both.

24. William Shakespeare used in many of his plays the motif that Fate, or predestination, ruled our lives. Do you believe in Fate, meaning that everything that happens is predetermined? Why/why not?

25. Who is the funniest comedian—Dana Carvey, Jerry Seinfeld, or Eddie Murphy? Why? Use this also to practice comparison and contrast and to review the elements of exaggeration (hyperbole), imitation (parody), and characterization—the same elements that appear in fiction.

Purpose: To improve skills at writing and analyzing poetry

26. Which of the following is the most important technique to use when writing poetry:

    * Using figurative language?
    * Avoiding wordiness?
    * Creating imagery with sensory language?
    * Selecting the type of verse (free verse, rhyme, couplets, etc.)?

27. Refer to William Wordsworth, whose poems often taught us to appreciate nature, and Rod McKuen, whose poems were simple and amusing verse and ask: Should poems entertain or teach a reader?

Purpose: To begin or conclude a drama unit

28. Distribute **Form 4-7** and ask: Who has contributed more to contemporary American drama/theater—Thornton Wilder or Paul Robeson? Use this possibly as a research project.

Purpose: To review research skills

29. Which President was the more experienced politician—James Monroe or James Buchanan?

> **James Monroe served in the Virginia House of Delegates and as a United States Senator, Governor of Virginia, and Secretary of State under James Madison, heading diplomatic missions to England and Spain, before being elected to two terms as President and establishing the Monroe Doctrine.**

> James Buchanan represented Pennsylvania in the U.S. House of Representatives and served as a diplomat to Russia, a U.S. Senator, the Secretary of State under James K. Polk, and President when seven states seceded from the Union.

30. Which President made the more dramatic contribution to U.S. government *before* he became President—Thomas Jefferson, who produced the Declaration of Independence, or Ulysses S. Grant, who forced the surrender of the Confederate army during the Civil War?

31. When gathering research, which is a more useful source—dated information from a famous authority or more recent information from a less-known authority? What determines effective research?

> Strong points can be made for using both information from a source who is considered an expert in the field although the material might be dated, and data that is the most current although it comes from a lesser-known individual. The best research overall is very recent and comes from a well-known authority.

32. Refer to the Presidents who have birthdays this month and ask: What would be the most effective source to learn about the President's political life—an encyclopedia, a reference book, a biography, newspaper articles, or a history textbook? What are the advantages and disadvantages of each?

> An encyclopedia article usually is composed from the notes and research of several academic individuals, and a reference book is comprehensive and thoroughly edited but both may lack updated information.
>
> A biography would be the most thorough and insightful source but could reflect the bias of the biographer.
>
> Newspaper articles and recent history textbooks would probably be the most updated, concise, and objective sources, but they are usually less detailed, offering only highlights instead of insights.

Purpose: To expand skills at word selection/vocabulary

33. Is it better to *accept* a law or *adopt* it? Why? Refer to the Civil Rights Bill passed by Congress over the veto of President Johnson in 1866.

© 2001 by The Center for Applied Research in Education

> When asked to accept a law, a person must receive it with both approval and satisfaction; a person who adopts a law follows and receives it as his own although he might not naturally do so.

Purpose: *To introduce a speech unit*

34. Refer to the Presidents who have birthdays this month and the annual State of the Union Address. Then ask: Which is more beneficial—to read a speech or hear a speech? How does the presentation of the speech add to its message? What are the benefits of having the speech script available to read?

WRITING ACTIVITIES

Purpose: *To review brainstorming as a prewriting strategy*

35. Have students list descriptive modifiers and concrete nouns that describe April and spring.

36. Ask students to list the difficulties they think Ponce de Leon experienced on his voyage to Florida before landing at St. Augustine in 1513 (e.g., bad weather, food and water shortages, lack of supplies, etc.).

Purpose: *To improve writing description*

37. Refer to John Muir who helped establish the national forest system and to Earth Day and have students write a descriptive paragraph about a forest they've hiked. Use this also to connect to a science unit on ecology.

38. Ask: What does April smell like? Have students list some of the modifiers that are useful for describing scents—for example, musty.

39. Direct students to use an atlas or any other source to write a brief descriptive essay about the terrain, bodies of water, and landscape of Louisiana. Use **Form 12-5** to evaluate them.

40. Refer to Billie Holiday, Duke Ellington, Ella Fitzgerald, and Emmylou Harris and have students describe the voice of their favorite singer/performer in a coherent paragraph, using sensory language (sound).

41. Refer to Hairstylist Appreciation Day and have students write detailed paragraphs about a hairstyle or haircut they have observed or received.

> Assist by writing on the board the following terms: scalp, teased, tinted, blow-dried, curled, braided, cowlick, red, blond, pigtails, cornrow, dreadlocks, ponytail, auburn, flattop, pageboy, black, and others as needed.

Purpose: To expand skills at persuasive writing

42. Have students write an editorial defending or challenging the need for forest conservation. Refer to John Muir who helped establish the national forest system and to Earth Day.

43. Refer to World Health Day and Olympic athlete Evelyn Ashford and have students write a one-page essay defending or challenging the importance of physical fitness where they cite the organs and parts of the body that are strengthened or weakened by physical exercise.

44. Ask students to write an editorial challenging or defending the importance of the Olympic games. Refer to the first modern Olympics held in Athens in 1896, the problems with terrorists, steroid use by athletes, Olympic boycotts in 1980 and 1984, and Evelyn Ashford.

45. Have students compose an editorial challenging or defending the importance of Earth Day.

Purpose: To introduce the plays of William Shakespeare

46. Distribute **Skill Sheet 4-8,** a survey on William Shakespeare, before reading one of his plays.

Purpose: To begin or conclude a poetry unit

47. Distribute **Skill Sheet 4-9,** a survey on poetry, for National Poetry Month.

48. Ask students to write a poem about spring. Have them consider images of nature (flowers, trees, insects) and weather (rain, wind, sunshine).

49. Have students pretend to be editors of a poetry magazine (devise a name) and list the criteria they will follow to publish poems that poets submit.

50. Refer to Rod McKuen and read some of his poems. Then have students write an editorial challenging or defending the quality of his poems.

51. Have students write an editorial that declares a preference for free verse or rhyme. Students must take a stand on which type of verse is better. Direct them to examine the works of William Shakespeare, William Wordsworth, and Rod McKuen first.

Purpose: To expand skills at characterization

52. Refer to Kindergarten Day and to the birthday of Friedrich Froebel, the founder of the first kindergarten in 1837, and have students write character sketches of real or imaginary kindergartners.

53. Refer to the playwrights who have birthdays this month and have students write an obituary for a character who dies in a play one of them wrote—such as *Romeo and Juliet.* Students could study newspaper obituaries first before writing their own.

54. Distribute **Skill Sheet 4-10**—the Washington Irving caricature example and explain the relation between caricature and characterization.

> **Washington Irving is considered by some to be our country's first important story writer. He created unusual characters like Rip Van Winkle, Ichabod Crane, and Brom Bones in stories he termed "sketches."**

Purpose: *To create brief, historical fiction*

55. Have students create a brief narrative about the Pony Express. Challenge their creativity and understanding of historical fiction.

Purpose: *To expand research skills and an appreciation of other cultures*

56. Refer to the Syrian Arab Republic and prompt students to discover the origin, use, and style of veils worn by women in the Middle East.

> **Veils, small rectangles of light cloth, were introduced in several regions of the world, but primarily, are known to have begun in Persia, which is now Iran. At first, only married women could wear veils, and the Islamic religion, which emphasizes physical modesty, encouraged this. In the early 20th century, the wearing of a veil indicated high social status; however, now they are more associated with less-educated women.**

Purpose: *To expand letter writing skills*

57. Refer to President William Howard Taft throwing out the first baseball to mark the beginning of the major league baseball season and have students write to a professional sports team, requesting information about its players or schedule.

58. Refer to Dana Carvey, Eddie Murphy, Emmylou Harris, or any of the celebrities who has a birthday this month. Have students write a fan mail letter to a celebrity (actor, singer, performer).

59. Have students write a formal letter to a college requesting information about admissions, housing, tuition, etc. Use this also as part of a careers unit.

Purpose: *To conclude a novel unit*

60. Have students write a 50-word advertisement about an author, promoting his/her works. Ask: Why does this writer deserve recommendations? What makes his/her work appealing? How can you encourage others to read his/her novel?

Purpose: To teach writing comparison/contrast

61. Refer to the first modern Olympics held in Athens, Greece in 1896, Evelyn Ashford, and other Olympic athletes and have students compose an essay comparing two or three Olympic sports.

Purpose: To review reflective writing

62. Prompt students to pretend to be Jackie Robinson and write a diary entry after he joined the Brooklyn Dodgers in 1947, becoming the first African-American in major league baseball.

63. Prompt students to pretend to be Yuri Gagarin, the Russian cosmonaut who became in 1961 the first human to orbit the earth in the 108-minute voyage of Vostok 1, and write a diary entry upon his return to earth.

Purpose: To review the format of news articles

64. Refer to the 1906 San Francisco earthquake which killed 4000 people and destroyed 10,000 acres of property and have students write the news lead that organizes the five Ws.

> **Example: Four thousand people died and 10,000 acres of property in and around San Francisco were destroyed when an earth-quake occurred yesterday.**

65. Have students write a news article about the sinking of the *Titanic*. Use this to work on organization in writing as the students focus on the five Ws.

> **Example: The luxury liner *Titanic* sank in the icy waters of the North Atlantic approximately 95 miles south of Newfoundland, just before midnight yesterday, killing 1500 of 2220 passengers and making this the worst maritime disaster in history. The ship of the White Star Line, although labeled as unsinkable and on its maiden voyage from Southampton, England, to New York City, sank in less than three hours.**

Purpose: To teach economy in writing

66. Explain that economy in writing refers to avoiding wordiness and repetition in sentences and refer to the license plates that were installed on automobiles for the first time in 1901. Then direct students to list amusing and/or interesting license plate messages they've seen on cars. (IMB4U, 4SALE, IMAQT, etc.)

Purpose: To expand skills at writing reviews (movies)

67. Refer to the first motion picture shown in New York City in 1896 and have students write a movie review of a movie they have seen on television, on video, or at the theater.

Purpose: To expand skills at writing reviews (restaurant)

68. Refer to the first McDonalds which was opened in 1955 in Des Plaines, Illinois by Ray Kroc. Currently, 15,000 McDonalds operate in seventy countries. Ask students to select a McDonalds and write a detailed review of its service and food.

DISCUSSION ACTIVITIES

Purpose: To promote reading and the use of the library

69. How important are community libraries? How would our lives change if public libraries did not exist? How often do you use the library? What do the books in libraries offer us? Refer to Thank You School Librarians Day.

70. If you could read the biography or autobiography of any of the individuals who has a birthday this month, who would you select? Why?

71. What are the best books you have read? Why that book(s)? What makes a book interesting to read? Refer to Thank You School Librarians Day.

Purpose: To begin or conclude a fiction unit

72. Refer to Eudora Welty, Beverly Cleary, and Scott Turow and ask: How can a reader identify the climax of a story or novel? Why is the climax sometimes considered the turning point? What have been the most dramatic climaxes that you have read?

> Typically, readers should look for the highest point of action in a narrative, the most dramatic event, as the climax. Here, as well, characters change relationships, attitudes, direction, or lifestyle; or a solution or secret could be revealed.

73. Explain the differences between Realism and Romance as literary genres. Then ask: What authors are classified under these genres? Which do you favor? Why?

> Realism = attempts to represent people and places as they really are, as shown in the works of John Steinbeck and Maya Angelou.
>
> Romance: presents life as we would like it to be, often full of love and adventure, as in the works of Barbara Taylor Bradford and Danielle Steele.

74. How important are honesty and reconciliation as social skills? What literary characters are especially noted for this? How often are they themes in literature? Refer to National Honesty Day and Reconciliation Day and use this also to improve students' social skills.

Purpose: To begin or conclude a poetry unit

75. Write on the board Booker T. Washington's quote: "No race can prosper until it learns that there is as much dignity in tilling a field as in writing a poem" and discuss its meaning.

76. Write on the board William Wordsworth's definition of poetry: "Poetry is the spontaneous overflow of powerful feelings; it takes its origin from emotion recollected in tranquility" and discuss its meaning.

77. Why is there a strong connection between poetry and April? Consider John Masefield's lines: "it comes from the west lands, the old brown hills,/And April's in the west wind, and daffodils," among other poems.

78. Explain that April and spring typically prompt poetry and that the following poetry terms are often used. Allow students time to locate the definitions from their literature text or dictionary and then discuss the differences between

   - alliteration and assonance
   - metaphor and simile
   - rhyme and free verse
   - a ballad and an ode
   - a couplet and a quatrain

> *Alliteration* is the repetition of the same consonant sound while assonance refers to the repetition of vowel sounds.
>
> *Metaphor* is an implied comparison—*He has rubbery legs* implies a comparison between rubber and legs while a simile uses *like* or *as* to make the comparison, as in *His legs were like rubber.*
>
> *Rhyme* is verse based on similar sounds, syllables, and meter in lines of poetry while *free verse* has no meter or rhyme.
>
> A *ballad* and an *ode* are both narrative, lyrical poems, but the ballad has verse that is simplistic and sentimental while the ode is more elaborate with a loftier theme.
>
> A *couplet* is two rhyming lines of poetry while a *quatrain* is a four line stanza with a rhyme scheme usually of *abab.*

79. What are the qualities of poetry that appeal to you? What makes a good poem? What makes a poem interesting to read? Refer to Shakespeare, Wordsworth, and McKuen.

Purpose: To begin or conclude a drama unit

80. Refer to the playwrights and authors who have birthdays this month. How is the setting typically introduced to the reader? What is the relationship between setting and plot? Who has written the most unusual settings in plays you have read before?

81. Refer to the first theatrical performance in North America which took place in 1598 on the banks of the Rio Grande River near El Paso, Texas and ask: What plays require the actors to wear costumes? How do the costumes influence our perception of characters? How can costumes identify the time period of the play?

82. Vanity is an important issue in Shakespeare's play "King Lear." Several characters, especially Lear, allow it to influence many of their decisions. How can vanity hurt a person? What could be the consequences for a person who is vain? What other examples of vanity in characters have you observed? Use this also to improve students' social skills.

83. Of all of Shakespeare's plays, *Romeo and Juliet* has been produced on film the most times. Why do you think it still remains so popular? What other Shakespearean plays were turned into movies?

> **Among the plays that have been made into movies are *King Lear, Hamlet, Macbeth, A Midsummer Night's Dream, Henry V, Much Ado About Nothing, Othello, Richard III, Julius Caesar,* and *The Taming of the Shrew.***

84. Refer to the playwrights and authors who have birthdays this month. Which of their characters has the most unusual personality? How would you describe his/her actions and behavior?

85. Refer to the Flag Act which was approved by Congress in 1818, creating the first flag for the United States, and explain that the flag had thirteen stripes, representing the 13 original colonies, and one star representing each state. Clarify the flag stands as a *symbol* for the United States and ask: What are some other examples of symbolism? What plays have characters, a setting, or events that are symbolic? What abstract concepts are represented by the characters or objects in Samuel Becket's play *Waiting for Godot?*

86. William Shakespeare borrowed some of the plots of his plays from other writers. Is he a plagiarist? Why/why not?

Shakespeare did borrow key plot elements and characters from other writers, like Geoffrey Chaucer, but this was, in fact, a common practice in the 16th and 17th century (as it is today). He looked to history, mythology, other plays, and fictional tales for his story lines, but the dialogue and characterizations are uniquely his own.

Purpose: To begin a composition unit

87. Refer to Jerry Seinfeld, Dana Carvey, and Eddie Murphy and ask: How does a comedian set up the punchline to a joke? How does a good joke resemble the organization of an essay, as in introduction, body, and conclusion? How can humor be used in a composition?

88. How is writing like sprinting, marching, climbing, rolling, or crawling? What kind of writing shouts? Whispers? Whines? Drones?

Purpose: To expand skills at word selection/vocabulary

89. Why do you think Indonesia President Sukarno in his opening speech at the Bandung Conference attended by nearly thirty African and Asian countries in 1955 labeled one section of the planet the "Third World"?

Generally, the *first* world was Europe, the *second* was North America, and the *third* world in terms of economic and military power were the nations located on the African and Asian continents.

Purpose: To encourage the reading of newspapers and news magazines

90. What makes watching television news or reading a newspaper difficult for some students? How often do you read a news magazine or newspaper? How often do other family members? Refer to William Randolph Hearst and challenge students to read newspapers and news magazines more often. In fact, prompt them to locate the type of news originated by Hearst and others termed "sensationalism," which focused on death, accidents, and tragedies, as found in the tabloids.

Often, the answers here are that students don't have the time, aren't interested, or find no benefit in knowing current events. However, students should recognize the importance of knowing the news and, second, the appeal of being a news reporter.

Purpose: To expand critical thinking skills

91. Distribute **Form 4-11** and discuss the importance of Branch Rickey's quotes regarding Jackie Robinson.

92. Refer to World Health Day and ask: What are the best ways to maintain health and physical fitness? Use this also to promote students leading a healthy lifestyle.

93. Write the following quote from Buddha on the board: "To conquer oneself is a greater task than conquering others" and discuss its meaning.

94. Write Anne Sullivan's quote on the board: "Language grows out of life, out of its needs and experiences" and discuss its meaning.

95. Refer to the first personal computer introduced in 1981 by IBM and write the following quotes on the board:

    • "I do not fear computers. I fear the lack of them." (Isaac Asimov)

    • "Computers are incredibly fast, accurate, and stupid; humans are incredibly slow, inaccurate, and brilliant; together they are powerful beyond imagination." (Albert Einstein)

    Then ask: What do Asimov and Einstein suggest about the influence, power, and usefulness of computers? How do you view the importance of computers? How much importance does society place on computers?

96. Distribute **Form 4-12** which explains the background of April Fool's Day, which encourages us to play pranks on other people. Then ask: What literary characters are famous for their pranks? (Tom Sawyer, Huckleberry Finn, the Fool in *King Lear*). When is it inappropriate to play a prank on another person? How could a prank harm someone? Use this also to develop students' social skills.

Purpose: To begin or conclude a careers unit

97. Have students consider Susan Salter, the first woman mayor, and ask: What are the duties of a mayor? Why would any person seek to be elected to that position? Why do you think Susan Salter wanted to be mayor? Would you want to be a mayor? Why/why not?

AUDIO/VISUAL ACTIVITIES

Purpose: To improve writing description

98. Distribute Hershey chocolate "kisses" and have students compare this chocolate taste with other brands. Refer to Choco-Mas Day and use this as an exercise in sensory language (taste).

99. Show selected scenes from the movie *Sleepy Hollow* starring Johnny Depp and direct students to list modifiers and phrases that describe characters and scenery.

100. Show a videotape of selected scenes from the television program "General Hospital" and have students list details related to the appearance, traits, and behavior of the characters.

101. Show pictures about Rome taken from travel brochures which can be easily obtained from any travel agency. Then have students write descriptions, as if for tourists in 753 BC or today. Challenge their creativity.

102. Refer to Moment of Laughter Day (to recognize the physical, emotional, and spiritual benefits of laughter) and have students laugh. Then have them describe the differences in sounds they hear. Use this to improve students' use of sensory language (sound).

103. Play recordings of Duke Ellington and have students write a list of sensory words/phrases the music inspires.

104. Play recordings of Paul Robeson and have students describe the tone, mood, and feelings they get from listening. Ask students to identify the pitches and rhythms of music.

105. Show the scene from the videotape *The Lion King* where Scar and the hyenas have decimated the land because Scar has not taken care of Pride Rock. Have students write descriptions of the terrain. Also refer to John Muir and Earth Day.

Purpose: To expand skills at word selection/vocabulary

106. Refer to John Muir and play a recording of Willie Nelson's "Everything is Beautiful." Then discuss the meaning of the word *beautiful* and how we could apply it to nature.

107. Play recordings of Emmylou Harris and have students list the lyrics they find especially interesting or effective.

Purpose: To develop speech/oral interpretation skills

108. Ask selected students to role-play kindergarten students, especially students who enjoy drama or theatrics. They should portray kindergarten students in terms of their behavior, mannerisms, and attitudes.

109. Ask selected students, especially those who enjoy drama or theatrics to role-play any scene from a play found in their literature text or available anthology. Allow them to work alone or with a partner. Lines could be memorized and their actions, voice, posturing, and props should be keys to their evaluation. Use this for the kinesthetic learner. Students should focus on how the scene and dialogue reveal tone, characterization, and mood.

110. Ask selected students, especially those who enjoy drama or theatrics, to role-play General Robert E. Lee, commander of the Army of Northern Virginia, surrendering to General Ulysses S. Grant, Commander-in-Chief of the Union Army, at Appomattox Court House, Virginia.

Purpose: To begin or conclude a poetry unit

111. Play a recording from Emmylou Harris or Billie Holiday. Ask: In what ways are their lyrics poetry?

112. Show selected scenes from the movie *A Merry Widow* starring Richard Grant as a poet in 1930s London. Use this to introduce or review the genre of poetry and the life of a typical poet. Ask: What do readers usually expect from poets? Who is your favorite poet? Why?

Purpose: To expand critical thinking skills

113. Play any scene from a "Rocky" film where Sylvester Stallone is training and refer to World Health Day. Then discuss the necessity for physical fitness and America's dramatic interest in health.

114. Refer to the first personal computer by IBM and show scenes from the movie *You've Got Mail* starring Tom Hanks as an introduction to discussing the influence of technology on verbal and written communication.

Purpose: To begin or conclude the reading of Romeo and Juliet

115. Play a recording of "Just like Romeo and Juliet" by the Reflections. Ask: How do the lyrics relate to the famous tragedy?

116. Show selected scenes from the movie *Shakespeare in Love* and have students identify the structure of the theater and the type of costumes along with the language of the time period.

117. Show selected scenes from the movie *Titanic* starring Leonardo DeCaprio to connect the film's theme to that of Shakespeare's *Romeo and Juliet*.

Purpose: To begin or conclude the reading of The Grapes of Wrath

118. Show the movie *The Grapes of Wrath* starring Henry Fonda to illustrate the characters, conflict, and resolution of the novel.

Name _____

Excerpt from *Jane Eyre*
by Charlotte Brontë

In the course of the day I was enrolled as a member of the fourth class, and regular tasks and occupations were assigned me; hitherto, I had only been a spectator of the proceedings at Lowood, I was now to become an actor therein. At first, being little accustomed to learn by heart, the lessons appeared to me both long and difficult; the frequent change from task to task, too, bewildered me; and I was glad, when, about three o'clock in the afternoon, Miss Smith put into my hands a border of muslin two yards long, together with a needle, thimble, etc. and sent me to sit in a quiet corner of the schoolroom, with direction to hem the same. At that hour most of the others were sewing likewise; but one class still stood around Miss Scatcherd's chair reading, and as all was quiet, the subject of their lessons could be heard, together with the manner in which each girl acquitted herself, and the animadversions or commendations of Miss Scatherd on the performance.

Questions

1. How would you describe the narrator's school day?

2. What is her attitude toward her school work?

3. What would you want to learn about the narrator?

4. What do you think happens next?

5. How would you explain Brontë's writing style?

Name _____

"The Midnight Ride of Paul Revere"

by Henry Wadsworth Longfellow

Listen, my children, and you shall hear
Of the midnight ride of Paul Revere,
On the eighteenth of April, in Seventy-five;
Hardly a man is now alive
Who remembers that famous day and year.

He said to his friend—"If the British march
By land or sea from the town tonight,
Hang a lantern aloft in the belfry-arch
Of the North Church tower, as a signal-light—
One if by land, and two if by sea;
And I on the opposite shore will be,
Ready to ride and spread the alarm
Through every Middlesex village and farm,
For the country folk to be up and to arm.

Questions

1. What kind of verse does Longfellow use here?

2. What event in history does the poem glorify?

3. How does the poem's introduction inspire the reader to continue reading?

4. What imagery is seen in the poem?

5. Why has this poem remained one of our country's most well-known poems?

Name _____

William Wordsworth and his Poetry

- Found comfort, joy, and pleasure in nature.

- Inspired by the extremes of Nature, especially storms, mountains, lightning, and waterfalls and by strong emotions.

- Stressed nature's harmonious relationship with humanity—for example, wind and breezes could be linked to human breath as seen in "Lines written in Early Spring."

- Concerned with beauty and aesthetics, especially of nature and pastoral scenes.

- Often sought escape from the limitations of civilization or city life.

- Found enlightenment and revelations in solitude which was a positive experience to provoke contemplation.

- Focused on the *sublime*—elevated thought as seen in awe, wonder, or imagination— "a flash that has revealed."

- Followed the philosophy and literary genre of transcendentalism.

- Emphasized an optimistic outlook as a theme in his poetry.

- Concerned with freedom for common people as seen in his descriptions of beggars and hermits in his poetry. Heroes were beggars, shepherds, peasants, outcasts like the "Old Cumberland Beggar."

- Used metaphor, hyperbole, and symbolism in his poetry—"As in the eye of Nature, he has lived,/So in the eye of Nature, let him die." The "eye of Nature" = the sun.

- Composed poems mentally while walking, especially in circles. The structure of his poems often resemble walking, and he saw poetry to be a natural language with no real difference between prose and poetry.

- "And I have felt/A presence that disturbs me with the joy/Of elevated thoughts; a sense sublime/Of something far and more deeply interfused,/Whose dwelling is the light of setting suns./And the round ocean and living air,/And the blue sky, and in the mind of man;/A motion and a spirit, that impels/All thinking things, all objects of all thought,/And rolls through all things."

267

Name _____

Famous Dialogue from Shakespeare's Plays

Directions: Paraphrase the following lines taken from the plays of William Shakespeare.

1. "All the world's a stage,
   And all the men and women merely players;
   They have their exits and entrances;
   And one man in his time plays many parts."
   (*As You Like It*—Act II, Scene 7—Jaques)

2. "What's in a name? That which we call a rose
   By any other name would smell as sweet."
   (*Romeo and Juliet*—Act II, Scene 2—Juliet)

3. "This above all; to thine own self be true,
   And it must follow, as the night the day,
   Thou canst not then be false to any man."
   (*Hamlet*—Act I, Scene 3—Polonius)

4. "Life's but a walking shadow, a poor player,
   That struts and frets his hour upon the stage,
   And then is heard no more. It is a tale
   Told by an idiot, full of sound and fury,
   Signifying nothing."
   (*Macbeth*—Act V, Scene 5—Macbeth)

5. "Some are born great, some achieve greatness,
   and some have greatness thrust upon them."
   (*Twelfth Night*—Act II, Scene 5—Malvolio)

Name _____

Overcoming Gobbledygook

Directions: References in this order to any order shall be construed as referring to that order as amended by any subsequent order, whether made before or after the making of this order, and if any order referred to in this order is replaced by any such subsequent order, the references shall be construed as referring to that subsequent order.

1. How many words are in this sentence?

2. How and where would you break up this sentence?

3. What problems does the use of the word *order* cause?

4. What phrases are awkward or clumsy?

5. What words could be eliminated?

6. How would you write this sentence?

Name _____

Thomas Jefferson
and the Declaration of Independence

Directions: Paraphrase each passage taken from Jefferson's "Declaration of Independence" and define each of the underlined terms.

1. "We hold these truths to be *self-evident:* That all men are created equal; that they are endowed by their Creator with certain *inalienable* rights . . ."

2. ". . . that among these are life, *liberty*, and the pursuit of happiness"

3. ". . . to secure these rights, governments are instituted among men, deriving their just powers from the *consent* of the governed . . ."

4. "that whenever any form of government becomes destructive of these ends, it is the right of the people to alter or to *abolish* it"

5. "[and] institute a new government, laying its foundation on such *principles*, and organizing its powers in such form, as to them shall seem most likely to effect their safety and happiness"

Thornton Wilder vs. Paul Robeson

Thornton Wilder
(1897–1975)

- Educated at Oberlin College and Yale University

- Published novel *The Bridge at San Luis Rey* (1927)

- Won Pulitzer Prize for Fiction in 1928.

- Wrote *Our Town* which was an experimental play with no scenery (1938).

- Won Pulitzer Prize for Drama in 1938.

- Wrote drama *Skin of our Teeth* (1943)

- Won Pulitzer Prize for Drama in 1943.

- Wrote *Matchmaker* (1954) which became the musical *Hello, Dolly!*

- Published novel *The Eighth Day* (1967).

- Won National Book Award in 1968.

Paul Robeson
(1898–1976)

- Educated at Rutgers University and Columbia University Law School.

- Began appearing on stage in New York City in 1924 in *All God's Chillun Got Wings*.

- Noted for his baritone-bass voice.

- Appeared on stage in *Black Boy* (1926) and *Porgy* (1928).

- Praised for his work as Othello.

- Appeared in eleven motion pictures, such as *Show Boat* (1936).

- Known also as a popular concert artist.

Name _____

William Shakespeare Preview Questions

I True or False

1. _____   William Shakespeare was very concerned about making money.

2. _____   Ann Hathaway, Shakespeare's wife, was many years older than he was.

3. _____   Although he was a well known actor, Shakespeare never had the opportunity to perform in front of Queen Elizabeth.

4. _____   Shakespeare was an actor first before he became a playwright.

5. _____   The Globe Theater, which was Shakespeare's first theater, still stands in part today in London.

6. _____   Shakespeare wrote over forty plays in his lifetime.

7. _____   Shakespeare died a wealthy man.

8. _____   Of all of Shakespeare's plays, none has been produced on film more times than *Romeo and Juliet*.

9. _____   Critics believed Shakespeare to be the best playwright of his time period.

10. _____   The famous balcony scene between Juliet and Romeo is in actuality a falsehood. Juliet did not have a balcony.

11. _____   Shakespeare plagiarized some of his plays, stealing scenes and dialogue from other playwrights.

12. _____   Shakespeare's plays were the only ones performed during the plague of 1591–1593.

13. _____   Shakespeare's plays were designed to teach Elizabethan audiences about morals.

14. _____   Shakespeare was born in London but lived in Stratford.

15. _____   Shakespeare's favorite subject in college was literature.

Poetry Survey

Directions: Circle the letter of the correct answer.

1. Interpreting a poem is the same as
   A. analyzing a poem.
   B. describing a poem.
   C. paraphrasing a poem.

2. A sonnet has
   A. 8 lines.
   B. 10 lines.
   C. 12 lines.
   D. 14 lines.

3. Poetry is
   A. a dying art form.
   B. more popular today than ever before.
   C. associated only with the highly educated.

4. A ballad and an ode are narrative poems.
   A. True
   B. False

5. Free verse and blank verse are the same.
   A. True
   B. False

6. All poems must have titles.
   A. True
   B. False

7. Poems appeared as literature before drama and fiction.
   A. True
   B. False

8. A poem could tell a story.
   A. True
   B. False

9. Haiku is a form of
   A. Chinese poetry.
   B. Korean poetry.
   C. Japanese poetry.
   D. American poetry.

10. A limerick has
    A. three lines.
    B. four lines.
    C. five lines.
    D. six lines.

Name _____

Caricatures and Washington Irving

Directions: Examine the following example of a caricature from Washington Irving. A caricature is a distorted representation of a person in which a physical feature, mannerism, or habit is exaggerated to produce a comic effect. Although a caricature is most common in a cartoon, it can also be seen in prose.

"He was tall, but exceedingly lank, with narrow shoulders, long arms and legs, hands that dangled a mile out of his sleeves, feet that might have served for shovels, and his whole frame most loosely hung together. His head was small, and flat at top, with huge ears, large green glassy eyes, and a long snip nose, so that it looked like a weathercock perched upon his spindle neck, to tell which way the wind blew."

(Irving's description of Ichabod Crane, the schoolmaster in "The Legend of Sleepy Hollow")

Now create your own example:

Name _____

Branch Rickey and Jackie Robinson

Background: Branch Rickey throughout his life strongly advocated for the rights of African-Americans. As the General Manager and President of the Brooklyn Dodgers he believed intensely in (1) the inclusion of black players, (2) fair play, and (3) profits for the Dodgers.

According to baseball historians, Rickey felt integration would be good for America, good for major league baseball, and especially good for the Dodger organization. He had scouts monitor the Negro Leagues and broke the color barrier of major league baseball by signing infielder Jackie Robinson.

Directions: Read the following statements from Branch Rickey and be ready to explain how they relate to his decision to sign Jackie Robinson as the first African-American major league baseball player.

1. "Problems are the price you pay for progress."

2. "The greatest untapped reservoir of raw material in the history of the game is the black race. The Negroes will make us winners for years to come, and for that I happily bear being called a bleeding heart and a do-gooder."

3. "Jack, I've been looking for a great colored ballplayer for a great many years. I have some reason to believe you might be that man. But what I need is more than a great player. I need a man that will take abuse, insults, in other words, carry the flag for the race."

Name _____

April Fool's Day—The History

In 1562 Pope Gregory changed the calendar for the Christian world, declaring the new year would now be observed on January 1, instead of April 1. Some French people, however, who either had not heard or did not believe the date had been changed, continued to celebrate the new year on April 1. Others began to play tricks on them and term them "April fools." A typical prank was to send them on a foolish errand or try to make them believe a falsehood was true. Today in France, April first is called "Poisson d'Avril," and children try to tape a paper fish to a friend's back. When the prank is discovered, the child yells out, "Poisson d'Avril."

Americans also play tricks on friends on April 1. In the 19th century, teachers would tease students by pointing to the sky and saying, "Look! A flock of geese" where there was none. In turn, students would tell classmates that school had been canceled.

Other common tricks include putting salt in a sugar bowl, setting a clock one hour behind, or sending a friend on a silly errand. Some practical jokes are kept up the whole day before the victim realizes he or she has been an April fool. Most April Fool jokes are not meant to harm anyone, and, in fact, the most clever of jokes prompts all parties to laugh.

Directions: Describe an April Fool joke you have played on someone or experienced in your life.

APRIL
Answer Key

#1 SKILL SHEET 4-1—EXCERPT FROM *JANE EYRE* BY CHARLOTTE BRONTË

1. The narrator's school day seems to be very routine, a little difficult, quiet, and somewhat long for her. The teacher is a firm authority.

2. She sees herself as an actor here. She's pretending to be mentally involved in her academics.

3. Answers will vary.

4. Answers will vary, but typical responses would be that she has a conflict with the teacher or another student, she goes home, etc.

5. Brontë's writing style is very formal.

#7 SKILL SHEET 4-2—"THE MIDNIGHT RIDE OF PAUL REVERE" BY HENRY WADSWORTH LONGFELLOW

1. Rhyme

2. Paul Revere's ride to warn the Minutemen of the advance of the British army

3. The poem's introduction inspires readers to continue reading by telling them to listen to a tale about a "famous day."

4. "lantern aloft in the belfry-arch of the North Church tower," "opposite shore," "alarm"

5. Answers will vary.

#10 SKILL SHEET 4-4—FAMOUS DIALOGUE FROM SHAKESPEARE'S PLAYS

1. Jaques's "The Seven Ages of Man" speech defines life as being predictable and temporary. Nothing lasts because the pattern repeats and repeats. We go through seven stages (or ages) or roles in a lifetime.

2. Juliet speaks these lines on her balcony as she ponders a relationship with Romeo, whose family name is an enemy to her family. Does it really matter, she wonders, what names we give to things or each other? Only appearances and personalities truly matter.

3. Polonius offers his son advice here on the proper conduct of a man, especially with respect to understanding personal limitations and avoiding deception.

4. Macbeth sees life as empty, short, and emotional. It is a meaningless charade.

5. Some are born great (royalty), some achieve greatness (as in a military or political triumph), and some have greatness thrust upon them (acknowledgment of a personal achievement).

#14 SKILL SHEET 4-5—OVERCOMING GOBBLEDYGOOK

1. 58

2. Answers will vary.

3. The word *order* is repeated 8 times.

4. Some awkward or clumsy phrases include "subsequent order," "shall be construed." among others.

5. Answers will vary.

6. Answers will vary.

#15 SKILL SHEET 4-6—THOMAS JEFFERSON AND THE DECLARATION OF INDEPENDENCE

1. We believe it to be true and unquestioned (self-evident) that all men are equal, that their Creator has given them certain inherent (inalienable) rights.

2. which are life, freedom from oppression (liberty) and the opportunity to have happiness.

3. It is the job of the government, which is made up of officials elected by the people (consent of the governed) to be sure all citizens have those rights.

4. And if that government becomes oppressive or abusive, the people have the right to change it or to get rid of it altogether (abolish)

5. and create a new government that will accept those rights (principles), and give its citizens the maximum freedom to pursue happiness in a safe environment.

#46 SKILL SHEET 4-8—WILLIAM SHAKESPEARE PREVIEW QUESTIONS

1. True

2. True—She was eight years older.

3. False—He performed in front of her as a member of the acting troupe Lord Chamberlin's Men.

4. True

5. False—It burned down in 1613 when a cannon was shot during a performance of King Henry VIII and ignited the theater's thatched roof.

6. False—only 39.

7. True

8. True—There have been nearly 10 films made from the play.

9. False—Christopher Marlowe was considered the better playwright of the day; *Romeo and Juliet* was criticized because the lovers died at the end.

10. True—In the original performance, Juliet leans out a window.

11. False

12. False—No plays were performed during the plague.

13. True

14. False—He was born in Stratford and moved to London before retiring to Stratford near the end of his life.

15. False—Shakespeare never went to college.

#47 SKILL SHEET 4-9—POETRY SURVEY

1. A.	2. D	3. B	4. B	5. B
6. B	7. A	8. A	9. C	10. C

MAY

MAY

Origin: The most commonly accepted legend is that May gets its name from Maia, the Roman goddess of spring and growth. Typically, the Romans held ceremonies in May in her honor and to praise Flora, the goddess of flowers.

Holidays: Memorial Day is observed in the United States to honor all those who died while serving the nation in war. Mother's Day and Armed Forces Day are also observed this month in the U.S.

Mexico celebrates Cinco de Mayo, a national holiday to recognize their victory over the French in 1862.

Children's Day is celebrated in Japan and Korea.

Argentina, Croatia, Jordan, Norway, and Paraguay all celebrate Independence Days this month.

Gemstone: Emerald

Flower: Lily of the Valley

Poetry: Here's to the day when it is May
And care as light as a feather,
When your little shoes and my big boots
Go tramping over the heather.
   by Bliss Carman

Hail, bounteous May, that doth inspire
Mirth, and youth, and warm desire;
Woods and groves are of thy dressing,
Hill and dale doth boast thy blessing.
   by John Milton

BIRTHDAYS

May 1	Joseph Heller, author of *Catch 22* (1923) [#11, 54]; Kate Smith, singer who recorded more songs than any other performer (3000) including "God Bless America" (1909) [#81]
May 4	Horace Mann, author/educator/"father of public education in the U.S." (1796) [#15]; Randy Travis, singer (1959) [#56, 69, 80]
May 5	Karl Marx, father of modern communism (1818) [#18]
May 6	Sigmund Freud, founder of psychoanalysis (1856) [#47]
May 7	Archibald MacLeish, Pulitzer Prize winning poet and playwright (1892) [#5, 32, 50, 58, 61]
May 8	Harry Truman, 33rd President (1884) [#25, 53, 55, 70]
May 12	Florence Nightingale, English nurse (1820) [#26, 54, 68]
May 13	Joe Louis, world heavyweight boxing champion (1914) [#23, 35]
May 15	Katherine Anne Porter, Pulitzer Prize and National Book Award winner (1890) [#22, 60, 66]; Paul Zindel, author (1936) [#10]
May 19	Lorraine Hansberry, playwright and youngest American and first black writer to win Best Play Award from the New York Critics Circle (1930) [#12, 17, 22, 84]; Malcolm X (El Hajj Malik Al-Shabazz) (born Malcolm Little), civil rights activist (1925) [#14, 39, 73]
May 20	Alexander Pope, English poet (1688) [#6, 32, 50, 61]
May 22	Arthur Conan Doyle, writer and creator of Sherlock Holmes (1859) [#9, 11, 77]
May 25	Ralph Waldo Emerson, poet/essayist/philosopher (1803) [#1, 19, 32, 50, 54, 63, 65]; Robert Ludlum, bestselling author (1927) [#8, 11]
May 28	James Thorpe, Olympic gold medalist in 1912 and pro baseball and football player (1888) [#23, 75]
May 29	Patrick Henry, American revolutionary leader (1736) [#39, 54, 71]; John F. Kennedy, 35th and the youngest President ever (1917) [#2, 25, 55, 67, 70]
May 30	Countee Cullen, poet (1903) [#4, 21, 32, 50, 61]
May 31	Walt Whitman, poet (1819) [#3, 20, 21, 32, 50, 54, 59, 61]

MEMORABLE EVENTS

May 5   Alan Shepard became America's first man in space in 1961 [#38, 57].

May 8   No Socks Day [#29, 49].

May 11 Minnesota was admitted to the Union as the 32nd state in 1858 [#28, 83].

May 12 Limerick Day [#64].

May 14 Jamestown, Virginia was founded by English settlers led by Captain John Smith in 1607 [#46].

Meriwether Lewis and Captain William Clark left St. Louis with the mission to find a route to the Pacific in 1804 [#48, 78].

May 16 Biographers Day [#13, 31].

May 17 The U.S. Supreme Court ruled that the segregation of public schools "solely on the basis or race" denied black children "equal educational opportunity [and] Separate educational facilities are inherently unequal" after hearing Brown vs. Board of Education in 1954 [#52].

The first running of the Kentucky Derby took place at Churchill Downs in 1875 [#43, 82].

May 20 Charles Lindberg began the first solo flight across the Atlantic in 1927 [#24, 37].

Amelia Earhart landed in Ireland, completing the first solo flight across the Atlantic by a woman in 1932 [#37, 74].

May 21 Clara Barton founded in 1881 the American Red Cross which currently has over one million volunteers [#26, 34, 51, 68].

May 22 "Mister Rogers Neighborhood" hosted by Fred Rogers premiered in 1964 on PBS [#79].

May 27 The Golden Gate Bridge opened in San Francisco in 1937 [#30, 42].

May 29 New Zealand explorer Sir Edmund Hillary reached the summit of Mt. Everest, the world's highest mountain, in 1953 [#24, 45].

Wisconsin was admitted to the Union as the 30th state in 1848 [#28, 83]

LEARNING ACTIVITIES FOR MAY

READING ACTIVITIES

Purpose: To expand critical thinking skills

1. Distribute **Skill Sheet 5-1** and have students read and respond to the quotes from Ralph Waldo Emerson.

2. Distribute **Form 5-2** and have students read and respond to the quotes from John F. Kennedy.

Purpose: To expand skills at analyzing poetry

3. Have students read selected poems of Walt Whitman found in their literature text or available anthology to study where his personal life connects to his topics/themes.

> Walt Whitman lived as an outcast for most of his life. Although he was anti-government, he was a patriotic American ("I Hear America Singing") and served as a nurse for Union troops during the Civil War. He hated materialism and supported the endeavors of all common men. He found spiritual insight in the contemplation of nature and joy in the menial work of laborers, with whom he identified himself. He said in "Song of Myself," "I celebrate myself and sing myself, and what I assume you shall assume, for every atom belonging to me as good belongs to you," lines meant to form a relationship between reader and poet.

4. Have students read selected poems of Countee Cullen found in their literature text or another available anthology to study his use of language, type of verse, and themes.

> Countee Cullen avoided the dialect used in poems by other black poets, and instead wrote lyrical poetry that most often dealt with themes that explored the African roots of black Americans.

5. Have students read selected poems of Archibald MacLeish found in their literature text or another available anthology to study his use of type of verse and themes.

> Archibald MacLeish's poetry was considered so original it earned him two Pulitzer Prizes (1933, 1953) and a National Book Award in 1953. His poems, which occasionally were written in free verse, had a strong narrative quality and reflected the Imagist technique.

6. Have students read selected poems of Alexander Pope found in their literature text or another available anthology to study his use of language, type of verse, and themes.

> Alexander Pope's highly didactic verse was most often both satirical and harsh, especially when he dealt with other writers and artists. He excelled especially in the use of the heroic couplet.

7. Have students locate and read limericks found in their literature textbook or an available anthology. Refer to Limerick Day and use **Skill Sheet 5-3**.

Purpose: To begin or conclude a fiction unit

8. Distribute **Form 5-4**—the titles of Robert Ludlum novels—and ask: How does each title interest the reader? What is revealed or suggested by the title? How effectively does Ludlum introduce the premise of the story and encourage you to continue reading? What does the novel seem to be about?

> Ludlum's titles refer to European names like Osterman, Rhineman, Bourne; documents like Matlock Paper, Chancellor Manuscript, Scarlatti Inheritance; mythology as in Icarus, Parsifal, Hades; signs of the zodiac, Gemini and Scorpio; Biblical terms like covenant and apocalypse; and locations like Gandolfo, Matarese, and Omaha.

9. Read orally excerpts from any Arthur Conan Doyle novel, especially one involving Sherlock Holmes, and ask students to identify his use of characterization, plot, and setting to set a mood of suspense.

10. Encourage students to select for independent reading a novel by Paul Zindel. Use **Skill Sheet 5-5** to preview this reading and **Form 11-8** to evaluate them.

11. Encourage students to read a book of historical fiction. Refer to Joseph Heller, Robert Ludlum, and Sir Arthur Conan Doyle as potential authors and remind students to study the book for its historical details. Ask: Were the details accurate? Was any event exaggerated? Were some key events omitted? Use **Form 11-8** to evaluate them.

Purpose: *To begin or conclude a drama unit*

12. Have students read dialogue from Lorraine Hansberry's play *A Raisin in the Sun,* the story of an impoverished black family in 1950s Chicago. The play often appears in various literature texts. Ask: What is revealed about characters? How does the dialogue seem to advance the plot?

> Walter Younger is a chauffeur who is frustrated by his position in life, and his wife Ruth exhausts herself each day cleaning her apartment and the homes of white people. Beneatha, Walter's sister, is struggling to complete her studies to be a doctor, which makes Walter jealous. They all eagerly anticipate the $10,000 check Beneatha and Walter's mother, Lena Younger, is to receive as payment for the life insurance policy of her dead husband.

Purpose: *To encourage the reading of a biography*

13. Refer to Biographers Day and assign the reading of a biography. Preview this by asking: Why might a biographer choose to write about that person? What could be the relationship between the biographer and his/her subject? Distribute **Form 12-1** when they finish.

> Generally, the subject of any biography is well-known or a historical figure who has significant achievements. This person might have an unusual or extraordinary background.
>
> The biographer could be a relative, a close friend, or an accomplished writer who the subject has asked to write his/her story. Sometimes, the biography could be unauthorized.

14. Refer to Malcolm X and his impact on the civil rights movement. Then distribute **Form 5-6**—his most noted quotes—and ask students to read and discuss them. Also direct students to locate biographies about Malcolm X.

> Biographies about Malcolm X include *Malcolm X: His Life and Legacy* by Kevin Brown; *Malcolm X and Black Pride* by Robert Cwiklik; *Malcolm X* by David Shirley; *Malcolm X* by Jack Slater; *Malcolm X: A Fire Burning Brightly* by Walter Dean Myers; *Malcolm X: A Voice for Black America* by Arthur Diamond; *The Autobiography of Malcolm X* by Malcolm X; among others.

DEBATING ACTIVITIES

Purpose: To strengthen critical thinking skills

15. Do you agree or disagree with Horace Mann's statement: "A human being is not, in any proper sense, a human being till he is educated"? Why?

16. What are the true signs of maturity? How can we be certain we have matured? What authors deal best with presenting mature characters?

17. In *A Raisin in the Sun*, Beneatha, one of the characters, says, "Money is life." Do you agree? Why/why not?

18. Should high school libraries provide copies of Karl Marx's book *The Communist Manifesto*? Is this appropriate reading material for American young people? Why/why not? Is this a book that should be censored? Why/why not?

Purpose: To begin or conclude a poetry unit

19. Do you agree or disagree with Ralph Waldo Emerson's quote: "All men are poets at heart"? Why/why not?

20. Walt Whitman in his poem "Song of Myself" writes: "I celebrate myself and sing myself." Is he being egotistical? Why/why not?

21. Who contributed more to American poetry—Walt Whitman or Countee Cullen? Use this also to compare/contrast the writing styles of these poets and to develop research skills.

Purpose: To practice comparison/contrast

22. Who contributed more to American literature—Katherine Anne Porter or Lorraine Hansberry? Distribute **Form 5-7** to compare/contrast the writing styles of these two famous women writers who wrote in different time periods.

23. Who was the better athlete—Jim Thorpe, who was an Olympic gold medalist in the pentathlon and decathlon, a two-time All-American in college football, a professional football and baseball player, a member of the football Hall of Fame, and the athlete sportswriters named the all-around best athlete of the first half of the 20th century; or Joe Louis, who went 68-3 as a professional boxer with 54 knockouts and defended his title 25 times, holding the title longer than any other boxer and entering the Boxing Hall of Fame in 1954? Use this also to develop research skills.

24. What was the more important historical event—Sir Edmund Hillary reaching the top of Mt. Everest in 1953 or Charles Lindberg crossing the Atlantic in 1927?

25. Which President was the more experienced politician—Harry S. Truman or John F. Kennedy?

> **Harry Truman was a judge in Missouri before representing that state as a United States Senator. He was the Vice President under F.D.R. and President from 1945–1953.**
>
> **John F. Kennedy represented Massachusetts in the U.S. House of Representatives and a U.S. Senator before becoming the President from 1961–1963.**

26. Who contributed more to the nursing profession—Florence Nightingale or Clara Barton? Use this also to develop research skills.

WRITING ACTIVITIES

Purpose: To improve writing description

27. Have students write a descriptive one-page essay about working in the yard—mowing the grass, weeding the garden, avoiding frogs or snakes. Use **Form 12-5** to evaluate them.

28. Have students compose a travelogue about northern states Minnesota and/or Wisconsin, concentrating on descriptive details. Use **Form 11-11** as a model.

29. Refer to No Socks Day, ask students to remove their shoes and socks, and direct them to write paragraphs describing their bare feet. Ask: How are your feet different?

30. Refer to the Golden Gate Bridge and direct students to write a detailed paragraph describing that or another bridge they've observed or traveled on.

Purpose: To encourage the reading of biographies

31. Have students list a series of comprehensive questions they would ask a famous person from history. Refer to Biographers Day.

32. Refer to the poets who have birthdays this month and then assign students to locate and read one of their biographies. Ask students to complete a project from **Form 12-1**.

33. Have students write a mini-autobiography of one of the writers who has a birthday this month or another favorite author. Students should assume the identity of the writer and include their name, best works, hobbies, personal life, close friends, influences on their writing, and recurring themes in the mini-autobiography.

Purpose: To review speech skills

34. Have students write the speech Clara Barton might have given to solicit volunteers for the Red Cross.

35. Consider Joe Louis, who boxed professionally from 1934 to 1951, becoming the world heavyweight champion and defending his title 25 times before retiring after being knocked out by Rocky Marciano. Ask students to write his speech that announces his retirement.

Purpose: *To write creative short fiction*

36. Have students create a brief, humorous narrative about a picnic, a baseball game, or a Memorial Day parade using sensory language and specific details.

37. Have students create a brief narrative about Charles Lindberg on his solo flight across the Atlantic in 1927 or Amelia Earhart on her solo flight across the Atlantic in 1932.

Purpose: *To review dialogue*

38. Have students create the dialogue between Alan Shepard and Mission Control over the radio during his space flight in 1961.

39. Direct students to create the imaginary dialogue between Patrick Henry and Malcolm X, two different revolutionaries. Possibly have students do some research first.

Purpose: *To review letter writing skills and format*

40. Encourage students to write a letter to an employer asking for a job (summer employment), a promotion, or a raise in salary (business letter). This activity could also be used as part of a careers unit.

41. Encourage students to write a letter to a company or business, requesting employment or career information. This activity could also be used as part of a careers unit.

Purpose: *To review news writing style*

42. Have students write the news lead about the opening of the Golden Gate Bridge in San Francisco in 1937. Be sure you review news article format (the five Ws).

Example: The Golden Gate Bridge opened yesterday linking San Francisco with Marin County . . .

43. Have students write a news article about the Kentucky Derby—either a straight article or a feature. Refer first to sports articles about the race and suggest feature articles about their favorite horse, jockey, or trainer.

Purpose: To improve an appreciation of other nationalities and cultures

44. Ask students to explain the life of a teenager who lived in a city in Argentina, Croatia, Jordan, Norway, or Paraguay. Direct them to an atlas to identify the city name.

Purpose: To expand reflective writing

45. Have students write the diary entry of Sir Edmund Hillary, the New Zealand explorer who reached the summit of Mt. Everest, the world's highest mountain, in 1953.

46. Have students write the diary entry of Captain John Smith the day after he landed at Jamestown, Virginia in 1607. Use this also to connect writing to historical events.

47. Refer to Sigmund Freud, who introduced the concept of dream analysis, and have students write an essay where they describe a dream they've had either using short, tense sentences or lengthy, complex sentences to create the mood or tone of that dream (possibly a nightmare). Use this also to improve their understanding of sentence structure.

48. Have students write the journal entry of Meriwether Lewis or Captain William Clark after they left St. Louis with the mission to find a route to the Pacific in 1804. Prompt students to write in military language and use this as an exercise in clarity and chronology.

Purpose: To begin or conclude a poetry unit

49. Ask students to create a poem involving socks. Refer to No Socks Day.

50. Distribute **Skill Sheet 5-8**—a survey on poetry and the poets who have birthdays this month—and then discuss the responses.

DISCUSSION ACTIVITIES

Purpose: To expand critical thinking skills

51. Refer to Clara Barton and the Red Cross whose goal is to assist those who are sick, injured, or unhealthy. Then ask: Why are more and more *healthy* people getting plastic surgery these days? What are the benefits and/or risks of this type of surgery? What does the popularity of plastic surgery suggest about our society?

52. The United States Supreme Court decided in 1954 that the segregation of public schools "solely on the basis of race" was unconstitutional. Are there examples of segregation today in public places that are non-race related? In what other ways does segregation still occur? How would you end segregation totally?

53. President Harry Truman said: "The buck stops here." What did he mean? What was his intent?

54. Refer to the persons below and challenge students to learn the major historical event(s) (wars) that occurred during their lifetime and influenced their writing. Use this also to improve research skills and connect history to literature.

    • Joseph Heller [WW II]
    • Ralph Waldo Emerson [Civil War]
    • Florence Nightingale [Crimean War]
    • Walt Whitman [the Civil War]
    • Patrick Henry [the American Revolution]

55. Refer to Presidents who have birthdays this month and ask: If the President of the United States walked in, what would you ask?

56. Refer to celebrities like Randy Travis and ask: What aspects of a person's life should *not* be in the news?

57. Consider Alan Shepard, who was America's first man in space in 1961 and ask: Why do you think he was chosen among all the other astronauts?

58. Write on the board Archibald MacLeish's sentence, which originally appeared in the 1968 *New York Times* after the Apollo mission returned from space with a photograph of the earth: "To see the earth as it truly is, small and blue and beautiful in that eternal silence where it floats, is to see ourselves as riders on the earth together, brothers on that bright loveliness in the eternal cold . . ." Then ask: What descriptive words and phrases does MacLeish use to describe the earth? What analogy does he use? How would you describe the earth if you were looking at it from space?

Purpose: *To begin or conclude a poetry unit*

59. Refer to Walt Whitman who traveled across America observing all types of people. How would you interpret his personal description: "I am the poet of the Body and I am the poet of the Soul"?

60. Write the following quote about reading poetry from Katherine Anne Porter on the board and ask students to interpret her perception of poetry.

    "If I read a book and it makes my whole body so cold no fire can warm me, I know that it is poetry. If I feel physically as if the top of my head were taken off, I know that it is poetry."

61. How can punctuation influence the meaning of a poem? Refer to the poets who have birthdays this month.

62. Why do poets use punctuation and capitalization differently than essayists and story writers?

63. Explain that Ralph Waldo Emerson was editor of the *Dial*, a transcendental magazine. Then ask: What does *transcendental* mean? What kind of poems and articles do you think he published? Would you find this an interesting magazine to read? Why/why not?

> *Transcendental* and *transcendentalism* refer to the philosophy that rejected the strict Puritan religious codes and, in fact, the dogma of all religious institutions in favor of a celebration of individualism and self-examination. Writers, like Emerson, who were transcendentalists, connected the creative process with the spiritual and natural world.

64. What is the rhyme scheme of a limerick? What is the usual tone of a limerick? Why do people often favor these types of poems? Refer to Limerick Day.

> Limericks, which originated in Ireland, are most often humorous poems with a rhyme scheme of *AABBA* that are inspired by humorous situations or people. People enjoy them typically because they are humorous, short, and whimsical.

Purpose: *To begin the reading of any book*

65. Ralph Waldo Emerson said: "Talent alone cannot make a writer. There must be a man behind the book." Do you agree or disagree with his statement? Why?

66. Katherine Anne Porter said: "If I didn't know the ending of a story, I wouldn't begin. I always write my last line, my last paragraphs, my last page first." What is she declaring about the way she writes a book? Why do you think she begins with the last page first? What process would you follow if you decided to write a book?

Purpose: *To review speech skills*

67. Refer to John F. Kennedy's inauguration speech when he said: "And so, my fellow Americans: ask not what your country can do for you—ask what you can do for your country. My fellow citizens of the world: ask not what America will do for you, but what together we can do for the freedom of man." Then ask: What is Kennedy suggesting to American people? What was he recommending to the citizens of the world? What was his intent here?

Purpose: *To conclude a careers unit*

68. Refer to Florence Nightingale and Clara Barton and ask: What are the advantages and disadvantages of a career in the nursing profession?

69. Refer to Randy Travis and ask: Who are some other country/western singers? How does any person interested in singing professionally get started in this field? How can a person rise to stardom as a singer?

70. Refer to the Presidents who have birthdays this month and the attention the media gives to their private lives. Then ask: What other professions or jobs deserve to be covered by the press on a regular basis?

Purpose: To teach parallelism and emphasis in sentences

71. Explain parallelism in writing and then refer to Patrick Henry's famous comment to the Virginia Convention: "Give me liberty or give me death." Ask: How does this sentence serve as an example of parallelism in writing? What is being emphasized? Why has this quote remained so famous?

> If two or more ideas are expressed in a sentence, they should be expressed in parallel form—that is, single words should be balanced with single words, adjective-noun constructions with another adjective-noun, phrases with phrases, clauses with clauses. A prime example would be Thomas Jefferson's "In matters of principle, stand like a rock; in matters of taste, swim with the current."
>
> The two clauses that begin "Give me" is the parallelism in Henry's statement. He is emphasizing his preference for death, rather than bondage. It became the battle cry for our revolution.

AUDIO/VISUAL ACTIVITIES

Purpose: To encourage an appreciation for other nationalities and cultures

72. Show a videotape of people of various nationalities or cultures and have students identify the characteristics of those people. Refer to Argentina, Croatia, Japan, Jordan, Korea, Mexico, Norway, and Paraguay.

Purpose: To begin or conclude a biography unit

73. Show selected scenes of the movie "X," about the life of Malcolm X, starring Denzel Washington, and direct students to locate the various biographies about his life.

Purpose: To improve writing characterizations

74. Show pictures, if available, or the videotape of the movie *Amelia Earhart: the Final Flight* starring Diane Keaton and then have students identify the characteristics, behavior, and attitude of the first famous woman pilot.

75. Show selected scenes from the movie *Jim Thorpe, All American* starring Burt Lancaster and have students list the characteristics and traits revealed about Jim Thorpe. Also use this to preview a biography unit.

76. Play a song about a person, such as "Barbara Ann" by the Beach Boys or "Billy Jean" by Michael Jackson. Ask: What is revealed about the person in the song?

77. Show selected scenes from a Sherlock Holmes movie starring Basil Rathbone and have students write descriptions of his appearance, behavior, and mannerisms.

78. Show selected scenes of the movie *Far Horizons* starring Charlton Heston which tells the story of Lewis and Clark and their journey to survey the Louisiana Purchase and have students write descriptions of the appearance, behavior, and mannerisms of these two explorers.

Purpose: To review diction/vocabulary skills

79. Show a videotape of a "Mr. Rogers Neighborhood" program and have students analyze his vocabulary and diction.

80. Play recordings from Randy Travis and have students analyze the lyrics for the type of diction and poetic qualities.

81. Play a recording of Kate Smith singing "God Bless America" and have students analyze the lyrics for the diction.

82. Refer to the Kentucky Derby, show illustrations and pictures of horses, and direct students to list words and phrases that describe them, especially those related to the breeding and training of race horses.

83. Distribute travel brochures about Minnesota and Wisconsin and have students identify the descriptive phrases and words used to describe the attractions in these states.

Purpose: To conclude the reading of Raisin in the Sun

84. Show the movie *Raisin in the Sun* starring Sidney Poitier and have students identify the traits and behaviors of the characters.

Name _____

The Wisdom of Ralph Waldo Emerson

Directions: For each quote from Emerson, first paraphrase in modern terms his statement and then explain why you agree or disagree with his belief.

1. "Good and bad are but names . . . the only right is what is after my constitution; the only wrong is what is against it."

2. "Who so would be a man, must be a nonconformist."

3. "Society everywhere is in conspiracy against the manhood of every one of its members."

4. "No law can be sacred to me but that of my nature."

5. "What I must do is all that concerns me, not what people think."

6. "That which each can do best, none but his maker can teach him."

7. "Imitation is suicide."

8. "None but he knows that which he can do, nor does he know until he has tried."

9. "It is easy in the world to live after the world's opinion."

10. "If you love me for what I am, we shall be the happier."

Name _____

The Words of John F. Kennedy

Directions: Read and respond to the following statements from President John F. Kennedy.

1. "If this nation is to be wise as well as strong, if we are to achieve our destiny, then we need more new ideas for more wise men reading more good books in more public libraries. These libraries should be open to all—except the censor."

2. "This nation was founded by men of many nations and backgrounds. It was founded on the principle that all men are created equal, and the rights of every man are diminished when the rights of one man are threatened."

3. "There is always inequity in life. Some men are killed in a war and some men are wounded, and some men never leave the country, and . . . some men are stationed in San Francisco . . . Life is unfair."

4. ". . . if more politicians knew poetry, and more poets knew politics, I am convinced the world would be a little better place to live . . ."

5. "And we must face the fact that the United States is neither omnipotent nor omniscient—that we are only 6 percent of the world's population—that we cannot impose our will upon the other 94 percent of mankind—that we cannot right every wrong or reverse every adversity—and that therefore there cannot be an American solution to every world problem."

Skill Sheet 5–3   Name _____

Limericks

Directions: Read and study the two examples of limericks and then create your own.

Limerick = verse that follows an AABBA rhyme scheme to convey most often a humorous tone or image.

Example #1

There was a young lady from Niger,

Who smiled as she rode on a tiger.

They came back from the ride

With the lady inside,

And the smile on the face of the tiger.

Example #2

A bridge engineer, Mister Crumpett,

Built a bridge for the good River Bumpett.

A mistake in the plan

Left a gap in the span,

But he said, "Well, they'll just have to jump it."

Now create your own limerick:

Name _____

The Novels of Robert Ludlum

The Osterman Weekend (1972)

The Matlock Paper (1973)

The Rhineman Exchange (1974)

The Road to Gandolfo (1975)

The Gemini Contenders (1976)

The Chancellor Manuscript (1977)

The Scarlatti Inheritance (1977)

The Holcroft Covenant (1978)

The Matarese Circle (1979)

The Bourne Identity (1980)

The Parsifal Mosaic (1982)

The Aquitaine Progression (1984)

The Bourne Supremacy (1987)

The Icarus Agenda (1988)

Trevayne (1989)

The Road to Omaha (1992)

The Scorpio Illusion (1993)

The Apocalypse Watch (1995)

The Cry of the Halidon (1996)

The Matarese Countdown (1997)

The Hades Factor (2000)

Skill Sheet 5–5   Name _____

A Preview of Paul Zindel

Directions: Answer the following questions in detail on a separate paper.

1. Paul Zindel's novels commonly involve a teenage romance. How does a teenage romance differ from an adult romance?

2. These romantic relationships typically involve problems between the partners. What problems can affect a high school romance/relationship?

3. The characters, however, do work to make the relationship succeed. What helps any relationship grow or improve?

4. Examine the title of the novel. What makes it unusual or different from other young adult novel titles?

5. Many characters in Paul Zindel's novels typically have eccentric or unique personalities. What does *eccentric* mean?

6. These characters often experience difficulties that make their life feel temporarily out of control. When have you felt as if things were temporarily out of control?

7. The dialogue in a Zindel novel often is humorous. Skim the novel you have and write an example of some humorous dialogue.

8. Another motif in a Zindel novel is the problems teens face with the generation gap. When people refer to a generation gap what do they mean?

9. Sometimes the resolutions in a Zindel novel are not positive ones. Is this satisfactory? Why/why not?

10. What do you expect to read about in the novel you've chosen?

Name _____

The Words of Malcolm X

Directions: Read and respond to the following statements from Malcolm X.

1. "Education is our passport to the future, for tomorrow belongs to the people who prepare for it today."

2. "Don't let people put labels on you—and don't put them on yourself. Sometimes a label can kill you."

3. "You can't separate peace from freedom because no one can be at peace unless he has his freedom."

4. "Without education, you're not going anywhere in this world."

5. "If we don't stand for something, we may fall for anything."

6. "Anytime you see someone more successful than you are, they are doing something you aren't."

7. "I believe in the brotherhood of man, all men, but I don't believe in brotherhood with anybody who doesn't want brotherhood with me. I believe in treating people right, but I'm not going to waste my time trying to treat somebody right who doesn't know how to return the treatment."

8. "Power in defense of freedom is greater than power in behalf of tyranny and oppression."

9. "I believe in human rights for everyone, and none of us is qualified to judge each other and that none of us should therefore have that authority."

10. "We declare our right on this earth to be a human, to be respected as a human being, to be given the rights of a human being in this society, on this earth, in this day, which we intend to bring into existence by any means necessary."

Name _____

Katherine Anne Porter vs. Lorraine Hansberry

Katherine Anne Porter

(1890–1990)

- Published *Flowering Judas* (1930)—a collection of short stories praised for their psychological insights and technical excellence.

- Published other story collections:
  Hacienda (1934)
  Noon Wine (1937)
  Pale Horse, Pale Rider (1939)
  Collected Stories (1965)

- Pulitzer Prize for Fiction in 1966.

- Published novel *Ship of Fools* (1962) which was made into a movie.

- Focused on the theme of the individual's search for freedom against oppression.

Lorraine Hansberry

(1930–1965)

- Worked as a reporter for a black newspaper *Freedom* 1950–1953.

- Wrote *Raisin in the Sun* and saw it become the first drama by a black woman on Broadway and win the Drama Critics' Circle Award in 1959.

- Wrote *The Sign in Sidney Brustein's Window* (1964) which was about a white intellectual in Greenwich Village, NY.

- Also wrote numerous articles about racism, homophobia, world peace, among other social issues.

A Survey on Poets & Poetry

Directions: Answer YES or NO to the following:

1. _____ Was Robert Frost, who won four Pulitzer Prizes for Poetry, a college graduate?

2. _____ Do most poems have only four line stanzas?

3. _____ Did Emily Dickinson write poems about her love for a married man?

4. _____ Are blank verse and free verse the same thing?

5. _____ Is a ballad a narrative poem?

6. _____ Did Carl Sandburg, who won two Pulitzer Prizes, work as a dishwasher, milkman, and carpenter to support himself?

7. _____ Must all poems have titles?

8. _____ Was English literature Shakespeare's main subject in school?

9. _____ Were nursery rhymes based on political and historical events?

10. _____ Were the first oral stories told in the form of poems?

11. _____ Does an epic poem typically tell the story of a romantic relationship?

12. _____ Were poets ever accused of treason by their governments because of their poems?

13. _____ Do governments pay people to write poems?

14. _____ Were any poets war heroes?

15. _____ Did poetry originate on the Asian continent?

MAY
Answer Key

#1 SKILL SHEET 5-1—THE WISDOM OF RALPH WALDO EMERSON

[Answers will vary somewhat.]

1. Personal morals are more important than the morals of society.

2. It is the mature person who does not follow the crowd.

3. Society wants to dictate to each individual how to act and behave.

4. No law should be followed unless I accept it as reasonable.

5. I don't care what other people think about my actions.

6. We should pursue our individual talents, not the goals or directions of others.

7. To imitate someone else is to destroy your own identity.

8. Each individual has to determine alone what direction to take in life. Each individual will never know his true talent until he has tried his best at it.

9. It is easy in the world to follow the crowd and to accept the opinions of others as your own.

10. We both can be happy if you accept me as I am.

#50 SKILL SHEET 5-8—A SURVEY ON POETS & POETRY

1. No—Robert Frost briefly attended Harvard but dropped out.

2. No—The number of lines in stanzas varies from 2, 3, 4, 5, 6, etc.

3. Yes—Emily Dickinson did fall in love with the Reverend Charles Wadsworth, but never pursued him because he was married.

4. No—Blank verse, like free verse is unrhymed poetry, but unlike free verse, it has traditionally the meter of iambic pentameter.

5. Yes—A ballad is a narrative poem, typically in the form of a song.

6. Yes—Carl Sandburg did work as a dishwasher, milkman, and carpenter to support himself. He also was a reporter, housepainter, stage hand, brickmaker, and salesman.

7. No—William Shakespeare, Emily Dickinson, Stephen Crane, and e.e. cummings were some famous poets who did not title their poems so the first lines became the way to identify them.

8. No—Latin was Shakespeare's main subject in school, and the literature he studied was Greek and Roman.

9. Yes—For example, "Little Jack Horner" was based on Thomas Horner, steward to the abbot Thomas Whiting, who sent Horner with a pie filled with the deeds to twelve estates as a Christmas present to King Henry VIII. On his trip, Horner opened the pie and extracted the deed to one estate (a "plum") before delivering the pie.

10. Yes—Historians believe ancient fables were in the form of poems.

11. No—An epic poem typically tells the story of a hero and his adventures.

12. Yes, the English authorities accused William Wordsworth of spying for the French because he took so many walks in the countryside they thought he was mapping the areas for the French army; Ezra Pound was arrested by the Allied army in Italy in WW II; and e.e. Cummings spent time in a French prison because he would not denounce Germany during WWI.

13. Yes—For example, the United States government pays a stipend to the U.S Poet Laureate. Many local, state, and international governments, in fact, fund the work of poets.

14. Yes—George (Lord) Byron fought and died in the Greek revolt against Turkey in 1823; Ben Jonson fought with the English army at Flanders; Carl Sandburg fought in the Spanish-American War of 1898; Randall Jarrell flew with the U.S. Army Air Force in WW II.

15. No—No one is certain about its origin, but historians point to the ancient Greeks and Romans as creators of fables and dramas which were written in poetic language and style.

JUNE

INTRODUCTORY PAGE

LEARNING ACTIVITIES

REPRODUCIBLES

QUICK LOCATOR FOR JUNE LEARNING ACTIVITIES

JUNE

Origin:

According to the Gregorian calendar, June is the sixth month and has 30 days as designated by Julius Caesar in 46 B.C. Some historians cite the Roman goddess Juno, the patron goddess of marriage, as the name origin for the month, while others point to the important and powerful family name of Junius. Either way, the beautiful weather prompted the ancient Romans to see June as an ideal month for marriages.

Holidays:

United States citizens observe Flag Day (June 14) and Father's Day in June. Flag Day is also celebrated this month in *Sweden* and *Finland*.

Congo, Djibouti, Ghana, Iceland, Madagascar, Mozambique, Philippines, Russia, Samoa, Tonga all celebrate their Independence Day in June.

Gemstone: Pearl and Moonstone

Flower: Rose

Poetry:

And what is so rare as a day in June?
Then, if ever, come perfect days;
Then Heaven tries earth if it be in tune,
And over it softly her warm ear lays;
Whether we look, or whether we listen,
We hear life murmur, or see it glisten.

   by James Russell Lowell

I knew that you were nearing, June, and I knew
   that you were nearing—
I saw it in the bursting buds of roses in the
   clearing;
The roses in the clearing, June, were blushing
   pink and red,
For they had heard upon the hills the echo of
   your tread.

   by Douglas Mallock

When June is come, then all the day
I'll sit with my love in the scented hay;
And watch the sunshot palaces high,
That the white clouds build in the breezy sky.

by Robert Bridges

BIRTHDAYS

June 1	Marilyn Monroe, actress (1926) [#15, 88]; Brigham Young, leader of the Mormon church (1801) [#38]
June 3	Charles Drew, African American physician who organized the first blood bank (1904) [#53]; Allen Ginsberg, poet of the Beat Generation (1926) [#9]; Larry McMurtry, Pulitzer Prize winner for *Lonesome Dove* (1936) [#3, 91]
June 10	Judy Garland, singer/actress who was Dorothy in *The Wizard of Oz* (1922) [#14, 15, 70]
June 11	Ben Jonson, English playwright/poet (1572) [#8, 49, 66]; Vince Lombardi, coach of the Green Bay Packers and winner of the first Super Bowl (1913) [#11, 13]
June 12	George Bush, 41st President (1924) [#16, 43]; Anne Frank, author of *Diary of Anne Frank* (1929) [#5, 97]
June 13	Tim Allen, comedian/actor (1953) [#84]; William Butler Yeats, Nobel Prize-winning Irish poet (1865) [#10, 49]
June 16	John Griffin, author of *Black Like Me* (1920) [#4, 94]
June 17	Gwendolyn Brooks, poet—"We Real Cool"—and first African American to receive a Pulitzer Prize (1917) [#9, 49, 68]
June 18	Paul McCartney, singer/song writer for the Beatles (1942) [#23, 70, 75, 78, 82]
June 19	Paula Abdul, singer/dancer (1962) [#23, 70]; Lou Gehrig, Hall of Fame baseball player (1903) [#6, 11, 17, 87]
June 25	George Orwell, author of *1984* and *Animal Farm* (1903) [#2, 55, 72, 78]
June 26	Pearl Buck, Nobel Prize-winning author (1892) [#18, 19]
June 27	Helen Keller, deaf and blind author/lecturer (1880) [#18, 33, 63, 95]

MEMORABLE EVENTS

June 1   Kentucky was admitted to the Union as the 15th state in 1792 [#35].

Tennessee was admitted to the Union as the 16th state in 1796 [#35].

June 3   "Casey at the Bat" was printed in the *San Francisco Examiner*, written by Ernest L. Thayer, in 1888 [#7].

June 5   National Family Day [#40, 96].

June 6   D-Day—Allied forces landed at Normandy on the north coast of France during WW II 1944 [#41, 71].

June 7   First VCR, which was a Betamax, was introduced by the Sony Corporation in 1975 and sold for $995 [#14].

June 14   Family History Day [#32, 40].

June 15   Arkansas was admitted to the Union as the 25th state in 1836 [#89].

June 18   Sally Ride became the first woman in space aboard the space shuttle Challenger in 1983 [#18, 25, 51].

June 20   West Virginia was admitted to the Union as the 35th state in 1863 [#35].

June 24   Kenneth Arnold of Boise, Idaho reported seeing "flying saucers," labeled Unidentified Flying Objects by the government, in 1947 [#21, 25].

June 25   First television program in color was broadcast by the Columbia Broadcasting System (CBS) in 1951 [#45, 76].

June 27   "Happy Birthday to You," considered to be the song most often sung, had its melody composed by Mildred J. Hill, a school teacher, in 1859 and its lyrics by her younger sister Patty Hill in 1893. It is believed the song is sung somewhere in the world every minute and generates $1 million a year for its copyright owner [#30, 81].

June 29   The Globe Theater caught fire during a performance of Shakespeare's "Henry VIII" and burned to the ground in 1613 [#90].

June 30   The 26th Amendment to the Constitution was ratified by Congress in 1971, granting voting privileges in all federal, state, and local elections to all persons 18 and older [#20].

LEARNING ACTIVITIES FOR JUNE

READING ACTIVITIES

Purpose: To promote independent reading (summer)

1. Introduce summer reading. Offer a plan and/or incentives for students to read books, magazines, and newspapers over the summer. Also, inform parents about the importance of summer reading. Use **Form 6-1** as a model.

Purpose: To improve analysis of fiction

2. Have students read either *Animal Farm* or *1984* by George Orwell to study the characters, symbolism, and satire of these classic novels. Use **Skill Sheet 6-2** to preview this reading.

3. Distribute **Form 6-3** to preview the works of Larry McMurtry and assign students to read one of his novels. Use **Form 11-8** to evaluate them when they finish.

Purpose: To improve analysis of nonfiction

4. Have students read the book *Black Like Me* by John Griffin to improve their understanding of segregation, racism, and discrimination. The book also serves as an excellent example of an autobiography.

5. Review the characteristics of an autobiography and assign students *The Diary of Anne Frank* by Anne Frank. Use this also to teach the tragedy of the Holocaust.

Purpose: To review speech skills

6. Distribute **Form 6-4**—Lou Gehrig's final speech in Yankee Stadium and ask students to identify how he connects with his audience and where he demonstrates sincerity in his comments.

Purpose: To improve skills at analyzing poetry

7. Distribute **Skill Sheet 6-5**—"Casey at the Bat" by Ernest L. Thayer to study this example of a narrative poem, a ballad. Have students analyze its rhyme scheme, story line, and amusing resolution. Casey Jones, the baseball player portrayed in the poem, was in reality John Luther Jones.

8. Have students read the poetry of Ben Jonson that appears in their literature text or available anthology and then analyze his for poetic language, the type of verse, and the content of his poems.

Ben Jonson's verse was traditional and classic, and the content was often satirical and witty.

9. Have students locate, read, and compare the poetry of contemporary poets Gwendolyn Brooks and Allen Ginsberg in any available anthology to study their poetic language and writing styles.

> **Gwendolyn Brooks used short verse lines and casual rhythms to portray the black struggle, especially involving racial discrimination. Allen Ginsberg's poems are characterized by long, overflowing lines and informal, colloquial words that reflect his feelings of social and political protest.**

10. Have students locate and read the poetry of William Butler Yeats that appears in their literature text or available anthology to analyze his poetic language, the type of verse, and the content of his poems.

> **Irish nationalism, the occult, and mythology were key topics for many poems by William Butler Yeats. These poems were often lyrical and symbolic.**

DEBATING ACTIVITIES

Purpose: To expand critical thinking skills

11. What is America's *national* sport? Baseball? Football? Students should consider the longevity, attendance, and acclaim of the major American sports. Refer to Lou Gehrig and Vince Lombardi. Possibly have students complete some research first.

12. Refer to Flag Day and ask: Should citizens who burn the American flag in protest be arrested and prosecuted? Or are they just expressing Freedom of Speech rights? What does our flag represent?

> **Songwriter George M. Cohan once wrote, "You're the emblem of the land I love, the home of the free and the brave." Others see the flag as a symbol for opportunity and unity. Still others attach no political importance to the flag.**

13. "Winning isn't everything, it's the only thing," said Vince Lombardi, who coached the Green Bay Packers to three National Football League championships. Never has one statement been used by so many coaches to emphasize the importance of winning games. Is Lombardi correct? Why/why not?

14. Which form of entertainment is more popular—watching the *Wizard of Oz*, starring Judy Garland, which still appears frequently on television, or videotapes in a VCR?

15. Who was the better actress/performer—Marilyn Monroe or Judy Garland? Possibly show videotapes of them and ask students to research their backgrounds.

16. What determines the effectiveness of a President? Refer to George Bush and use this also to practice research skills.

17. Refer to Lou Gehrig, Hall of Fame baseball player, and ask: Which current baseball player(s) deserve to be in the Hall of Fame? Why? Use this also to explore sports reporting and current events.

18. Who demonstrated the most physical courage—Sally Ride, who flew on two shuttle flights; Pearl Buck, who worked with missionaries in communist China; or Helen Keller, who although deaf and blind graduated from college with honors?

19. Write Pearl Buck's following quote on the board: "If you want to understand today, you have to search yesterday." Is she correct? Why/why not?

20. Is 18 old enough to vote? Refer to the 26th Amendment and use this especially in an election year to review our responsibilities as citizens.

21. Do UFOs exist? Refer to Kenneth Arnold of Boise, Idaho who reported seeing "flying saucers," labeled Unidentified Flying Objects by the government, in 1947. Students may want to research this before debating.

Purpose: *To improve social skills*

22. Because many marriages take place in June, possibly some of the students' relations, marriage and all its activities can be an appropriate topic to develop students' social skills. Ask: What are the signs of true love (vs. puppy love)? Other than love, what other traits should a couple share before marrying? (For example, trust, dependability, loyalty)

23. Refer to Paula Abdul, Paul McCartney, and the subject of censorship as it relates to song lyrics. Then ask: Should tapes or CDs with questionable lyrics be sold to teenagers? Why/why not? Who should judge these lyrics? What criteria should they follow?

Purpose: *To review skills at word selection/vocabulary*

24. How would you rank the following types of diction from most to least important? Students must select from these types of diction-slang, informal, jargon, formal, or profanity.

25. Refer to Sally Ride and Kenneth Arnold and ask: What are the various terms used to identify spaceships?

Terms include Unidentified Flying Object, shuttle, spaceship, spacecraft, satellite, interplanetary vehicle, missile, rocket, rocketship, among some others.

Purpose: To review skills related to letter writing

26. If an applicant submits an application and resume, is a letter even necessary?

Yes—a letter is more formal; the letter officially establishes date and intent of the correspondence; a letter can provide additional information.

No—a letter could bog down the personnel director or manager with additional reading; sometimes managers prefer phone, e-mail, or personal interviews only; the company might prefer a more informal approach.

Purpose: To improve skills at analyzing fiction

27. What was the best novel we read this year? Why that one? Use this also to assess the various novels read by students during the school year.

WRITING ACTIVITIES

Purpose: To review listing as a prewriting activity

28. Have students brainstorm a list of modifiers associated with summer vacation: warm, breezy, barbecue, etc.

29. Have students list those items they would put into a "Time Capsule"—a wonderful way to discover students' insights and values. Students should also decide what the capsule should look like and where it should be buried. Finally, they could describe the reactions of the people who find the time capsule in the future. Challenge their insights and creativity.

30. Refer to the traditional song "Happy Birthday to You" and direct students to list all the items typically associated with a birthday party.

Purpose: To review research as a prewriting activity

31. Assign students to list the climates and general terrain of Tonga, Madagascar, and the Philippines to possibly use as the setting of a fictional narrative. This also will increase students' knowledge of other nations.

32. Refer to Family History Day and ask students to list all their ancestors as far back as they have information and a brief background on each individual as an exercise in primary research.

33. Refer to Helen Keller and ask students to write details about the devices used by deaf or near-deaf people to hear and/or communicate, signing, or the physiology of the ear.

Purpose: To review organization skills in writing

34. Ask students to write a detailed essay describing their ideal summer vacation. Ask: How would you travel? Where would you go? What would you do?

35. Have students write a travelogue about Kentucky, Tennessee, and West Virginia—states that border each other. This also could prompt a review of research skills. Use **Form 11-11** as a model.

36. Put a timeline on the blackboard. It could be structured 8 AM to Midnight; Monday–Friday; September–June. Students then write the important events—imagined or real—in chronological order on the timeline.

37. Ask students to write a narrative about a trip or journey that had a dramatic influence on them, such as a vacation to the Grand Canyon or to another country. Use this to review chronology in writing as well. Use **Form 12-7** to evaluate them.

38. Direct students to compose the itinerary of Brigham Young as he left Illinois with his fellow group of 5000 Mormons and traveled west to Salt Lake City, Utah.

Purpose: To review writing character sketches

39. Have students write a character sketch that describes any person at work on his/her last day before retirement.

40. Refer to National Family Day and Family History Day and have students write brief, descriptive essays about their most interesting family member.

41. Refer to the allied soldiers or the German counterparts who were involved at the battle of D-Day and challenge students to write a character sketch that describes a soldier's actions, behavior, and attitude on that day.

Purpose: To review writing personal narratives

42. Ask students to write a brief narrative about their most memorable experience they had in school during the past year. Use **Form 12-7** to evaluate them.

Purpose: To review letter writing skills

43. Prompt students to write a detailed letter to any public official about a community issue like cleaning up the park. Refer to the correspondences George Bush received when he was President.

44. Ask students to pretend to be a groom writing a letter to his bride-to-be or a bride writing to her groom and have them write the first paragraphs of a letter. Refer to June as a common month for marriages.

45. Refer to CBS, which was the first network to broadcast in color, and have students write a letter to the president of any television network giving an opinion on the content of current children's cartoons. Are they too violent? Students must cite specific examples.

46. Have students write a letter that has recommendations and advice for the class behind the students. They should deal with specific preparations the younger students should make toward their academics. Give these letters later to those younger students.

47. Ask students to write a detailed letter to an anonymous student in the elementary school or to any student who will be entering their school in the fall. They should pass on what they think the younger students should know about the school, the key points about succeeding at the secondary level. The salutations should simply be Dear Elementary Student (or Dear Middle School Student). Later, distribute these letters to those students.

48. Ask students to write a standard, formal business letter where they explain their most memorable high school experience and their future plans. This letter can be written to a parent, a teacher, a relative, or an employer. Use this also as a closure exercise.

Purpose: To review skills at analyzing poetry

49. Have students locate a poem or story whose theme reflects the importance of graduation or moving on in life. Ask: How effectively has the poet presented that theme? They should copy the poem and write at least a paragraph that explains its theme. Refer to Jonson, Yeats, and Brooks.

Purpose: To create a poem

50. Have students compose a poem about graduation and/or moving on. They can read these in class—an excellent closure activity.

Purpose: To practice reflective writing

51. Have students create the diary entry of Sally Ride after she became the first woman in space aboard the space shuttle Challenger in 1983.

52. Ask students to consider essays that are poorly written and to pretend to be a teacher who must respond to them. Ask: What comments should a teacher make to a student who has produced an ineffective essay? Then they should write their comments.

© 2001 by The Center for Applied Research in Education

Purpose: To review skills at word selection/vocabulary

53. Refer to Charles Drew who organized the first blood bank and have students define the terms related to blood, like plasma, platelets, clotting, and transfusion and then use these terms in a coherent paragraph.

Purpose: To review composition skills

54. Distribute *Skill Sheet 6-6* and *Skill Sheet 6-7* and then discuss the students' responses.

Purpose: To conclude a fiction unit

55. Ask students to list moral values (at least 10) such as honesty. For each value, students must cite one character they have read in their literature text or assigned novels who has that value (with an explanation). Refer especially to the works of George Orwell.

Purpose: To conclude a careers unit

56. Distribute **Skill Sheet 6-8** to enhance students' knowledge of job skills related to the letters of application, the resume, and interviewing.

57. Distribute **Skill Sheet 6-9** to review the students' knowledge of interviewing. Of course, several students could already have experienced an interview so use their input.

Purpose: To assess course content/lessons

58. Ask students to write a persuasive essay that assesses the course content and lesson plans. Use this to maintain and/or improve any aspects of the course just completed.

59. Have students list what they learned this past week, past month, past two months to assess the course.

60. Ask students to list their favorite learning activities in each of the following categories: fiction, poetry, biography, composition, and speech.

DISCUSSION ACTIVITIES

Purpose: To review research skills

61. Refer to the Roman goddess Juno, the patron goddess of marriage and ask: The statistics say fifty-two percent of marriages today end in divorce and that more men and women are waiting until they are over thirty and forty years of age to get married—How do we know that? What sources could give us that information?

Court records, church records, interviews with newlyweds and lawyers, marriage announcements in newspapers, some census statistics

62. What can be done to make schools safer? What sources would you use to locate information on this issue? Use this also to assess your own school safety issues.

63. Refer to Helen Keller and direct students to explain the advantages and disadvantages of each of the following types of communication: telephone, fax machines, signing, e-mail, and letters. Also ask: What do you imagine Helen Keller's response would be to each type of communication format?

64. What are some interesting tourist spots in our town or city? What could make our city an enjoyable vacation spot for travelers? How would you use primary research here?

Purpose: To expand critical thinking skills

65. Write Helen Keller's quote on the board: "Keep your face to the sunshine and you cannot see the shadow" and have students analyze its meaning.

66. Write Ben Jonson's quote on the board: "To speak and to speak well are two things. A fool may talk, but a wise man speaks" and have students analyze its meaning.

Purpose: To improve skills at analyzing poetry

67. Write on the board Matthew Arnold's reflection on poetry: "Poetry is simply the most beautiful, impressive, and widely effective mode of saying things." Is he correct? Why/why not?

68. Refer to Gwendolyn Brooks who wrote the classic poem "We Real Cool" and ask: How would you interpret these lines from the poem?

> We Sing sin. We Thin gin.
> We Jazz June. We Die soon.

Gwendolyn Brooks uses alliteration, capitalization, and rhyme effectively to portray the lifestyle and attitude of urban youths. Profanity, alcohol, heat, freedom, and early death all seem to be a part of their daily lives.

Purpose: To begin a careers unit

69. What careers interest you? What fields or occupations seem interesting? Why those?

70. Refer to Paula Abdul, Judy Garland, Paul McCartney, and Tim Allen. Other than talent, what makes a person successful in theater, comedy, and performing? What characteristics should this type of person have? How have these performers gained success?

Purpose: *To begin or conclude a fiction unit*

71. Refer to D-Day and ask: What novels have been written about WW II? Who are some major authors who have made WW II the setting of their fiction? What makes these books interesting to read? Use this also to connect history with literature.

72. Refer to George Orwell and his famous satire *Animal Farm*. Have students identify other book or story titles that have animal references, for example, *One Flew Over the Cuckoo's Nest* by Ken Kesey and *P.S. Your Cat is Dead* by James Kirkwood. Also ask: Why would these authors use such references?

Purpose: *To conclude a composition unit*

73. What is the most important stage/step in the writing process? What is the most important criteria for judging or evaluating a composition?

74. Who is your favorite professional writer? Why? Who is the best writer in the class? What are the traits of a successful writer?

AUDIO/VISUAL ACTIVITIES

Purpose: *To begin or conclude a fiction unit*

75. Play the lyrics of a song by Paul McCartney then ask: Based on those lyrics what could be the premise of a story's plot? What kind of narrative would you create from the lyrics?

76. Refer to the first television program in color that was broadcasted by the Columbia Broadcasting System (CBS) in 1951. What is your favorite television program? Why? What is special about its characters or plot?

77. Have students draw or paint a picture of any scene from a novel they read. Or they could make a collage of events and characters from the novel they read.

78. Play a recording of "Revolution" by the Beatles. Relate this to George Orwell's satire about the Russian Revolution *Animal Farm*.

Purpose: *To begin or conclude a poetry unit*

79. Sing "Take me out to the Ballgame." The lyrics were written by Jack Norwooth, a vaudeville song-and-dance man who had never been to a major league game and supposedly wrote the lyrics while riding the New York subway in 1908. Use **Form 6-10** and ask students to respond to the poetic quality of the lyrics.

80. Show a video clip or picture of any major league or college baseball player at the plate while students read the poem "Casey at the Bat" **(Skill Sheet 6-5).** Also discuss the poem's diction, imagery, and theme.

81. Have students sing the song "Happy Birthday to You" and then ask: What makes this a poem? How effective are these lyrics? Why has it remained so popular and included with every birthday celebration?

82. Play recordings of Paul McCartney and discuss the poetic qualities of his lyrics.

Purpose: *To review writing character sketches*

83. Show pictures of interesting or unusual-looking people (either in magazine ads, on a transparency, or on pictures on the bulletin board). Ask: What kind of backgrounds do you think they have? What is interesting about them? Use this as part of a unit on writing profiles of people and also challenge students' creativity.

84. Show selected scenes from a videotape of "Home Improvement" starring Tim Allen and then have students write a detailed profile about the appearance, behavior, and traits of any character.

85. Examine yearbook pictures taken during the school year and have students list the traits of the people on the pages.

86. Assign students to watch any news programs for events that involve Russia. Have them write a brief report on what they learn about the people who live there.

87. Show selected scenes from the movie *Pride of the Yankees* starring Gary Cooper, which profiles the life of Hall of Fame baseball player Lou Gehrig, and have students list details related to his appearance, behavior, and traits for a character sketch or as an exercise in biography.

88. Show selected scenes from any movie starring Marilyn Monroe and have students list details related to her appearance, behavior, and traits for a character sketch or as an exercise in biography.

Purpose: *To improve skills at writing description*

89. Distribute travel brochures or pictures related to Arkansas and have students write paragraphs about specific places or areas that could highlight this state.

90. Refer to William Shakespeare's Globe Theater and either take a field trip or ask students to visit a local stage theater to write a brief essay describing it, focusing especially on its dimensions, appearance, and atmosphere. Possibly have students also research the original Globe Theater and compare it to the one they visit.

91. Show selected scenes from any movie based on a novel by Larry McMurtry and instruct students to describe the land, a character, or a place portrayed in the film. Possible movies include *The Last Picture Show, Lonesome Dove,* and *Terms of Endearment.* Use **Form 12-5** to evaluate.

Purpose: *To review skills related to speech/oral presentation*

92. Have students bring in an object that represents them, such as a uniform for an athlete, a musical instrument for a band member, a stuffed animal, etc., and then explain the connection to classmates.

93. Have students make a two to three minute oral presentation to their classmates where they explain in order their most memorable high school experience; read a favorite poem, quote, or article related to the end of the school year; and explain their plans for the summer. Use this also as a closure activity.

Purpose: *To begin or conclude a biography unit*

94. Show selected scenes from the movie *Black Like Me* starring James Whitmore, which portrays some of the experiences John Griffin wrote about in his book.

95. Show selected scenes from the movie *The Miracle Worker* starring Anne Bancroft and Patti Duke, which portrays the early life of Helen Keller as documented in her various biographies.

96. Refer to National Family Day and ask students to bring in pictures of family members they think could be the focus of a biography. Direct them to explain why in one or two paragraphs.

97. Show the movie *The Diary of Anne Frank* to correspond to the reading of her autobiography.

Form 6–1 Name _____

Letter for Summer Reading

School Address _____

Date _____

Dear Parent/Guardian:

It is my understanding that your child has registered for _____ for the _____ school year. As part of this course curriculum, students have a summer reading requirement designed to sharpen their reading skills and introduce them to two important authors. I am very appreciative of your efforts in supporting this summer reading program, now required for _____ students by the school administration and curriculum for this course.

Students must select *one* book by _____ and *one* book by _____ for a total of two books. Students should expect an evaluation on these two books during the first week after Labor Day. Both authors have published multiple books, which are readily available in most libraries and book stores.

We also recommend students regularly read a daily newspaper and a favorite magazine to stay updated on current events, which could appear in lessons in the coming school year.

If you see a problem in completing this reading, please call me at the school. I frequently check my voice mail messages during the summer.

Thanks again for support. Enjoy your summer.

Sincerely,

Name _____

George Orwell—A Preview

1. Orwell's novels, like *Animal Farm*, are in some ways modern fables. Why would Orwell choose the format of a fable for his novels?

2. Fables have predicaments. What predicaments might you expect in the novels *Animal Farm* and *1984?*

3. In his books, Orwell offers some paradoxical statements:

   "All animals are equal, but some animals are more equal than others." (*Animal Farm*, Chapter 10)

   WAR IS PEACE
   FREEDOM IS SLAVERY
   IGNORANCE IS STRENGTH

   (*1984*—the slogans of the Party engraved on the Ministry of Truth building)

   How can these statements be interpreted?

4. Orwell observed the abuse of citizens by Joseph Stalin's communist government in the former U.S.S.R. He satirized these events in his books. Why would Orwell, an English author, choose to criticize Stalin and communism?

5. Orwell wrote satires. What is satire?

Larry McMurtry

Background

- Taught at Texas Christian University, Rice, George Mason University, and American University.

- Uses characters and setting (most often Texas) associated with the American West.

- Has become an authority on Western geography, culture, and people.

- Shows a realistic depiction of frontier life in both his fiction and nonfiction works.

- Has also written various screenplays.

- Expresses often themes of alienation and struggles related to small town and ranch life on the frontier.

Major Works

- *Leaving Cheyenne* (1963)

- *The Last Picture Show* (1966)

- *Terms of Endearment* (1975)

- *Lonesome Dove* (1985)—Pulitzer Prize winner

- *Texasville* (1987)

- *Anything for Billy* (1988)

- *Buffalo Girls* (1990)

- *Commanche Moon* (1997)

- *Crazy Horse* (1999)

Name _____

Lou Gehrig's Speech
Yankee Stadium—July 4, 1939

Background: Lou Gehrig had just learned he had an incurable disease.

Fans, for the past two weeks you have been reading about a bad break I got. Yet today I consider myself the luckiest man on the face of the earth. I have been in ballparks for seventeen years and I have never received anything but kindness and encouragement from you fans.

Look at these grand men. Which of you wouldn't consider it the highlight of his career just to associate with them for even one day? Sure I'm lucky. Who wouldn't have considered it an honor to have known Jacob Ruppert? Also, the builder of baseball's greatest empire, Ed Barrow? To have spent six years with that wonderful little fellow, Miller Huggins? Then to have spent the next nine years with that outstanding leader, that smart student of psychology, the best manager in baseball today, Joe McCarthy?

Sure, I'm lucky. When the New York Giants, a team you would give your right arm to beat . . . sends you a gift, that's something. When everybody down to the groundskeepers and those boys in the white coats remember you with trophies, that's something. When you have a father and mother who work all their lives so that you can have an education and build your body, it's a blessing. When you have a wife who has been a tower of strength and shown more courage than you dreamed existed, that's the finest I know.

So I close in saying that I might have had a bad break, but I have an awful lot to live for.

Name _____

"Casey at the Bat"

It looked extremely rocky for the Mudville nine that day;
The score stood two to four, with but one inning left to play.
So, when Cooney died at second, and Burrows did the same,
A pallor wreathed the features of the patrons of the game.

A straggling few got up to go, leaving there the rest,
With that hope which springs eternal within the human breast.
For they thought: "If only Casey could get a whack at that,"
They'd put even money now, with Casey at the bat.

But Flynn preceded Casey, and likewise so did Blake,
And the former was a pudd'n, and the latter was a fake.
So on that stricken multitude a deathlike silence sat;
For there seemed but little chance of Casey's getting to the bat.

But Flynn let drive a single, to the wonderment of all.
And the much-despised Blakey "tore the cover off the ball."
And when the dust had lifted, and they saw what had occurred,
There was Blakey safe at second, and Flynn a-huggin' third.

Then from the gladdened multitude went up a joyous yell—
It rumbled in the mountaintops, it rattled in the dell;
It struck upon the hillside and rebounded on the flat;
For Casey, mighty Casey, was advancing to the bat.

There was ease in Casey's manner as he stepped into his place,
There was pride in Casey's bearing and a smile on Casey's face;
And when responding to the cheers he lightly doffed his hat,
No stranger in the crowd could doubt 'twas Casey at the bat.

Ten thousand eyes were on him as he rubbed his hands with dirt,
Five thousand tongues applauded when he wiped them on his shirt;
Then when the writhing pitcher ground the ball into his hip,
Defiance gleamed from Casey's eye, a sneer curled Casey's lip.

And now the leather-covered sphere came hurtling through the air,
And Casey stood a-watching it in haughty grandeur there.
Close by the sturdy batsman the ball unheeded sped;
"That ain't my style," said Casey. "Strike one," the umpire said.

From the benches, black with people, there went up a muffled roar,
Like the beating of the storm waves on the stern and distant shore.
"Kill him! Kill the umpire!" shouted someone on the stand;
And it's likely they'd have killed him had not Casey raised his hand.

With a smile of Christian charity great Casey's visage shone;
He stilled the rising tumult, he made the game go on;
He signaled to the pitcher, and once more the spheroid flew;
But Casey still ignored it, and the umpire said, "Strike two."

"Fraud!" cried the maddened thousands, and the echo answered "Fraud!"
But one scornful look from Casey and the audience was awed;
They saw his face grow stern and cold, they saw his muscles strain,
And they knew that Casey wouldn't let the ball go by again.

The sneer is gone from Casey's lips, his teeth are clenched in hate,
He pounds with cruel vengeance his bat upon the plate;
And now the pitcher holds the ball, and now he lets it go,
And now the air is shattered by the force of Casey's blow.

Oh, somewhere in this favored land the sun is shining bright,
The band is playing somewhere, and somewhere hearts are light;
And somewhere men are laughing, and somewhere children shout,
But there is no joy in Mudville—mighty Casey has struck out.

by Ernest Lawrence Thayer

Questions

1. How does the poet develop a sense of tension?

2. What words/phrases provide a picture of this baseball scene (the imagery)?

3. How does the name Mudville itself affect our attitude toward Casey?

4. How is the poem like a short story?

5. What are some themes?

How Good Are Your Composition Skills?

Directions: Circle the letter of the correct answer.

1. A type of nonstandard language is
   A. excessive word choice.
   B. humorous sayings.
   C. slang.
   D. all of the above.

2. Formal language is often
   A. confusing.
   B. polysyllabic.
   C. just like informal language.
   D. none of the above.

3. It is never appropriate to use nonstandard language in an essay.
   A. True
   B. False

4. Newspapers and popular magazines usually use
   A. formal language.
   B. dramatic language.
   C. informal language.
   D. didactic language.

5. Descriptive writing improves if the writer uses
   A. sensory language.
   B. specific word choice.
   C. concrete details.
   D. all of the above.

6. Which of the following is the most specific word?
   A. blue
   B. aqua
   C. colorful
   D. sky

7. Which of the following is the most sensory word?
   A. rough
   B. touch
   C. clammy
   D. flat

8. Diction can be defined as
   A. the type of words used in writing.
   B. descriptive words.
   C. foul language.
   D. nonstandard words like graffiti.

9. Selecting the appropriate words depends on
   A. the audience for the written work.
   B. the reader's background.
   C. the topic of the written work.
   D. all of the above.

10. A descriptive essay should be based on
   A. sensory details.
   B. a funny observation.
   C. something in nature.
   D. all of the above.

11. Prepositional phrases are usually not helpful for descriptive writing.
   A. True
   B. False

12. Compositions can be organized through the use of
   A. a first draft.
   B. webbing.
   C. an outline.
   D. topic sentences.

13. The concluding paragraph should
   A. offer new, dramatic information for the reader.
   B. be two paragraphs usually.
   C. reflect a concise summary of main points.
   D. do all of the above.

14. Essay coherence is achieved by
   A. following paragraph unity.
   B. the use of descriptive words.
   C. using transitions and following the thesis.
   D. doing all of the above.

15. The key difference between a topic sentence and a thesis is
   A. the thesis has more meaning.
   B. the topic sentence has a shorter length.
   C. the topic sentence announces an essay topic.
   D. the thesis announces the essay topic.

16. Paragraph unity
    A. means every sentence relates to the thesis.
    B. refers to one topic being the focus of the paragraph.
    C. equals paragraph coherence.
    D. is violated when incorrect grammar occurs.

17. For shorter compositions a first draft isn't required.
    A. True
    B. False

18. Slang is never appropriate in persuasive essays.
    A. True
    B. False

19. Clarity in writing refers to
    A. the type of outline that is used for the essay.
    B. selecting a topic.
    C. being specific and direct in word choice.
    D. revising and editing paragraphs.

20. Prewriting is a stage where
    A. a topic is selected, details are listed, and a thesis is written.
    B. the outline is transformed into paragraphs.
    C. a peer editor proofreads and edits the first draft.
    D. the writer changes grammatical constructions in sentences.

Name _____

Assessment of Composition Work

Directions: Complete the following questions about the writing projects we completed during the school year.

1. What was your favorite writing project? Why?

2. Which project didn't you like? Why?

3. What writing project would you add?

4. What have you learned about writing skills that you didn't know before?

5. What writing skills would you like to have dealt with in greater depth?

6. How would you improve the peer editing sessions?

7. If I only knew (or evaluated) you based on your writing folder, what would it reveal?

8. General reactions to our writing activities?

When It's Time to Get a Job!

Directions: Answer True or False to each of the following.

1. _____ In a letter of application, always have a date.

2. _____ In a letter of application be as brief as possible.

3. _____ A business letter should be characterized by professional language.

4. _____ Put all hobbies on a resume.

5. _____ Young people should put volunteer work in a resume.

6. _____ Health status is important for a resume.

7. _____ Generally, for a young person's resume, quantity is more important than quality.

8. _____ Bringing food or drink is acceptable at an interview.

9. _____ By law, companies must publish the salary when they advertise a job opening.

10. _____ In today's business dealings, a cover letter should accompany the application.

11. _____ Almost all jobs offered in newspaper classifieds apply only to high school graduates.

12. _____ At the first interview, it is acceptable to discuss salary.

13. _____ The only purpose of an interview is to test the applicant's personality and knowledge.

14. _____ Any job held for six months or less should not appear on a resume or application.

15. _____ Previous or expected salary should appear on a resume.

Bonus

16. _____ It is best to introduce your interest in the job before writing about your background in a letter of application.

Name _____

Preparing for an Interview

List five things to do *before* interviewing for a job:

1. _____

2. _____

3. _____

4. _____

5. _____

List five things to do *during* an interview:

6. _____

7. _____

8. _____

9. _____

10. _____

List five things to do *after* the interview has concluded:

11. _____

12. _____

13. _____

14. _____

15. _____

Name _____

"Take Me Out to the Ballgame"

by Jack Norwooth

Take me out to the ball game,

Take me out with the crowd.

Buy me some peanuts and Cracker Jack,

I don't care if I never get back,

Let me root, root, root

For the home team,

If they don't win it's a shame

For it's one,

two,

three strikes you're out,

at the old ball game.

JUNE
Answer Key

#2 SKILL SHEET 6-2—GEORGE ORWELL—A PREVIEW

1. Orwell chose the format of a fable for *Animal Farm* to educate both youths and adults. He used a different approach from other writers.

2. Answers will vary.

3. "All animals are equal, but some animals are more equal than others" suggests that true equality among the animals does not exist anymore. WAR IS PEACE, FREEDOM IS SLAVERY, and IGNORANCE IS STRENGTH—These slogans of the Party engraved on the Ministry of Truth building in *1984* can only be explained when citizens accept the government's authority without thought or complaint.

4. Orwell observed the abuse of citizens by Joseph Stalin's communist government in the former U.S.S.R. and satirized those events in his books because he feared dictators like Stalin, the spread of communism in the rest of Europe, and totalitarianism.

5. Satire is a form of literature where society, individuals, vices, or government are ridiculed with the intent to bring about change or reform.

#7 ACTIVITY 6-4—"CASEY AT THE BAT"

1. The first two batters made outs; the crowd threatens the umpire; Casey gets two strikes on him.

2. "multitude a deathlike silence sat," "when the dust had lifted," "joyous yell, it rumbled in the mountain tops, it rattled in the dell," "lightly doffed his hat," "rubbed his hands with dirt," "writhing pitcher ground the ball into his hip," "a sneer curled Casey's lip," "leather covered sphere," "benches black with people," "his face grew stern and cold," "pounds with cruel vengeance his bat upon the plate."

3. The name Mudville suggests a very small town; Casey is the most prominent person there; in the end, Casey's name is mud.

4. The poem is like a short story because it has characters and a conflict—Casey vs. the pitcher; it has a climax—Casey strikes out; it has a resolution—"there is no joy in Mudville."

5. The problems that can result from overconfidence (Casey's self-confidence is the cause of both his popularity and failure; our "eternal" belief in hope; the drama of athletic contests—a small town baseball game in this case; fans should be more careful in their choice of a hero.

#54 SKILL SHEET 6-6—HOW GOOD ARE YOUR COMPOSITION SKILLS?

1. C	2. B	3. B	4. C	5. D
6. B	7. C	8. A	9. D	10. A
11. B	12. C	13. C	14. C	15. D
16. B	17. B	18. B	19. C	20. A

#56 SKILL SHEET 6-8—WHEN IT'S TIME TO GET A JOB!

1. TRUE	2. TRUE	3. TRUE	4. FALSE	5. TRUE
6. FALSE	7. TRUE	8. FALSE	9. FALSE	10. TRUE
11. FALSE	12. TRUE	13. FALSE	14. FALSE	15. FALSE
16. TRUE				

#57 SKILL SHEET 6-9—PREPARING FOR AN INTERVIEW

Five things to do *before* interviewing for a job:

1. Research the company/business
2. Decide salary expectations
3. Prepare a resume
4. Rehearse potential interview questions and answers
5. Confirm date and time of the interview
6. Seek potential references

Five things to do *during* an interview:

1. Answer questions honestly
2. Be direct and sincere
3. Smile
4. Try to stay relaxed
5. Show enthusiasm
6. Have all necessary forms/papers

Five things to do *after* the interview has concluded:

1. Follow up with a letter of thanks and interest
2. Phone several days later to ask about the status of the position
3. Critique the interview
4. Explain interview to current employer/references
5. Send out more letters of application
6. Arrange more interviews

NOTES

NOTES

NOTES

NOTES

NOTES

NOTES

NOTES

NOTES

NOTES

NOTES